NAVIGATING THE BUSINESS SWAMP

A treasure map through the murky waters of business.

by STEVE POORMAN

A Lock Haven University Honoree
Stephen Poorman College of Business

PUBLISHED BY TRIMARK PRESS, INC., DEERFIELD BEACH, FLORIDA.

LIBRARY OF CONGRESS CATALOGING-IN-PUBLICATION DATA
NAVIGATING THE BUSINESS SWAMP
STEPHEN POORMAN
P. CM.
ISBN: 978-1-943401-62-8
LIBRARY OF CONGRESS CONTROL NUMBER: 2019909073

H-19
10 9 8 7 6 5 4 3 2 1
FIRST EDITION
PRINTED AND BOUND IN THE UNITED STATES OF AMERICA

A PUBLICATION OF TRIMARK PRESS, INC.
368 SOUTH MILITARY TRAIL
DEERFIELD BEACH, FL 33442
800.889.0693

WWW.TRIMARKPRESS.COM

DEDICATION

This book is dedicated to all of those hopeful entrepreneurs brave enough to step into a world where they provide goods and services, create employment, and fuel the economy.

Thanks to my friends whose persuasion led me to write this book, and to my clients and business partners who placed confidence in my advice. Thanks to Sarah McCracken for her persistence in urging me to write.

But mostly, I want to thank my loving wife of 35 years, Pamela Ann, who is always there to share my life.

ACKNOWLEDGEMENTS

I would like to thank my editorial team and The Lock Haven University of Pennsylvania for their support:

Publishers: TriMark Press, Deerfield Beach, Florida
                       Lock Haven University of Pennsylvania Press

Senior Editor: Richard Westlund, MBA, Miami, Florida
Junior Editor: Michael Seemuth, Hollywood, Florida
Junior Editor: Richard Morris, Lock Haven, Pennsylvania
Copy Editor: Joyce Moed, Coral Springs, Florida
Composer: Good Book Developers, Atlanta, Georgia
Designer: GD Design Studios, Fort Lauderdale, Florida
Photographer: Tiffany Studios, Fort Lauderdale, Florida
Caricaturist: D. Mark Stevenson, Lock Haven, Pennsylvania
Indexer: Allegheny Writing & Publishing
                       Pittsburgh, Pennsylvania
Accounting Review: Timothy C. Marshall, CPA,
                       State College, Pennsylvania
Legal Review: R. Thompson Rosamilia, Esquire
                       Lock Haven, Pennsylvania
Literary Publicist: Randee Feldman

Table of Contents

Leaving the Swamp
  Exiting Your Business   **333**

FOREWORDS

Dr. Stephen P. Neun, Dean
Co-Author, *Health Economics: Theories,
Insights and Industry Studies, 4th. Edition*
The Stephen Poorman College of Business,
Information Systems & Human Services
Lock Haven University of Pennsylvania

If you are an aspiring entrepreneur with an idea and the dream of starting your own business, then this book is a must read. *Navigating the Business Swamp* provides the reader with a clear and concise roadmap for growing your own company.

Becoming an entrepreneur can be both a challenging and rewarding experience, and this book will help you navigate around many unexpected roadblocks you will face in your career. It is based on the author's years of experience as an entrepreneur and management consultant; and, as such, it is filled with an innumerable number of insights and tips.

Dr. Petru Sandu
Author and Professor of Entrepreneurship
& Management
Elizabethtown College

The journey of writing a highly practical book on this topic is as challenging as creating a business. Mr. Poorman's passion to prepare young people for the business world enticed him to crystallize a life-long experience into *Navigating the Business Swamp*.

Each chapter of this teaching manual is an essential piece of the exciting business game puzzle. Through real life stories, the reader will learn that it is a high contact sport. And, to succeed, one must practice. This message has been enthusiastically preached by Steve to my budding students during his numerous lectures.

Entrepreneurship is a journey to find your true self within the realm of opportunity. The relentless motivation to keep learning is the sign of a great entrepreneur. Wherever you are in your swamp journey, reading this book is a wise decision. It will gain you more confidence, discipline and independence.

Dr. James L. Norrie, Dean, LL.M.
Author of Five Business Books
Fortune 500 Consultant
The Graham School of Business
York College of Pennsylvania

Wow! *Navigating the Business Swamp* is about the most practical view of entrepreneurship and small business management I have ever read. Using his obvious expertise and stories drawn from decades of experience, Steve will help generations of those who aspire to be self-employed accomplish their dream.

PREFACE

This book contains hundreds of tips designed to save you time, trouble and money. Most of these strategies and "survival stories" are not found in textbooks. Trade journals are hesitant to publish "survival tactics" because they could offend industry advertisers who shun negative news, or want to suppress tactics that could be diametrically opposed to their agendas. But the truth is that these tips could save you thousands of dollars each year, if not your business.

This book serves as a primer for students, start-ups and small business owners. Its purpose is to dodge the expensive "school of hard knocks." Conveyed with actual experiences, it may harden you just enough to protect you from the attacks and losses that dominate the small business arena.

If you want to make enough money to actually pay your taxes and buy some toys, then read this book. If you want to play the game of business to win, and understand that money is how we keep score, read this book. If you're trusting by nature and want to place your future in the hands of others, or if you believe "one good turn deserves another," you have no choice but to read this book. Conversely, if you're a trust-fund baby, easily offended or sport rose-colored glasses, then perhaps it's not for you. Or, is it?

This book may be too raw for some morality maniacs or lexicographers. Employing the same philosophy as in my consulting practice, I believe readers don't need someone to tell them something; they deserve to be shown something. **For that reason, asterisks are embedded in the chapters throughout the book. When you see an asterisk, it indicates that there is a template available at www.navigatingthebusinessswamp.com.**

Finally, this book is also the personal story of my life in business, real estate, investments and consulting. When I started out decades ago, technology was far less prevalent than today. Certainly, tools like computers, smartphones, and social media have dramatically changed the business landscape since my years in the swamp. So, if you're looking for the latest guide to using Facebook or Google or data analytics in your business, then you should look elsewhere.

But too often we pay attention to the gadgets rather than the underlying realities of business, which are as true today as they were in the past. You might be launching a new mobile app, planning a new farm-to-table restaurant or opening a laundry, warehouse or real estate business. In order to succeed in any venture, you will still have to navigate the complex relationships between your customers, investors, bankers, attorneys, accountants, the IRS, and anyone else who wants to have a stake in your business. That's why this book is so important!

The impetus to write arose after giving lectures to graduating university seniors who yearned to know more about navigating the swamp they were about to enter. It was their enthusiasm and positive reception to my talks that motivated me to write. So, here comes all the nasty stuff that no one else seems to want to talk about.

I'm So Very Sorry

Before I generalize on the entire human race and institutions, I'll apologize in advance. There are honest lawyers, dedicated government workers and excellent employees in this world. To those who qualify, I want to say, "I am truly sorry." But, sadly, after more than 45 years of doing business in 26 states, and after being "kicked in the head" a few thousand times, you'll have to forgive the cynicism that shines through my writing. After owning my own companies and consulting to hundreds of clients, I've reached a conclusion that traditional education simply doesn't prepare one for the hard work and courage needed for a successful business career. Most of the "nice" people in the business world live in shallow areas of the swamp. As you traipse into deeper water, their colors change.

If you want to own a very small business in a small town, you might not encounter too many alligators snapping at your feet. But if you hire people, borrow money, grow your company and take risks, then be prepared for the battle of your lifetime. The more business you do, the more vermin you will encounter.

So now that I've apologized . . . lets go wade in the swamp.

ENTERING THE SWAMP

Starting Your Business

Planning ahead is crucial to the success of any business venture. Use your intelligence, your experience, and your relationships to build a strong canoe that will carry you across the swamp.

1. THE ENTREPRENEUR

"All business proceeds on beliefs, or judgments of probabilities, and not on certainties."

Charles Eliot

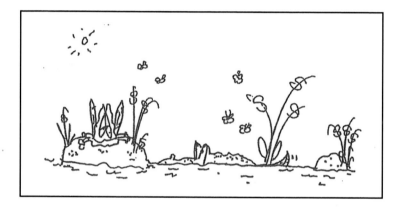

The word "entrepreneur" is a bit obscure. For some English speakers, the French origin may fog its meaning. One dictionary definition blandly declares that an entrepreneur "assumes the risk and management of business." This one describes an entrepreneur as a kind of transformer:

Entrepreneurship...

Is the act of being an entrepreneur, which is a French word meaning "one who undertakes innovations, finance and business acumen in an effort to transform innovations into economic goods."

But these lifeless characterizations don't capture the gritty reality. Here is my down-to-earth definition:

Entrepreneurship...

"is the act of trying to get rich in a business world where the odds are stacked against fortune seekers. A few succeed with relative ease. For most the trip is hazardous, comparable to wading in a swamp full of hungry alligators, all trying to eat their silly little asses for even daring to make the trip."

Entrepreneurs are leaders into the unknown, captains of uncharted waters. The best are innovators and risk-takers who inspire others to see their vision and earn big profits by combining capital and labor to deliver products and services. Sadly, most fall prey to the alligators. The best paddle past the rest by taking a more disciplined and educated approach to achieving success. You may not have been born rich, but you can learn how to unearth a fortune somewhere in that scary swamp.

Management consulting guru Peter Drucker demystified the art of entrepreneurship. "Most of what you hear about entrepreneurship is all wrong," Drucker wrote in *Innovation and Entrepreneurship*. "It's not magic; it's not mysterious; and it has nothing to do with genes. It's a discipline and, like any discipline, it can be learned."

While the personal motives that drive entrepreneurs vary, their common financial goal is to make lots of money and to avoid losses, the twin subjects of this book. Entrepreneurs are leaders who not only long to become rich but also devote themselves to learning how. As John Maxwell says, "Leaders must be close enough to relate to others, but far enough ahead to motivate them." Being an entrepreneur is a cultivated mindset. So with reasonable intelligence and ambition, many swamp navigators can stay afloat and succeed.

What Will Entrepreneurs Foresee That Others Won't?

To be a successful entrepreneur, you must envision yourself as one. It's never too early to start. As a young boy, I dreamed about my future, and those dreams came true.

I took my earliest inspirations from multiple sources, not just my parents. Notes in my "baby book" indicate that I wanted to grow up to be a salesman, a harbinger of my entrepreneurial future. My best childhood friend lived in a fancy new home overlooking a valley, which fueled my own dreams of luxury surroundings.

One especially inspiring fellow helped me to envision myself as a home owner in sunny South Florida. This renowned Fort Lauderdale keyboard artist would make summer trips to visit his sister, who happened to be my neighbor in Pennsylvania. He was my idol. He often said to me, "Stevie, you need to move to Florida to be successful."

Envisioning success makes achieving it easier when opportunity arises. When I was just 14, my musician brother became ill, and I substituted for him as the piano player in a musical group. It was my first performance in front of an audience. Thrown onto the stage with no experience, I struggled to read tattered music sheets, and relied on the guitar player to shout the chords to me all night long. Petrified? I sure was. But I took the risk and allowed my confidence to displace my fear.

At age 17, I bought my first Cadillac and soon cut my first record album, opened my first music store and, in my early twenties, bought a fancy home. Later in life I bought a second home in Fort Lauderdale, Florida, and then a summer residence. All these acquisitions materialized from early visions, experiences and desires. I wanted to live well. The thought of working in a corporate setting and getting stuck in a middle-class lifestyle never crossed my mind.

What is your vision of success?
Who Are YOU Anyway?

The Entrepreneur

You have the right mindset to survive in the business swamp if you have deep faith in your startup business when the rest of the world says it will drown. You know when your canoe is taking on water, and where to find the right person with a bucket and oars. You accept the fact it may take years to cross the swamp, yet you will not abort the trip until you reach the other side.

YOU recognize the need to delegate because you're not equipped to succeed alone. You thrive on positive stress and realize that success may come at a cost to your health or family. You know that when you listen, you learn, and when you talk, you only repeat things you already know.

So, you will listen to advice, but recognize that you have more insight than most of your advisers.

You will be self-confident, but not so cocky that you're blind to risk. You will temper your impulsiveness and keep your ego in check. YOU will learn to stay focused and ignore the little vermin nibbling at your ankles. And YOU will brace for possible failure as you plan for success.

YOU probably will possess a "Type A" go-getter personality and perhaps some narcissistic tendencies. You know you are a control freak and don't find anything distasteful about the trait. Events such as the 2008 financial recession can cause a failure beyond your control, so you will prepare for such anomalies and develop a way to restart your next venture without being devastated by your current one. You know a new venture takes time to make money.

YOU are creative. You have the guts to launch a concept no one else ever tried. You actually get turned on by proving others wrong. While money is a way of keeping score, your real reward is productively pursuing opportunity. As you succeed, money will follow you.

YOU must see yourself as successful and believe that you deserve what you hope to achieve. Your professional advisers can answer all kinds of questions, but they only carry out projects created by you. After all, if there were no successful companies, who would need lawyers or accountants? Just like the journey of becoming a musician, mastering entrepreneurship is a long, bumpy road, and you will not garner respect until you become a master performer. Critics will laugh at you and ostracize you. You will be in the minority. You'll be alone.

No one will truly share your own vision of personal success. You will constantly need to convince others to follow your lead, while worrying that you are taking them down a dead-end street. You will feel this emptiness because you've experienced the horror of rejection. But that won't stop you because you're actually addicted to success. You don't want to work for a big company that will never embrace your dreams. You need a new challenge. You fly above the crowd.

Does this sound like you? If so, beware: You may bankrupt yourself at least once. Many entrepreneurs must fight to win, making themselves vulnerable to knockout punches. You're no less vulnerable to a bankruptcy than Donald Trump, Chrysler or the corner grocer. So it makes sense to study and prepare to avoid the first hit. Whether you're still young and have time to recover, or you've been playing the game for a while, you'll find countless business-swamp survival tips in this book. My goal is to help you avoid an unnecessary plunge into the muck so you can enjoy the independence of controlling your own destiny sooner rather than later. Gird yourself, though. The shock of "being your own boss" may interrupt your lackadaisically content lifestyle as you begin to climb into the boat and push into the swamp.

Some people become entrepreneurs because they are simply dissatisfied with their career path or believe corporate America neither rewards nor appreciates their creativity. If you are young or broke or both, you're in a much better position to assume risk because you have little to lose and time to recover! You're standing on the green grass.

The Entrepreneur

Whether you are a serial entrepreneur or an unseasoned amateur, you'll constantly face threats. Like the vast population of pests and predators in a swamp, risk never disappears. Getting past all those alligators demands an unwavering faith in the financial theory that the greater the risk, the greater the potential reward. This book will help you become a "risk mitigator," but you must take the first step.

Philosopher Ralph Waldo Emerson said, "The step from knowing to doing is rarely taken." In life, you'll meet a lot of people who aren't as smart or creative as you, but they'll be more successful and wealthier. It's only because they "pulled the trigger," so to speak, and took their best shot at winning. They made their own luck . . .if there is any such thing.

What Do You Need?

Successful entrepreneurs have a need to achieve, an ability to tolerate stress, good judgment, adaptability, and self-confidence without arrogance. They have an appetite for hard work, discipline, and a sixth sense for opportunity while others see only problems. These leaders must master and perform multiple jobs at the same time — everything from marketing director, accountant and salesperson to chief financial officer, personnel manager, public relations specialist and lavatory attendant. As multi-tasking leaders expand and recruit additional help, they gain a basic understanding of the jobs they ask others to perform.

Some human needs are more deeply felt than others. In the 1940s, psychologist Abraham Maslow developed his classic hierarchy of six human needs, ranked by the intensity of each one. He theorized that the most powerful needs are such physiological ones as nourishment, oxygen, exercise, rest and sex. Safety is the second-ranked need in his hierarchy, followed in order by social satisfaction, self-esteem, self-actualization and aesthetic achievement.

Do all people really have needs in the same order? In my unscientific opinion, different people have different priorities. What drives entrepreneurial leaders, for example, may steer administrative managers the wrong way. What are your own personal needs and tendencies? In particular, ask yourself: Are you a leader or a manager? Which personality type is the most comfortable fit?

Leaders are proactive; managers are reactive. Managers seek compromise; leaders challenge the norm. Managers meet expectations; leaders create them. Leaders not only possess high energy, they can energize their followers. The smart entrepreneur recognizes that he or she is not the best listener and may not have the personality to enjoy mundane tasks. The repetitive tasks of a tidy manager are boring to an entrepreneur.

Not everyone has the stomach for a grueling trip through the swamp. Nevertheless, it can mean working 16-hour days, seven days each week. Even with today's technology, the successful entrepreneur is usually the last one to turn off the lights at night. He or she is the one pledging personal assets and sacrificing leisure and family time. That sacrifice will be a necessity. And you will need to ignore the critical comments: "You work too much . . .Life's too short . . . Don't you ever have any fun?" After all, closing a deal just might be fun — to you. The world belongs to passionate, driven leaders.

So Can Anyone Learn to be an Entrepreneur?

Some universities serve as swamp guides by offering entrepreneurship curricula. Academic preparation helps the early entrepreneur, but attending class and doing homework cannot compare with the raw experience gained from running a business. Studying financial theory is fine but it provides little preparation for the nasty emotional issues that inevitably surface in the real world. Schools may convey knowledge, but not necessarily how to apply it in the entrepreneurial landscape. The owner of a business degree has learned to research and think. That is a good thing – but those skills must be applied in the real world. Complex management models and formulas become useful as the entrepreneur blossoms and grows his or her company. That said, never pass up an education opportunity. Never. A college education is invaluable. Just don't expect it to fully prepare you for the perilous swamp you will enter after emerging from the academia jungle. Working or interning with a company in your industry of interest might better prepare you to launch a new idea or product than education alone.

I was fortunate because my middle-class family saved for my tuition to attend a private business college. I also had the unusual advantage of accumulating eight years' experience as a business owner before I was awarded a diploma. This allowed me to recognize the stark difference between the textbooks and the trenches. I once questioned what this empirical collage of theory had to do with running a business. I ultimately came to realize the real world is based upon theory and that schools teach the kind of abstract thinking that inspires the birth of theories when important facts are unknown, like unseen peril beneath the murky surface of a swamp. No education is perfect, of course. But wading into the swamp without a fundamental business background is very dangerous indeed. Too many entrepreneurs learn their lessons the hard way, blindly diving into risky ventures destined to explode. Accountants and other professionals attain continuing education credits and support their professional associations; dedicated business owners are no less professional. Brain exercise is mandatory for business success. Business management is a balance of art and science. It's dynamic, too. Entrepreneurs must pay close attention to innovative managerial theories as well as important changes in legal standards and accounting practices. Business management experience often is the difference between ventures that "swim" and those that "sink." Acquiring the insight of a seasoned entrepreneur can be as challenging as learning to litigate or perform surgery. A physician is expected to master one science; entrepreneurs master as many skills as their time and talent will allow. Management talent is easier to identify than to emulate. That's why a truckload of smart doctors and smart lawyers couldn't squeeze profits from a lemonade stand if the lemons were free. Squeezing out profits is your profession, not theirs!

Time and Money

Many entrepreneurs run out of money, but some just run out of time. One whose time ran out was a heroic fellow named Harry Raymond. When I was a young boy, Harry was a contractor who visited our home to bid for a job to install a tile floor in our kitchen. Fifty years later, he called my business consulting office for an appointment.

Long before "green" became a buzzword for environmental conservation, Harry founded RayCore®, a manufacturer of energy-efficient polyurethane panels for the building industry. He engaged in a 19-year struggle to convince people to accept his story: this product was much easier to install and it cut energy costs by 40 percent, compared with competitive products.

What went wrong? Harry painstakingly reminisced about funding cash shortages and relentless testing, certification and production challenges. I agreed to support his dream to achieve industry leadership. But it soon became obvious there were just as many people who wanted to keep his unique product off the market to protect their own selfish interests as there were people who wanted it on the market. Harry was aging. He had pitched the RayCore story a thousand times. He was tired and discouraged that no one enthusiastically embraced the product. But the moment the name RayCore left his lips, Harry sat up, re-energized himself, became positive and demanded we continue forward.

His tiny plant eventually closed. Harry later died. But his product did not. His grandson, Bryan Brusman, restarted the firm in Idaho, resumed production of the polyurethane panels, and in 2011, the business his grandfather founded was chosen as Idaho's Small Business of the Year.

The business swamp can be a frightening place. But almost no obstacle can deter dogged business owners like Harry who are destined to battle against long odds until their last breath. This entrepreneur pursued his dream for two decades and fully believed his business would ultimately succeed. I was honored to be a small part of the process. This, my friends, is a true entrepreneur.

What Might Stop You?

The essence of entrepreneurship is dealing with unknowns. So, what might kill your business are your intellectual and emotional reactions to the unseen, the untested, and the unimagined. Your real enemy is "FUD." It is the biggest roadblock to success. It feeds low self-esteem, insecurity and pointless anxiety. It may stop you from taking manageable risks. You must face "FUD" head on.

    F = **F**ear
    U = **U**ncertainty
    D = **D**oubt

FUD will kill your dreams. So, tame fear. Let those whom you encounter sense that you have no fear. Better yet, let them think you're half-crazed and dangerous. Learn how to intimidate people on the rare occasions it's necessary.

Nothing dissuades potential entrepreneurs, or "wanna-preneurs," more than FUD and the threat of humiliating failure. Surrendering the thrill of pursuing success for the mundane processing of tasks that other leaders assign can crush your spirit. An ancient Japanese saying describes fear as "the little death, death by a thousand cuts." Fear has no place in your long-term future.

FUD will stifle your career if you believe old adages such as "it takes money to make money" and all the other idiotic reasons people invent to discourage the ambitious and take comfort in their own fear and failure. If FUD becomes your roadblock, then you will need to study ways to manage it.

I never feared business risk or ever surrendered to FUD. I had more to worry about than the unknown. As a young man, I traveled the world and lived well. My fear was losing that lifestyle. But there was never a fear of business on my part, nor should there be for you.

What Is Your Weapon Against FUD?

If you're interacting with bright and successful people, you inevitably come away with unforgettable insights. For example, a man who served as mayor of Williamsport, Pennsylvania, took me to a hamburger joint one day and told me "three Bs" were necessary for success throughout your career:

B = Brains

B = Balls

B = Backing

If you're somewhat unintelligent, you probably network with people who are, too. If you don't own a set of balls (including the ladies), you'll never pull the trigger. And, if you don't have any backing or thrust, you won't get off the ground.

Know your personal needs hierarchy, and be aware that your

needs may change with age. Despite elderly magnates like Col. Hartman Sanders, who at 65 decided it was time to launch a national chicken restaurant chain, people's tolerance for risk tends to drop as they age.

So, if you want to roll the dice in a calculated way, start a business when you are single, a DINK (dual income/no kids) or while you're young, not when you're applying for admission to an assisted living facility. It is not true that only old, mean people get rich. Young leaders can make a lot of money, generate employment, tax revenue, excitement and opportunity for others and have fun in the process!

Trust No One

Lopsided deals tend to fall apart over time. The fast buck will sometimes fall on your lap, but generally speaking, the road to success is long. Entrepreneurs who are anxious to devour everything in front of them and take pleasure from slicing someone up ultimately learn that business is not a "win-lose" proposition. Instead, success comes from "win-win" deals. This is not to say that you are responsible for protecting the other guy; it isn't your job. But you do have an ethical responsibility to do the right thing. Fairness makes practical sense, too. Those who deal unethically, or who are aloof, brash, uncaring and unfair in business are long-term losers. Leaders face a monumental responsibility because many people depend on them.

There are plenty of books on professional ethics that make one thing clear: unethical business people never win for long. They just don't. While the tenor of my approach might suggest otherwise, there are lines you do not cross. Being fast, hard, efficient, focused and tough in business is requisite. But so is being honest and fair.

In my mid-20s, I met a sweet old lady, who was once an accomplished musician, and sold her a pipe organ. She was one of those special customers and my wife and I checked on her from time to time. Insisting we come for dinner one evening, she served a surprising statement, along with a meal that tasted like spoiled rat. She said, "Honey I'd like you to build your new home next door to me." This was one of the most desirable parcels around, atop a cliff with a spectacular view of a valley and with little nearby development. We agreed to her price and purchased the land.

Shortly thereafter, a major denomination preacher essentially told me that my plan to build a home on that parcel would punish orphaned children. He represented that my friend, that sweet old lady, had promised the land for my future cliff-top home to his church, which supposedly wanted to build an orphanage there. Certainly my wife and I could never be comfortable knowing we displaced underprivileged children, so we reversed the transaction. Soon thereafter, our friend, the sweet old lady, passed away, and the preacher and his family moved into her estate. The only children who ever resided on that cliff-top location mountain were his own. The preacher wanted it for himself. As crass as this may sound, you can't trust anyone. Not even the agents of Jesus Christ.

Ethics for Entrepreneurs

No matter what other people do, you should be ethical. Daily business decisions are immersed in the principles of appropriate conduct, and your decisions may affect many people who are already skeptical of your motives. A 1989 survey conducted by Louis Harris and Associates, based on 2,000 interviews, revealed that 42 percent of people felt that "most businessmen will do anything, honest or not, for a buck," and 77 percent regarded business as a "dog-eat-dog proposition." Young people share a strong opinion that businesspeople lack morality. A Purdue University panel found that one quarter of participating teenagers agreed that "most business concerns are out to make all the money they can, no matter who gets hurt." How could they not with the likes of men like Bernie Madoff, who concocted the largest Ponzi scheme in U.S. history?

Entrepreneurs, marketing people, purchasing agents and sales staff may be typically less ethical than, say a personnel director or accountant. But most people in business are viewed as being less ethical than in other professions.

Christian-based liberal arts colleges are more apt to require a course on this subject within their theology department, but most often it's an elective, if offered at all. Some believe it's not the job of universities to teach ethics. Every student should choose Ethics in Business over the Science of Superheros 101. Otherwise, they may find themselves ill equipped to dissect a decision because most come in shades of gray, rather than black or white.

There is a world of opinions on what is ethically or morally correct. Pure moralists say a good end never justifies a bad means, but just what is a bad means? I believe you must devise your own principles of conduct. You must learn how to reach the best ethical decisions, and appreciate the reality of your need to be morally good in business.

American professor Joseph Fletcher said there are only three alternative approaches to follow when making a moral decision:

- The Legalistic
- The Antinomian
- The Situational

The legalistic, or pure law without deviation, will fail on your first day at the office. The antinomian is the extreme opposite with no principals, so this won't work unless you want to sell placebo drugs via the Internet. This only leaves you with the situational, and thus, it is an important approach to understand.

Fletcher believes that situation ethics goes part of the way with natural law, by accepting reason as the instrument of moral judgment while rejecting the notion that the good is "given" in the nature of things, objectively. It goes part of the way with scriptural law, by accepting revelation as the source of the norm while rejecting all "revealed" norm or laws but the one command: to love God in the neighbor. The situationalist follows a moral law, or violates it, according to love's need. Only the commandment to love is categorically good. "Owe no one anything, except to love one another." (Rom. 13:8)

Your obligation is relative to the situation, but obligation in the situation is absolute. We are only "obliged" to tell the truth, for example, if the situation calls for it; if a murderer asks us his victim's whereabouts, our duty might be to lie. The core of the ethic is that it describes a healthy and primary awareness that "circumstances alter cases." Situational factors are so primary that we may even say "circumstances alter rules and principles." Situation ethics are sensitive to variety and complexity within the gray areas the businessman must operate.

The classic rule of moral theology has been to follow laws but do it as much as possible according to love and according to reason. Situation ethics, on the other hand, call upon us to keep law in a subservient place, so that only love and reason really count when the chips are down.

If a lie is told unlovingly it is wrong; if it is told in love it is good, right? If an entrepreneur chooses to do something good and not excusably bad, the situationalist holds that whatever the most loving thing in the situation is the right and good thing. It is not excusably evil, it is positively good.

I have always been guided by "situation ethics." As president of a large snack food company that was losing money for reasons unveiled in this book, I engaged a consulting firm to study production and identify areas of waste. One was a container cost and one a transportation cost. I concluded that if I did not stop the container production, change the packaging, and terminate West Coast distributors, the company could not survive. Not only would this decision shake the foundation of the image upon which the company was built, it would result in an immediate loss of production, trucking and sales jobs. Based on that situation, I concluded that it was more important to save all of the other workers and distributors than to avoid hurting 300 people. I pulled the trigger. Given that situation, it was the only ethical principle that I could adopt.

Being ethical is a wise practice for other reasons. If you treat people fairly, your subordinates will mimic your ideals, and your customers will return.

Be Ethical, But Harden Up

Success breeds envy, gossip and revenge, so plan for all of that and more. Harden your emotional shield against mindless personal attacks. When I drove my new Caddy to senior high school, even the teachers believed I must be a drug dealer. That local hometown rumor stayed with me for a long time, despite my filing a slander lawsuit against a disgruntled former employee who fostered the myth. Sadly, perception can become reality in the idle minds of others. So harden up because you will never succeed if you care what gossipers say.

The bigger your business becomes, the more people you employ and the more projects you undertake, the more potshots you'll need to fend off. Which newspaper headline do you think will pique interest?

IRS FILES LIEN ON PROMINENT BUSINESSMAN'S ASSETS
or
LOCAL COMPANY SUPPORTS CANCER CENTER

No matter how much good you do, the nature of news is to report the dirty stuff because it sells. When things go well, you might get a public pat on the back, but when things go south, expect hate mail. As you mature, these attacks will cause you less emotional distress. But they probably will never stop.

It's good that Facebook's entrepreneur extraordinaire Mark Zuckerberg is a fencing enthusiast; he's already been attacked several times. There was even a movie portraying him as a thief. Worse, the Department of Justice sued Bill Gates' company in 1999 (U.S. v Microsoft) because it had "become a monopoly and stifled competition." The DOJ said it was acting in the best interest of consumers. We don't need protection from Bill Gates, who bequeaths $3 billion each year to people in need; we need protection from the DOJ! Gates believed that if he worked hard he would be successful. But, Uncle Sam is always watching over your shoulder and he is not always fair-minded.

What Will Give You An Edge?

Not every entrepreneur can muster the mastery of Bill Gates or Apple legend Steve Jobs. But almost any entrepreneur can commit to daily habits that reduce his or her reliance on sheer luck to get rich. Here are seven habits I strongly recommend:

1. Get things done on time.

2. Pay attention to detail.

3. Do your business homework.

4. Delegate to others all that they can comfortably handle.

5. Take decisive action with facts and common sense.

6. Employ a little showmanship in your presentations.

7. Reinvest profits, but stay liquid.

The Entrepreneur

Some skills are harder to master. The typical entrepreneur has three weaknesses that demand more than just a change in daily habits: negotiating deals, documenting agreements and managing the use of their time.

Negotiation Skills

If you still want to enter the business swamp after reading this chapter, your excursion must be managed. If nothing will drown your enthusiasm and energy, then you can enjoy success beyond description. And to start, you must become a master of negotiation. Whether buying a diamond for your fiancé or a piece of equipment for your factory, or whether trying to convince someone to marry you in the first place, nothing is more important than learning how to get what you want. Nothing.

The art of negotiation is rarely taught in universities. Nevertheless, negotiating is a learned art. It is governed by the same psychological and sociological principles of other social interactions. So, like any art, it can be studied and rehearsed. Lawyers attend negotiation classes and so can you. Just as entrepreneurship is a discipline and learned mindset, you can learn to negotiate. One simple negotiating tip in this book could save you tens of thousands of dollars every year. But that will be a minuscule gain after you master the skill.

This is a skill that you must practice and polish. Your entire success will depend on your ability to subtlety convince others to achieve what you need in order to move forward. This is your job and you should seldom rely on third parties, especially lawyers and other professionals, to do it for you. Rarely will they achieve your goals.

Your weapons will be knowledge, details and preparedness. It is critical that you memorize the deal issues and practice what you intend to say – all the time having alternate plans in mind. No matter how strong your opponents might be, your preciseness, focus and command of the situation will weaken them. Preparation is a competition killer. Sloppy, lazy people neglect to rehearse for a negotiation as if it were a public performance.

Before performing a musical concert, I typically rehearse 10 hours for each hour of stage time. When I touch the keyboard, I want to know that I'm totally in command of the work. And, I treat an important negotiation session with the same preparedness. Even more so because I am often representing the interests of my clients, not just my own.

Researching the opposing negotiator is part of this preparation. Lawyers often contact other lawyers to learn the demeanor of a judge, or the style of an opponent. I've often run a Dun & Bradstreet report to learn the financial condition of the opposing party. How badly do they want or need the deal and can they come up with the money? This is what separates professional businesspeople from hackers.

If your surroundings are impressive or intimidating, bring others to your turf. And occasionally, you may need to rough them up a bit. But don't attempt serious negotiations electronically. That's why we have jets.

Never relax and take comfort thinking that your opponent is an honest, nice guy. He is the enemy so treat him accordingly, but respectfully. Or, not. Accusatory, arrogant and abrasive behavior sometimes will produce the intended result. Let the adversary know you are serious and intense. Whether your style evolves as aggressive or calm, you should first convey sincerity, credibility and confidence. Sometimes it just doesn't work. So, be sweet and nice or intimidate the hell out of them — whatever it takes.

Don't be delusional. Your opponents have no love for you. They are not your friends, even if they purport to be. Go ahead and act like you're buddies, but be mindful that you're not. They are not on your side of the desk. They do not care whether you meet loan payments or if you can fund your children's college educations.

It's OK to say things like, "Melanie, you know I respect your talent, but you also know damn well you just fed me a line of baloney and I came here to get the deal done so lets not play with each other." Then, don't smile.

Never make a concession unless you get something in return from adversarial negotiators. Speak at their pace. Listen, learn and ask questions more than you talk. And even if you live in the Carolinas, take the damn polo shirt off and dress like a professional.

Don't buy into your opponent's nonsense, which is mostly what they will feed you — especially if they're good. And take your time, because fast deals only shove further negotiations into the future as the need for details arises, and the deal you thought you negotiated comes undone.

Know when to invite others to attend negotiating sessions, especially if you're not comfortable with your own skill level. It is said that one requires 800 hours of negotiating experience to become proficient. So, there are times to bring in a highly trained third party, especially when you want to play "bad-guy, good-guy."

Generally speaking, he who speaks first loses. When you do make an offer, be aggressive; you can always come up. Start low and go high and — if the other negotiator accepts your first number — you just left money on the table. So be careful if you decide to show your hand.

Ultimate success typically is comprised of many small gains. You should never be too busy to negotiate for $50 off a monthly janitorial contract. Neither life, nor business, have many shortcuts. Thus, each and every time you purchase something, hire someone or make any other business decision, you must be committed to negotiating a good deal.

You may need to conjure up a little greed in the process. Treat money with respect. Whether greed is innate or not, walking away from the table feeling that you "got what you needed" can be a real high.

Never convey a dire need to complete the deal. Learn to walk away; there will be new opportunities if you create them (or old ones that will come around again). Walking away is simply another tactic. Recently I sold a large amount of real estate after the buyer took a two-year hiatus from negotiations. There are times to push hard for a close and times to wait it out.

Negotiating and selling whatever you have in your bag has got to be the cornerstone of your success. Read a dozen books and take some courses, because it's magic. And someday, when you finally figure it out, it will revolutionize your thinking. It will be a gift you earned, and it will bring you success. Read more about negotiation tactics in chapter 9.

Time Management

Another non-textbook skill to master is the art of time management. You must run your day; it cannot run you. This is a learned skill that many entrepreneurs seem to lack. Why should they care? They are idea people.

A college education forces one to be reasonably organized, which is every bit as important as gaining knowledge. But you need to learn more ways to preserve time once you're in the business swamp. Things happen at a much faster pace, so you will need to improve your timeliness as well.

Meetings are often a waste of time. Blah, blah, blah. If you must have a meeting, distribute an agenda and set a time limit. Always divert telephone calls to staff and review written, detailed messages and have your staff return the call. Telephone time wasters will clog up your day. Utilize "to-do" lists. STOP people from stealing your time.

Other time wasters include unnecessary communication, unimportant appointments, an inability to say no, excessive accessibility, needless interruptions, workplace disorganization, vague priorities and under-staffing. These are only a few factors that will erode your performance.

Excluding the world of electronics, my two best time savers have always been a simple recording device and the use of personal assistants. No need for word processing, carry a recording device and have staff type and implement your plans vis-à-vis emails, letters and directives. And, while we all may enjoy shopping for personal items, you should not be making a trip to the dry cleaner. Pay your assistants to handle mundane business tasks.

Time truly is money. As you begin to place a dollar value on your time and visualize the cost of spending it poorly, you will waste less of it. I'm astonished at how much time people manage to waste, including seasoned entrepreneurs with loads of

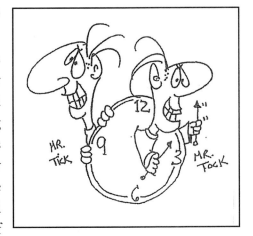

experience. You should pump out five times the amount of work that a newbie produces in the same amount of time.

Don't start your day like it's a social event. Start to win the game fast, hard and efficiently. Don't spend an hour looking at Facebook posts. Don't take long martini lunches. And sure as hell don't go out for a round of golf because you bought into the myth that "you can do a lot of business on the golf course." Once in my career, at the invitation of a bank president, I had an opportunity to meet important people on a golf course. But only once. This is a sport for players and partiers, not doers. When your financial ratios ultimately allow, you may want to enjoy the luxury of doing business at the club, but it probably isn't for you. I don't know anyone who embraces social time and hosts more parties than I do – but only after the work is done.

Beware of mixing business with friendship. While some of your revenue stream may be derived from solid personal relationships, don't depend on them, especially in large or complex transactions. Friends don't always pay for what they get, and you're the culprit when disputes and collection activities ensue. How can you enforce a contract with people who are your friends? Look elsewhere for business. Moreover, you will ultimately use up the potential of door openers and opportunities that your friends can provide. Meet new people.

The Internet is a popular route for professional networking via such websites as LinkedIn. But, networking too can quickly become a time waster. Students are now being told of the "ping" in business, and that networking with a lot of people is an important use of time. Certainly good contacts are invaluable. But if you want to network, then do it for kicks and don't expect anything in return. Your aficionado friends may give you moral support as they armchair quarterback, but their advice is usually wrong. If you want advice, pay your accountant, business adviser or lawyer, or contact people within your own industry. Well-intended folks can't help you. You'll do the "ping" and get none of the "pong."

Go to work instead of wasting your time building false hopes, hiding from FUD and taking comfort that your friends have a safety net. Work longer hours, call more prospects and cut another deal. That is how you'll grow your company. Then, after you're rich, invite your friends out on your catamaran for an evening. Temper your desire to make friends with the world and stay focused on your operation. If you want to network, do it with people who are already cutting you a check – or those who might cut one. Treat them to fine dining and wine. If you take care of them, they will take care of you. At least most of the time. Well, maybe sometimes.

Document Everything

Entrepreneurs simply must embrace written and electronic

contracts. Business disputes suck up valuable time. Handshake deals are dead; document everything. American culture, in contrast to other cultures, encourages a belief that the world should be perfect, fair and just. Well, it isn't. There is little justice. There is more law. And despite excessive business regulation, there are more despicable business operators today than ever. The government can't keep abreast of the complaints, and it is your job to protect your own assets.

Throughout the last several decades, business ethics have eroded dramatically. Sadly, your probability of getting screwed has increased. It isn't a question of whether it will happen, it's only when and how, and how much will it hurt.

Even under contract, people default on commitments. If you're not inquisitive enough to write your own contracts, then retain a lawyer or borrow one from someone else. But if you think you're going through this swamp on verbal deals, you're simply delusional. At the end of the day, nothing will matter except what you have in writing. That is, unless, you want to pay a lawyer to litigate over "he said, she said" with no sure outcome.

Recently one of my clients offered a sign-on bonus in a help-wanted advertisement. Two applicants refused to sign a non-compete agreement and in exchange, waived the sign-on bonus. After nearly a year of employment, both employees quit without notice, to open a competing business, sued my client's company for payment of the sign-on bonus, and won the case.

Why? Because the employment terms were not reduced to writing. One piece of paper with one sentence "I, George Greedy, hereby waive the 'sign-on' bonus offered in the newspaper" would have saved the day.

I once had lunch with the owners of a chain of hotels and told them a Perkins restaurant would work well in their operation. They told me to draw up a contract and contact Perkins. They did the proverbial "end-run" and immediately contacted Perkins themselves and purchased the franchise. No ethics and no paper. How many of these actual accounts would you like to read before you adopt the fact that you must do business in writing?

Contractor behavior is the best justification to paper everything. In my experience, you have an 80 percent chance of being cheated by almost every contractor you will ever retain. As former television talk-show host David Letterman once asked a contractor in his audience, "So, tell me, are all you guys crooks?" A pseudo-contractor with a pick-up truck, a tool chest and an account at Lowe's will screw you out of greed or stupidity. You will find some basic contract outlines to help prevent those losses in Chapter 17.

Naturally, cheating can move in more than one direction. Contractors who accept jobs with one-page proposals containing no specifications or terms will just as quickly be screwed. Everyone needs to paper everything because everybody wants to sleaze out of financial obligations.

Too cynical? Perhaps. But business owners who do not employ these skills are those who eventually will call consulting firms like mine, seeking a way to save their business from failure. So, document it – or lose it.

The Path to Profitable Exit Strategies

As a visionary and long-term thinker, you will operate your business as though you are going to sell it soon, so you will keep it clean and well organized. If you're a slob, your business will be a dirty mess. You must contemplate failure as much as success. Plan not only for an easy and profitable exit from your business if you succeed but also for a soft landing or bailout if you fail. Get used to the fact that most businesses ultimately are sold or liquidated, and acknowledge the possibility that you could become a serial entrepreneur, not just a one-business owner.

The right path to a profitable exit from business ownership is often unclear. As I warned in the preface of this book, my recommendations are full of generalizations. Perhaps you can toss some aside, beat the odds and luck out. But if you want to lower your risks and save yourself heartaches, you'll probably need to adopt many of the recommendations.

This book is about tap-dancing, tricking, maneuvering, dodging, blocking and beating down competitors, government bureaucrats, dishonest employees and other obstacle makers who complicate your business. Then, once you make a whole lot of money and wash off all the swamp gunk, you can throw rocks at all the other poor slobs trying stay afloat in the water, assuming you don't adopt situation ethics.

Most people want the safety of a guaranteed paycheck. They don't share your desire for personal achievement, independence and financial gain. Only you see the big picture. As the early 20th Century American steel industry leader Charles M. Schwab said, "A man to carry on a successful business must have imagination. He must see things as in a vision, a dream of the whole thing."

Seeking Safety or Risk?

Working for a paycheck is safer than pursuing an entrepreneurial dream, but it is less captivating for people who crave being their own boss. Self-employed people make up less than 20 percent of American workers but account for two-thirds of its millionaires. Despite the global financial panic and Wall Street debacle of 2008, the U.S. population of millionaires is still the world's largest at 10.4 million and counting. To be among them, you must develop a lifestyle of hard work, discipline, planning and perseverance. Are you ready? Do you want to try to succeed using cash as the yardstick? If the answer is yes, read on.

Tips To Keep You Afloat

> Make certain you have the stomach to be an entrepreneur.

> If confused about whether to start or finish business studies, don't be a fool and stay in school.

> Fear, uncertainty and doubt (FUD) will kill your dreams.

> Confront FUD with the Three Bs.

> Strive to create "win-win" deals.

> Unethical businesspeople are losers.

> The envious relish taking cheap shots at successful people.

> The cornerstone of your career is the art of negotiating.

> Success usually comes in small gains.

> Time management and multi-tasking are crucial to success.

> Don't rely on friends to solve your problems.

> Become a contract maniac or you'll lose every time.

> Pull the trigger and take a chance on entrepreneurial success or you could end up doing some mundane job for the rest of your life, or being walked out the door after 25 years of service because of down-sizing.

2. THE PLAN

> *"Our goals can only be reached through a vehicle of a plan, in which we must fervently believe, and upon which we must vigorously act. There is no other route to success."*
> *Pablo Picasso*

Make a map. The path to big money is usually murky. Plan carefully for your romp in the swamp. Maybe you're one of the lucky few. Maybe you don't need a business plan. Many successful entrepreneurs have started companies with nothing in writing. I've seen plans written on napkins. But if you need money from investors or lenders, you need a detailed, written plan. And besides, given the high mortality rate of small business, the odds favor planning. Unless you have more money than you really need, writing a formal business plan is rarely a waste of time. Rewriting is warranted sometimes, too, if your plan is flawed. My list of the 22 most common reasons for business failures, which appears later in this chapter, can serve as a guide to writing a new plan or fixing a flawed one.

Mission Statements – The Focus of Your Business

First, determine your true mission. Before you write a business plan, consider writing a brief Mission Statement. A good one answers big questions in few words. What is your business? Who will be your customers? What reputation do you seek? Why will your business survive? An effective Mission Statement clearly describes your company's purpose and goal and why your approach to the market will be superior to others. Post your mission statement for everyone to see. Declare where you are going and the values you will embrace to get there. If your business is a surgery center, for example, your mission statement may read something like this:

> We will fully educate patients about surgical procedures and will offer advanced, high-quality accessible care. We will deliver safe, consistent and supportive patient treatment. We will employ compassionate physicians and staff with a warm concern for individual dignity and uncompromising commitment to patient satisfaction. Our highly trained and personable technicians will do their job with integrity. This is our pledge of excellence.

As former Prime Minister Margaret Thatcher once said, "Plan your work, and work your plan." In other words, write your own plan and let it breathe. Don't treat a business plan as if it were cast in stone. Keep rolling with it until it gives the right answers to the five Ws of a business plan:

- Who are you? What is your experience? What are your credentials?
- What do you have to sell, and how will you sell it?
- When do you plan to start, or reboot, your business?
- Where do you plan to operate?
- Why will you succeed?

Specify your goals and objectives, and how you're going to get there. Explain to readers why your venture is interesting or exceptional. Include details such as industry trends and owner/management team expertise. Show off your experienced team, or access to expertise. You may want to do a SWOT analysis* of strengths, weaknesses, opportunities and threats. This, coupled with a Source & Use of Funds* will give potential investors an insight as to how their funds will be expended and how you plan to grow your business.

Some universities offer support for writing a business plan. Others host business plan competitions that give participants a great opportunity to learn from the judges. Another potential source of help is SCORE (Service Corps of Retired Executives), a nationwide nonprofit associated with the U.S. Small Business Administration and dedicated to entrepreneur education.

While you may need a plan to attract lenders or investors, you may also need it as a swamp guide. Business mistakes are costly. A comprehensive and accurate plan can help you avoid mistakes. The most critical section of your business plan is its financial projection. You must anticipate sales, expenses and profit. New entrepreneurs often get waterlogged at this juncture because they have never estimated revenue before. This will be of utmost interest to lenders and investors because they want to know how you intend to pay them back. You can learn to create a forecast of revenue*. If you are considering the purchase of an ongoing business, you will find a revenue-forecasting approach in the section on business valuations. I recently worked with a client from Iceland who had a wonderful sounding concept, but his plan was full of unverified assumptions... so his project was never funded.

Demonstrate that you have done your due diligence and that you keep abreast of industry changes, with references to trade journal articles and websites with industry research. There is most likely a state or national association that represents the best interests of your industry, and several monthly magazines filled with helpful, industry-specific information. Regional and national conventions provide relevant seminars. So get to work. There is no excuse for failing to do your homework.

First Plan the Pitch, Then Pitch the Plan

When your homework is done, it's time to pitch your plan. But first, you must plan your pitch. Your pitch is as important as your plan! Your sales presentation should be neat and organized, containing only information that is relevant and of interest to your audience. If you feel the need to provide great detail, add exhibits.

PowerPoint is an excellent way to present your plan to investors. Bullet point lists can be used to convey the most important pieces of information without making your presentation look too busy or unorganized. Elaborate on each bullet point topic with the facts, statistics, and research you have prepared. Lenders and investors always have people chasing after their money, so improve your chances by making your plan accessible and inspiring; use your presentation to show you are passionate about your potential business venture.

Practice your pitch. Remember that you're the lead actor in a play. Write your lines. Even if your project is to grow bean sprouts, put some pizazz into it. Rehearse by role-playing with your friends. Anticipate questions that might stump you, and have good answers prepared. Practice so much you simply can't be jittery. Never appear pathetically needy. Learn the names and backgrounds of the people to whom you will make your pitch.

Save your best pitch for the biggest hitter in the lineup. Identify the real decision makers to conserve your time. If further information is requested, provide it quickly. Remember, finding funds is a numbers game, so pitch early and often. The more balls you toss into the air, the better the chance that one will land right in your pocket.

How Healthy Must You Be?

Industry research can enable those of you already in business to compare your performance to others. Financial ratios are comparable indicators of health and performance. Financial reports* should be formatted to provide a clear view of operations. If your business is in the pre-startup phase, you can develop a projected balance sheet* to enhance your tap dance for investors and lenders. Generally, businesses stay healthy by maintaining five financial vital signs:

- Solvency: Comparing long-term debt to short-term debt. This indicates whether you will meet long-term obligations.

- Liquidity: Comparing short-term assets to short-term liabilities. The higher the ratio, the more likely you'll be meeting short-term obligations.

- Leverage: Measuring risk by comparing debt to equity or assets. A lower proportion of debt suggests less risk.

- Efficiency: Measuring costs through such comparisons as operating expenses to total sales.

- Profitability: Measuring your company's ability to generate operating profits and positive cash flow.

Good industry research also will allow you to compare your performance and size to others in the same business. Become acquainted with your industry's business activity code or SIC number* (which is shown on your tax return), and use those comparables to test your progress.

Is Bigger Better?

Bigger isn't necessarily better in business. Small is safe, and if you want to grow, you must commit to more time, resources and risk. Definitions of "small business" vary by source. The U.S. Small Business Administration, National Industrial Conference Board, Investment Banker's Association and other organizations have defined the term in somewhat different characteristics. The most widely used yardstick is the number of employees. Some definitions permit as many as 500 for a "small" business. Some make sales of less than $200,000 per year the defining characteristic. A business may be described as "small" when compared to larger firms, and "large" when compared to smaller ones. According to the SBA, there were 30.2 million small businesses in the United States in 2018, employing 58.9 million people.

By any definition, small businesses often have fleeting lives. Sadly, small business survival odds aren't great. Two-thirds of new employer establishments survive only two years and less than half are still around after four years. Unprepared entrepreneurs would be better off gambling in Vegas.

The existence of small businesses is every bit as important as the presence of large ones. All big businesses, after all, were once small. Many owners of small businesses invest far more in their communities than large chains. However, the big boys are treated differently. A small business will enjoy fewer public-policy perks and will encounter more governmental roadblocks to success than bigger, richer competitors. Yet blow-hard politicians continuously say how important small businesses are. It's enough to make you sick. But keep your head up. Become keenly aware of laws and politicians because they impact your ability to survive, though few lawmakers have ever walked in your shoes.

Most of our past presidents are pathetically unfamiliar with business. Most of the members of the executive and legislative branches have never been in your situation — even though they set policies and define the playing field for small business owners. But no public policy can eliminate the oversized disadvantages facing small business owners. Just as volume discounts and other economies of scale benefit big businesses, "diseconomies of scale" afflict the little guys.

Small Business Returns on Investment

Oftentimes, my clients ask why they are not earning the same percentage of profit as they open new markets. My first store with 800 square feet produced annual sales of $300,000 while my second store with 2,200 square feet only produced $175,000 in sales. But as I grew and took advantage of more buying power, cross-marketing economies, broader inventory and sharing of expenses, the total dollar profit grew rapidly. This is why a profitable Papa Johns franchisee may need a half-dozen outlets to make it a hot investment. Most diseconomies occur in the early-growth stages of a young company. The first three years are the dangerous growth years.

22 Reasons Your Business Might Fail

Businesses flop for any number of reasons. Being outsized and outmatched is just one. In my experience, the following 22 culprits are the most common:

1. Naivety.

Namby-pamby parents coddle their kids. These spoiled children become adult pushovers, so they're totally disarmed when they meet the first real culprit who strips them of the "balls" part of the 3Bs. If your parents are wimpy, hang out with some hard-core business owners and listen to how they scratched their way to the top.

2. Poor image.

People do judge a book by its cover. The same goes for companies and their names and logos. Before you name your bakery after your dog, invest a little time and money to develop your company's brand and image. This seemingly simple step can make or break a business operation.

3. Under-capitalization.

Credit can kill. Your friendly loan officer will give you just enough money to hang yourself. If your plan says you need $250,000 then, of course, they will want to negotiate down to $150,000. It's almost impossible to "go back to the well" to raise more cash when you unexpectedly run low. If you run out of capital mid-stream in the swamp, you're probably going under. Start-up artists tend to be too optimistic regarding potential revenue and the amount of capital they will require. Keep six months of operating capital in reserve for a new business because events and circumstances seldom evolve as anticipated.

4. Spending trust taxes.

Payroll and sales taxes are called "trust" taxes because the government entrusts employers to collect them and forward them on. This isn't your rainy-day slush fund. It belongs to the taxpayers, and if you don't pay it, you are a thief. Also, if you don't pay your taxes, the interest and penalties could put you out of business. Even if you file a Chapter 11 bankruptcy, trust tax obligations may not be discharged.

Always pay trust taxes first. If you fail to do so, file an appeal of the penalties; you might prevail the first time, if you come up with the right excuse. Mental problems are best. The IRS believes if both your legs are in a cast, you can still call an accountant to file. But being nuts is a much better excuse. A side benefit of retaining a firm to handle your payroll is that they demand all wages and taxes be paid each pay period.

5. Failure to negotiate hard for all of your purchases.

Everything is negotiable. Whatever you buy, negotiate the best deal. Here's a line to think about: "It isn't what you sell, it's about what you keep." Resist overspending instigators: laziness, failure to develop budgets, and a lack of respect for money.

6. My 92% Rule.

I have a concept that could save you tens of thousands of dollars each year. It's my "92% Rule." Shop around and obtain two or three quotes. Then, call the vendor with the lowest price. Explain that you want to do business because you like them, you like their product, you want to buy locally, a friend referred you, or whatever cheap reason you conjure up. But, then you say that the price is just a bit higher than other quotes and your partners, your budget or your spouse just won't allow you "to pay too much for that muffler." The vendor will drop your price by 8%, or more. Eight percent times your discretionary expenses each year will grow into a big sum of money. I am so very confident that a good negotiator will attain this reduction that I often offered to work for clients with my total fee being simply the money I could save on their purchases. This 8% savings could be more than your annual income!

7. Wrong target.

Get real. Your business plan is an intangible desire that must be realistic. Carefully craft a plan with hittable targets, not impossible ones. This is your swamp map, and since you can't see the bottom, you must exercise all due diligence to stay afloat, which means targeting the right niche in the right industry. Don't force things. Don't engineer circumstances and invent numbers to fit into your plan just because your ass is on fire to start a new company.

8. Overestimating cash flow and underestimating expenses.

You will need several tools in your bag to avoid this mistake. First, you must begin with an existing seller's trend or forecasted revenue*. Next, obtain industry ratios for each line item of expense, utilizing various sources. Your best barometer is a trade association; some compile financial data from all of their members. So if the industry says its members spend 6.3 percent of sales on advertising, then you should budget for that amount (and budget more in your first year).

9. Failure to develop a good management team.

If you are starting a business with minimal overhead and need an affordable source of expertise, form a corporation and recruit smart directors. Invite insurance agents, accountants and other professionals to sit on your board. Many will be honored when asked, and most decent entrepreneurs will want to support a newcomer. Your lenders will love this aspect of your plan.

10. Ineffective or non-existent marketing.

Create a marketing plan and stay within your budget. Incorporating social media can be an efficient way to generate awareness of your brand. So, utilize sites and applications that are "hot" and spend your money wisely. While marketing will be a crucial part of growing your business, be wary of alligators in the ad industry. Advertising salespeople will sell a bill of goods. They'll tell you anything to take a chunk of your budget, and in most cases, you're not going to get much bang for the buck.

11. Ignoring customer needs and preferences.

Communicate with your customers and learn what motivates them. You and your employees must have intense interaction with customers online, in the field or on your premises. Make certain you have the goods or services they want, not what some commissioned sales rep wants you to stock. Too many companies believe the crap vendors feed them instead of listening to customers. From delivery personnel to receptionists to IT technicians, everyone in the organization must be customer-oriented. This is your business lifeline.

12. Trying to sell from an empty wagon.

"Stack 'em high, price 'em low, out they go." Variety is the spice of business life. The more you have, the more you sell. While it's often said you get 80% of your sales from 20% of your products, your store or menu of services should be brimming with buying options for customers. If you sell products, make your suppliers fund the cost of a full store vis-à-vis better terms. Merchandise does them more good in your showroom than in their warehouse. But don't overdo it. Monitor your days-in-inventory ratio to achieve a turnover that is typical of your industry.

13. Poor location.

In my second store I paid $5 per foot for 2,200 square feet, including most utilities, and sold $175,000 per year in merchandise. I moved the store to a high-traffic location and paid $28 per foot, plus utilities, for 1,200 square feet and grossed $475,000 a year in sales. Sales per square foot rose from $80 to $395, while the need to advertise declined. Do you want to pay $5 or $28? A San Francisco client retained me to negotiate for space in high traffic Chinatown for a second-floor convenience store. There was no rent budget and he would even pay to install escalators. There are times to nickel-and-dime a landlord and other times to take the spot before your competitor does. You can avoid poor location decisions by temporarily putting aside day-to-day duties to pay closer attention to trends in your territory.

When expanding, do it to cover more people or target demographics. If you operate a yoga studio, instead of doubling the size of your current location, open a second in a different pocket of people to offer a "close to you" facility. It may be better to have three 1,500 square foot locations than one 4,500 square foot location. This is especially applicable to retail operations.

14. Failure to understand the competition and treat them as the enemy.

Occasionally my clients tell me what a good relationship they have with their competitors. "Oh Steve, we lunch together. She is so nice," and the competition is "healthy." Really? Well, to quote a clownish character from the old "In Living Color" comedy show on cable television, "Homie don't play that game." Unless you're Burger King sliding next to McDonald's, or operating in an airport food court, competition is generally unhealthy. You should be stealing ideas, suppliers, employees and customers from your competition. Those little piggies are eating a slice of your pie every day. Give them a "Homie" bang on the head every time you get a chance. I've been so fanatical in this regard I would often approve a sale at my cost because it crippled my competitor's ability to market and sustain their business. The sale gave me more buying clout with suppliers, allowed me to steal the customer, make them mine and sell to all their friends.

So, get chummy with your competitive rivals. Glad-hand them at the Chamber of Commerce dinner, or chat with them at a trade show. Buy them a few drinks. Who knows, they may spew out confidential things that can help your business. But don't ever think they mean anything to your success unless you can buy them out after you've crippled them. And if you think this is advice from a madman, get back to me in a few years after your "friendly" competitors have screwed you a few dozen times. You'll be up at night worrying about paying your rent, and trying to figure out how to get it from your competitors. Wake the hell up. This is war and they are the damn enemy!

15. Spending other people's money.

Banks call a revolving line of credit an "evergreen loan" because the balance grows on and on forever and never gets paid. A revolving line of credit should only be used for seasonal needs, special purchases or situations that arise where you can make a fast gain. If your cash flow is not allowing you to draw down and pay back a line of credit in the short term, convert it to a term loan credit facility. Remember, cash flow does not belong to you when you have debt! Never spend other people's money. You are only entitled to retain a small percentage of all those dollars that will flow through your fingers. After taxes, pay your lenders. Stiffing lenders is a very bad habit that will put you under. It is especially prevalent with newbies who never had access to significant cash. They start to believe it all actually belongs to them.

16. Procrastination.

Comedian "Larry the Cable Guy" is right. You just need to "Git 'er done!" Pull the trigger. After you've given an issue reasonable consideration, make a decision–right or wrong. In my role as a distressed-business turnaround consultant, delay is not an option. Walking into a company being foreclosed upon, it's necessary to change almost everything overnight. You can't vacillate in the business swamp, especially in a do-or-die financial emergency. The business world moves at a pace faster than you'll ever attain.

17. Fixing things that aren't broken.

I'll never understand why people feel the need to keep fixing things that already work. This compulsive behavior is an expensive way to satisfy your boredom. Functional obsolescence means that something is no longer viable or efficient and should be replaced. It's broken or it's not broken. Technological obsolescence means that old technology may not be efficient. It works or it doesn't work. If it works, spending money on more bells is foolish. Don't mess with success.

Upon selling my client's hotel and restaurant to a young couple, I gave them some "free advice" at the closing table. I said, "You just purchased a cash stream. It's been there for 10 years and it should be there for the next 10. Do yourselves a favor and don't fix anything. Nothing is broken. The chefs are happy, the employees are happy, the customers are happy and the owner was happy." Within 60 days after the sale, they changed the menu, hours, staff, and environment, and within six months, revenue dropped by 50 percent. Ultimately, some-one else bought it from them for 40 percent less than they paid! If you want your own image or feel the need to put your picture on the marquis, for God's sake, start from scratch or buy a junker. Certainly you can implement improvements over time, but just as people know what McDonald's has in its box, patrons return because they like it just the way it is.

18. Over expansion.

Jack Sundling took me out for a bowl of chili one afternoon. He was a 55-year-old manufacturer's rep, and I was an ambitious 25-year-old music dealer. At the time, I was opening a retail store location every six months. While this may sound prehistoric to some readers, older guys can offer wise advice. He said, "Steve, slow down. I know it's all good right now, and I love selling you more, but you're growing too fast, and if there's a cyclical dip, you could get caught in it." I didn't take the advice. Sure enough, Jimmy Carter managed to unmanage the economy to the point where the prime rate skyrocketed to 21.5% in 1980 — the highest in modern U.S. history. At the time, I was sitting on $4 million of inventory and paying high interest rates. Consumer borrowing rates were also high so big-ticket luxury sales stopped dead. I lost $1 million overnight. I learned a valuable lesson in macroeconomics: watch for shifts in the economy and political wind that will make the business swamp safer or scarier.

19. Getting spooked.

Fear is generally overrated. Face problems head on. The business world is the proverbial "school of hard knocks." Some people bury their heads in their hands and hope the alligators will creep past them, offering no more than a glassy eyed glare. They are spooked, and their boats are headed for the bottom of the swamp.

20. Poor internal controls.

Get a grip on your internal controls. Granted, accounting is boring. Insurance is worse. Who really wants to worry about monitoring petty cash? Come on, we're entrepreneurs! But if you don't have a penny-pincher numbers guy on your management team, you can quickly lose more money than you make. Financial statements are as important to you as x-rays are to a surgeon. Whether historical or projecting, they must be timely and accurate in order to avoid losses before they arise.

21. Lack of reserve funds.

Having nothing in reserve is a sure way to sink in the swamp. Stay liquid and you will stay afloat. I once had a friend in musical instrument retailing. He was far enough away that I didn't lose any sleep over the business threat he posed. Yet I was still competitive. One time, I hung a sign on his store's front door announcing he was closed and urged his customers to visit my stores instead. He gave me a valuable tip. He said, "Every time I sell a piano I put $50 in the safe and never touch the money." I followed suit, and when sales of luxury-goods virtually stopped during the Carter recession, I was able to weather the storm because of this tip, coupled with my real estate investment.

22. Trying to do it all on your own.

It's critical to carefully hire staff and delegate responsibility. Moreover, it's important to listen to employee input. It's your responsibility to motivate and manage people. Personnel problems left unresolved will destroy morale, productivity and profits. While the suggestions in Chapter 7 will be of help, the management of people will become your largest challenge in business.

Plan for the Best, but Prepare for the Worst

Like a homeowner in a flood zone, a business owner should prepare for costly calamities. A detailed analysis of the warning signs of financial disasters and what to do when they arise can be found in Chapter 14.

A small business owner needs to be competent, experienced, confident and a "jack of all trades." Unfortunately, many owners have limited education and experience, or they don't comprehend the time commitment required. In my first retail business, my store was the only one in my area open on Sunday, when we could work with what we called a "full house," meaning mom, dad and the kids. My restaurants were open 365 days a year, early morning to late night. Spanish siestas, summer hours and "I'm On Vacation" signs are for people who have no respect for the consumer.

Solicit feedback from customers. Encourage them to fill out comment cards and send email invitations to communicate with you. This information is irreplaceable. Have someone "shop" your business and report the results. One nasty clerk can destroy a retail store in six months.

I recently went into a Boston Market restaurant. I was conditioned to the rude, uncaring staff that slapped food on plates with no eye contact, agitated that customers were causing them to work. But this time they were neat, wore big cheerful smiles and offered a warm welcome. Pleasantly surprised, I placed my order. Then I noticed a trainer. I complimented him on the turnaround. He said, "We've built a great team." Then, in earshot of the staff, I said, "I don't know how to burst your bubble, but this staff is only congenial when you're here, and when you're not, they're miserable." Don't become as delusional as the trainer.

If your staff must sell for your business to succeed, you will need a comprehensive training and monitoring program, because the majority of noncommissioned retail clerks are "order takers" who are more interested in their date for the night than in your success.

How Rich Will Your Conscience or Philosophy Allow You to Be?

People go into business for all kinds of reasons, including generating tax losses to offset income, a desire to prove one's ability, to occupy one's time, and yes, even to get away from one's spouse. But of course you also should be doing it for the money. It can be a part-time endeavor, pursued while you are in school or gainfully employed. Perhaps you might start a virtual company with minimal risk and maximum flexibility. But it is really all about money. Come on, admit it. Say it with me: "I WANNA BE RICH!" And say it each morning when you wake.

Being one's own boss or enjoying freedom may be reward enough. But even when you work for yourself, you still have bosses such as your loan officer, partners, union heads, landlords, franchisers and Uncle Sam, to name a few.

Few acts express individualism better than starting a business. It is the antithesis of plodding corporate capitalism. Many of today's baby boomers abhorred corporate life when they joined the work-force in the 1970s. They wanted to "do their own thing" from the start, and they did so in spectacular style. The boomers made staggering electronic advances. They launched the Internet, the World Wide Web and the cell phone, to name a few. This is true capitalism.

If you, too, are a capitalist and all-American consumer, and don't feel guilty about living with a little excess, you probably have no choice but to start your own company. No truer words were ever written than those by Adam Smith, the Scottish economist, philosopher, educator and author of "The Wealth of Nations," in his classic book on capitalism. He argued that "opulence and freedom are two of the greatest gifts a man can possess." If you believe wealth is a corrupting influence that equates to conspicuous consumption of goods and nothing more, then admit it and don't buy a swamp canoe!

The Plan

Perhaps you can ease your conscience about ostentatious wealth by subscribing to the author David Brooks who makes the case that you can "make good" (having and spending a lot of money) while "being good" (doing what's right for society). There now, doesn't that make you feel a whole lot better?

So, if you really want to get your little share of the world's wealth, make generous estimates of your needs. If your assets are less than $4 million and you have less than a half million in cash, you're not rich. If your assets are less than $10 million, you're only a tiny bit rich. If you multiply your age by your pretax income, and divide by 10, you will know what your net worth should be. So, unless you've been in the swamp for a while, you have a hell of a lot of work ahead of you. Accept the fact you're a needy, greedy capitalist and get busy! Focus on goals that inspire you. Come on, you do want to be RICH, don't you?

One old wise guy gave me this acronym: YCMMSOYBFA. It means "You Can't Make Money Sitting On Your Big Fat Ass." So, get up, get out, make cold calls, mingle, investigate your industry, sniff around your competitors and work your plan. Make every day a learning experience.

Tips To Keep You Afloat

> You must develop a meaningful mission statement and comprehensive business plan.
> New business financial projections begin with a forecast of revenue.
> Industry associations and websites provide a wealth of knowledge.
> Plan the size of your business and project its growth trends.
> Keep the 22 reasons for failure gentle on your mind.
> Capitalism is not a bad thing and you're in this for the money. You want to be rich.
> This book not will only suggest ways to do business, the down-loadable documents will show you how.

3. THE OPPORTUNITY

> *"No student knows his subject; the most he knows is where and how to find the things he does not know."*
> *Woodrow Wilson*

There are opportunities to succeed in almost every business sector. While technology gets a lot of attention today, never forget that you can join the ranks of millionaires by operating a successful janitorial service, a coffee shop or a plastics molding company. Those are just a few examples of the ways you could apply your entrepreneurial skills and spirit to achieve your personal goals.

When looking for that promising opportunity, take a moment

to think about your own interests and desires. If you enjoy cooking or dining out, for instance, you might want to consider opening a restaurant or a health food store. If you drive along a street and wonder what could be built in a vacant lot, then you might want to start a real estate or construction business. For me, opening a music store was a natural step, since I enjoyed playing the keyboards.

If you don't yet feel an affinity for any type of business, that's perfectly okay. In fact, that can even be an advantage because you can look closely at a wider range of industries. For instance, I had a client who owned a Mexican restaurant and then decided to open a dry-cleaning facility. There are plenty of opportunities in the unglamorous business sectors — and fewer would-be entrepreneurs chasing after that same pot of gold.

But to seize that market opportunity, you must cross the treacherous business swamp. If you plan to exit enriched, choose the canoe that's right for you. Begin by deciding to build one or buy one, or to invent a business from scratch or acquire an existing one. Do you want a clean but untested canoe or a dirty one that is already floating? In this chapter, I will explain how to reduce business risk by affiliating with other companies via a strategic alliance or franchising (borrowing a canoe).

Canoes already afloat in the business swamp deserve special attention. Because so many shiny new start-ups sink to the bottom, much of this chapter is devoted to the mechanics of acquiring an existing business with a few dents but proven buoyancy. In particular, I will explain how to negotiate a business acquisition without spending thousands of dollars on legal fees.

Where in the business swamp is the best place to begin? Are you willing to enter a dark, swirling whirlpool of uncertain depth and danger? Or would you prefer a shallow spot near shore with a clearer view of the bottom? Different entry points have different entry barriers. Your ultimate profit will probably depend heavily on the type of business you enter and its barriers to entry. In the case of a restaurant, for example, barriers are minimal compared to those of a radiology center. The return on investment (ROI) for a 4,000-square-foot restaurant may be 6%, or $100,000, and the radiology center ROI may be 40%, or $500,000, in the same space. Yet the cost to open a radiology center may be five times greater than a restaurant. Conversely, the dollar-denominated barrier to entry for a new mobile app or social network business could be virtually zero.

Generally, the easier it is to enter a business, the lower the return on investment. The problem with low barriers is the competition they encourage. Tall barriers do the opposite. Permits, licenses, training, equipment and other upfront obstacles tend to discourage business formation in certain industries.

Remember this: You can own almost anything. While you can't practice medicine without a degree, you can own the technical component of a surgery center. While you may not hold a broker's license, you can partner in a real estate agency as long as you don't sell real estate. Having done both, I can assure you that you can capitalize on almost any type of operation if you are creative and persistent. However, be prepared to receive puzzled looks from everyone (even your lawyer) when you explain your proposed, nontraditional participation.

On Naming Things

One of your biggest creative decisions will be branding your business. Naming your company is an important beginning step. Many start-ups give this decision very little time or weight. If your plan is to acquire a business, would you keep its existing name or adopt a new one? Whether you build a business or buy one, settling on a name isn't something you can force. Invest adequate time in the process. It will directly affect your success.

Two things ensure that a name will be remembered: repetition and creativity. Repetition through marketing is a simple but expensive approach. If publicized often enough, even a name like "Anendums" will be remembered. But if a better name is created at the start, less exposure and less expense is required to build a profitable brand. That few memorable names arise is probably the result of owner-oriented labeling. Memorable business names are buyer-oriented brands that create distinctive images. Your trade name should induce a visual image. Whether this image relates to the product or market is almost immaterial as long as it elicits positive emotional feelings about your company and what it sells.

Acronyms are trendy in some industries, but mere initials often portray a lack of imagination and can leave consumers cold. "Ho- hum" names like Bob Smith's Storage Center are worse. Unless you're a celebrity, consumers could care less who you are.

By the time you've racked your brain to conjure up an effective name, you may have 10 candidates. Now, you should test them:

- Write all 10 names on a sheet of paper.
- Invite several of your friends into a room.
- Have them turn the sheets over and allow 20 seconds to read the names.
- Have them turn the sheet back over and write down the first three names that come to mind.
- If they remember names different from your personal prefer-ences, consider deferring to their judgment.

Make sure that the name has a certain amount of shock value. This forces targeted consumers to toss the name around in their minds.

If you locate in a large market and plan no geographical expansion, you may want to use your business's name to reflect its location and specialty, such as a restaurant known as "Waterfront Seafood." Your name might identify your market, as would a men's hair salon called "Gentleman's Quarters." Names that start with the first part of the alphabet appear first in many directories. Short names like Starbucks are better than wordy ones. Business names with words that sell such as "quality," "home" or "love" are likely to be winners.

I named my first business Hammond Organ Studios, trying to capitalize on the trade name of an organ manufacturer. The Hammond brand was important to me as a musician. But Charles Q. Public could care less. In front of each of my stores, I erected a 12-foot-tall musical note and painted it red. After we answered our phones with the name Hammond, callers would hang up immediately saying, "We wanted the Big Red Note!" That unique red note had become synonymous with my business, which I renamed The Big Red Note World of Music.

So I wasted several years marketing a brand name, making it more familiar for the benefit of the manufacturer of a product I eventually dropped, and even some competitors. I never embraced the name Big Red Note, but customers only had to hear it once to remember it. These are the kinds of blunders I hope my readers will avoid. They are expensive.

Your logo is every bit as important, if not more so, than your name. Your logo will project your image — and be assured that consumers respond to both the name and the look. It should be unique as to shape and color. Recognizable in today's logo landscape even without the actual trade name, such as Starbuck's "twin-tailed siren." Determine whether your logo will look great on a sign, website or billboard, especially at night. Will the colors show well and communicate the right message?

This may be an occasion to pay a marketing agency for advice, especially if the agency takes the time to understand your business and target market. Another way to develop a unique and memorable name is to steal it — just as your agency may do (and then charge you for the service). I retained one an agency to name a cosmetic surgery center and subsequently learned they stole not only the trade name but also the typeface! Another one stole the name and logo for a laundromat.

You can use an existing trade name so long as you undertake some verification. Start online by checking your Department of State to ensure the name is not registered. Even if it's taken, you may be able to use a variation of it. The law states it should not be "deceptively similar to" another name. Yet if "My Girlfriends' Place Hair Salon" is taken, you may still be able to use "Girlfriends." You should also check fictitious name filings. You don't need to file for a fictitious name if your corporation is the same as your trade name, but you may if your trade name does not contain your own name.

People may threaten you for trademark infringement. Verify the exclusivity of a name with the help of an attorney before you invest money it. I developed a mini-mall and named it Penny Lane. Soon, the Beatles' New York law firm sent me a cease and desist letter. I told them to go ahead and sue my corporation. I really didn't think Paul McCartney would care! I guessed right. Besides, I did enough research to know they couldn't stop me because Penny Lane is a street in London. I did stop playing the Beatles' recording of the song "Penny Lane" in my advertising jingles, but only for a while. You see, business owners simply cannot survive if they succumb to all of the pressures placed upon them. Complying with everyone is nice, but it isn't realistic in the business swamp.

Where to Locate Your Business

While location is relatively unimportant for many commercial enterprises, businesses such as retail stores, restaurants and hotels gravitate toward high-traffic sites. Before choosing between a busy downtown location and a more relaxed suburban address, recall history. Before the proliferation of malls, strip centers and warehouse-style "big box" stores, downtowns were vibrant. But most smaller local governments, with zero vision, failed to understand downtown revitalization needs and instead, chased shoppers away with things like parking meters and fines. And, there was no control over the product mix and uniform or extended hours.

Studies show that most people go into business to be their own boss. So predictably, in a downtown setting, when organized groups attempt to standardize hours of operation, there is always some idiot who wants to close at 2:30 p.m. so he can pick his kid up from daycare. These factors led to the widespread decay of downtowns. Commensurately, small-town local officials failed to understand their voting mass is better served when they foster commerce because it is more profitable than residential development. If you don't comprehend the need to accommodate the public on their terms, you will fail. The private sector did understand these factors. Developers of suburban malls gave people a climate-controlled environment with free parking, a varied product mix and uniform, extended hours. The score: private developers-10, town council-0.

After commerce migrated to the suburbs, governments began to throw tax dollars around in an attempt to revive central business districts. In a few cases they have succeeded, and the result is an inviting environment for a new coffee shop, boutique or bike rental store. But most downtowns have become service-oriented, which further lessens retail foot traffic. So, take a close look at your downtown to see if it may work for your type of business. Downtown landlords are oftentimes faster to strike a lease deal because many are struggling to pay an even higher tax burden back to the town council that chased their tenants away.

Strip centers are typically less expensive than malls, but the consumer is outdoors, and your entry doors create a mental barrier to keep them out. Strip center landlords are usually less aggressive than mall developer vultures. To understand a mall, you should understand the model developers use to maul small tenants. It started with this concept: Give Macy's, JC Penney's and two more big boys space for $2 per foot under a 50-year lease. Next charge the other 100 small businesses $18 per foot and require them to pay for all of the interior construction, right down to the concrete. Then, after their first renewal lease term has expired, force them out to take advantage of their make-ready improvements on the next small tenant and hike the rent to $28 per foot. Or, replace them with a chain store that will also sign with their other malls. Cute, huh? Once more the small guy gets a good, swift kick in the head.

Today, many of those vulture-developers that failed to acquire out-parcel space have begun to lose tenants to outlet malls and big box stores. The newest mall developer trend is to put shoppers back out in the rain with the new "outdoor mall" concept. But, wherever you choose to operate, do your research and choose well. Some industries exhibit unusual phenomena such as restaurants where the location has to pass through three or four sets of hands before there's a fit between the location and the market that's being served. This is going to be one of your major decisions, and it alone can require months of investigation.

In my youth, a very successful man, seemingly enamored with my energy, took me for a ride to lunch at his men's club. He owned 52 drug stores. He said, "Now son, when you expand, make sure you're in a county seat, a college town, a corner location and on a high-traffic road." I followed that advice with every location except one. It failed.

The next time I bumped into him, he was sitting in his limo in a small town where he owned a store, three hours away from his corporate office. It was 8:50 a.m. I stopped and said, "Mr. Widmann, what are you doing way out here so early?" His response: "When these people come to work in 10 minutes, I'm going to meet them. If you want to own faraway operations, you need to make frequent, unannounced visits." Once again, I heeded his advice, and it worked. I would announce to my staff that I was heading east, knowing they would make alert calls, and then drive west.

Many entrepreneurs want a familiar business location near their own backyard, regardless of the size of their local market, primarily for family reasons. But remember, if you enter a major market, you will make a lot more money with the same effort than in a rural area, which will usually demand more expertise and yield smaller rewards. It took me just as much time to acquire, develop and lease a building in Smalltown, Pennsylvania, than in Houston, Texas, for example. If you're young and mobile, the world is your market so select your venue with long-term goals in mind.

Consider the lifestyle you prefer. Do you crave urban access to hundreds of restaurants and entertainment options, or will the Saturday night Strawberry Festival in the town square suffice? Other non-business factors to consider in comparing an urban market to a rural market include the quality of education, crime rates, housing costs and a sense of community. Wealth isn't all money.

Let's Buy a Business!

Now let's get serious. Hopefully we lost all the lazy socialists in Chapter 1 or Chapter 2. Building a new business is exciting, but buying an ongoing or established business can be easier and more profitable than starting from scratch. Why buy an existing business? Here are some reasons an ongoing operation may avoid the hazards of a young start-up that struggles for years in the swamp:

- Existing operation and customers in place.
- Long-term revenue trend.
- Established supply sources.
- Immediate cash flow.
- Goodwill and recognized trade name.
- Potential lender in place.
- Transition support.
- Elimination of three-year start-up struggle.

Opportunities for buyers are endless, and target companies are easy to identify. Begin by profiling the type of business you're considering and then undertake market research to determine if your preference is viable. Don't rule out junk! I'd much rather pay a lower multiple of sales or cash flow for a tired dog, revitalize it and reap the return than pay full price for an energetic dog that can outrun anyone. Besides, it's more fun to wake a sleeping dog.

To find acquisition candidates, contact business brokers, bankers, accountants and attorney leads. Run a small ad in the targeted industry's website or trade magazine: "WILL PURCHASE Car Wash in Anytown, USA. Call Bill: 555-555-1234." Search www.businessesforsale.com or www.daltonbusiness.com. These are the types of sites professional business brokers use, so you can find sellers yourself instead of watching a broker add 12% to the selling price for his commission.

Buying an ongoing profitable business is no guarantee of success, of course. An acquisition may fail if the business has, what I call, "bad will." Perhaps existing customers are so disgusted with substandard service or inferior products that you won't succeed under the prior trade name. If you've inherited a company, especially in an industry that bores you, proceed cautiously. There's a phenomenon where under second-generation family business owners fail to build on their predecessor's success. If your parents do own a business, learn to love it and maintain the success because it could be a stepping-stone into your future.

Take an Airboat Across the Swamp and Dazzle Potential Sellers

Once acquisition targets are identified, send owners an introductory letter; send inquiries to multiple targets. Buying a business is a numbers game, so contact as many sellers as you can. What do you have to lose by making runs at possible deals? Here is an unconventional but effective strategy to negotiate a business acquisition and sidestep uncertain sellers:

1. Show potential sellers you are serious and professional. Arrive with a confidentiality letter* so you can obtain (1) three years of income statements, (2) a balance sheet, and (3) the last federal tax return. The remainder can be gathered if you move past preliminary talks.

2. Stabilize (adjust) the Income Statement, often referred to as "recasting" the Profit & Loss Statement*. What will your profit or loss be after adding your new loan interest expense, removing the current owner's personal expenses and adjusting other numbers based on your research and industry standards?

3. Ask the seller what he thinks his business is worth. Believe me, he has no idea. Instead, you're going to determine the right price (see the following) and show him in a Business Valuation*. You will establish the price you want to offer and maximum you might pay. Master this analysis and you'll save $5,000 to $9,000 in professional fees, and perhaps you'll be inspired to sell this capability to other businesses. You don't have to be licensed to sell personal property or receive a "finder's fee."

4. Later in the conversation, after you've bonded, mention that you may need some "owner financing." He will usually say, "No way, I want to sell it and move on." Don't argue. Just wait, because you may ultimately convince him otherwise. You will explain that he could double the interest he can obtain from a safe market investment, be fully collateralized and postpone capital gains taxes into the future. You also may be able to pay him more than he would receive under a cash deal. From your perspective, it's often easier to pay 5% more for the business than origination fees and other closing expenses to a bank, or to wait six months while some lending officer lies to you about their bank's interest in the deal.

5. You are going to assess accounts receivable and debt. Some debt you may assume, but seek to compromise with lenders. As will be explained later in this book, there is no faster way to make money than to convince creditors to accept less than what is due.

6. A client sent me to Manhattan to purchase a well-established transcription agency. After scouring the business, meeting staff, visiting the owners at their home and convincing them to finance the purchase, I reached a conclusion that the bond between the principals and the law firms they serviced for many years was rock-solid. Fearing a disruption of that relationship might quickly result in a drop of revenue post-sale, I inserted a sentence into the Sales Agreement: "In the event annual revenue should drop more than 10% during the first year after the closing date, then the selling price and monthly installments will be reduced by 20%." And, revenue did drop. Law firms "jumped ship" overnight and the adjusted selling price eased the sting. Introduce these concepts to the seller.

7. Find an abstractor who undertakes lien searches for local law firms and hire that person. Often the Register & Recorder's office will give you those names. The cost may be as little as $50 to run an initial lien search whereas a law firm might charge $500 or more. This will reveal whether lenders or creditors have encumbered the seller's assets. You'll do this because the seller is going to lie to you. Before

closing, you will complete a comprehensive Due Diligence Checklist*. Throughout the process, you will learn facts the seller intentionally withheld. Learn them early or you'll waste half a year working on a deal that will never survive the closing table.

8. After you pointed out all of the negative aspects of the seller's company over several months, and beat him down, weakening him to the point of sheer frustration, you've done your job. You're moving closer to the magic number. If an agitated seller insults me, it becomes my barometer to know if we are reaching his lowest selling price. You will also remind him that a typical seller of a business needs to court many potential buyers in order to close one sale and that most deals crumble. This is a great testing ground for your negotiation skills.

It is always best to compromise or accept less important terms to gain more important ones. However, it isn't always possible to avoid pressure. The bigger the deal, the more stressful the negotiations. During one session while representing a neurosurgeon, with he and his wife in the room, I made a tactical decision to pack up and end the talks. The adversarial party grew infuriated, stood up and pushed me in the chest, demanding that we remain. Of course, he paid dearly for that physical attack.

9. Next you are going to hand the seller a Term Sheet*. This sheet will outline all of the business terms and conditions you want. He will be impressed, even if he doesn't agree with it. Not only does it memorialize the deal, a comprehensive Term Sheet may reduce legal bills.

You can also mesmerize your new friend with a draft Asset Purchase Agreement*. It helps you to explore deal-stoppers early on. Presenting a Purchase Agreement will titillate him with the notion that this might be a real deal. He's already envisioning himself without that 30-year albatross. Perhaps he is bored, or as B. B. King sang, "The Thrill is Gone."

10. If you've convinced the business owner to sell, and you've become his target buyer, offer to sign a Letter of Intent* with a refundable good faith deposit and contingencies. Inform the seller that you're going to retain legal counsel. You may, or may not, want to suggest the seller get a lawyer too. You don't want your lawyer wasting time negotiating with someone who doesn't understand the mechanics of a transaction.

11. First read my later chapter on professionals, and then take your Term Sheet, Letter of Intent and/or Asset Purchase Agreement to your lawyer and explain that you wish to go forward with the transaction. You will now sign an Engagement Letter with your lawyer and limit the amount of money you will spend on legal fees to determine if the deal is real. Yes, you can also negotiate the lawyer's Engagement Letter, but intimidated clients rarely do. While your lawyer will not solely rely on your documents, those will be a good starting point for redrafting. Having this preliminary work completed will save you money, let your lawyer know you've got a brain and you're not going to blindly place your life and wallet in their hands.

You've arrived at this point in the process without paying a broker, CPA or attorney. You did your own solicitation, financial analysis, business valuation, negotiation and draft agreements. You are now 75% of the way home! And if your seller walks or you're not feeling his love, stop the legal clock, dump him like yesterday's trash and move on to the next deal. Never become emotionally attached to an acquisition.

You will need counsel to close. You simply should not acquire a business without proper legal advice. But by doing much of the work yourself, you could save $5,000 to $10,000. Incurring a big legal bill only to learn simple facts that will kill your deal is a bitter surprise worth avoiding. If you're moving forward, let your lawyer earn their fee by trying to sweeten the terms at the 11th hour as he plays the "bad guy" role while you befriend the seller.

If the seller is actually foolish enough to allow you to spend time in and around the business before closing, that may reveal more negatives he tried to conceal from you, unconsciously inviting a lower bid. Suppose the seller generally agrees to the terms but hesitates to close? A legal counsel who understands contract law and is also business savvy may be of great assistance to ensure that the deal does close.

What is the Right Price?

How much should you pay when acquiring a business? As we said above, the answer is simple: No more than necessary! So, first you have to get a solid estimate of the business's market value and then try to convince the seller to give you a bargain. There are several steps involved in getting a fair estimate of the business' value.

Step 1: Annualized Stabilized Income Statement

A seller will typically hold onto the business' tax returns, which are crafted to show poverty and low profits to minimize payments to Uncle Sam. However, the seller will be happy to hand you a Quick-

Books Income Statement prepared in house that boasts higher profits. You should ask for the tax returns and all other financial data for the past few years, so you can analyze the trends.

You will need to review the year-to-date income, expenses and profit. Then, you can create a Stabilized Income Statement* that reflects the business's anticipated performance after your purchase. This newly created statement of income and expenses may be adjusted up or down for some of these anomalies:

- Income could be less because the new owner won't have revenue from an asset that isn't being acquired in the deal, or perhaps a tenant lease will not be renewed. Buyers do not pay for better performance that they might enjoy because of their ingenuity, but should only pay for the seller's performance on the valuation date.

- Perhaps the owner paid insurance one year in advance, and so it could be a partial expense the buyer won't incur, or perhaps he pays for his personal life insurance premium from the business. Conversely, if you will need life insurance as a requirement for borrowing, then that new cost should be added into expenses.

- Perhaps there are trips to the spa or golf outings hidden in travel and entertainment expenses that should be removed.

- Suppose the seller fully satisfied his long-term debt, but intends to finance $500,000 of your purchase price (because you sold him on the idea). You will incur a new interest expense that is not on his statement, but will be on yours.

- If the owner's spouse is the company bookkeeper, you may need to hire an employee for that task and increase your payroll and employee benefit costs accordingly.

If you're stuck because you don't know what spa or golf trips might be hidden in expenses, turn to industry standards. For example, if data collection sources indicate that travel and entertainment for a typical jewelry store should be 0.7% of annual revenue, then ignore the seller's line item amount and simply multiply the adjusted revenue by that ratio. Our clients are often shocked after we hand them this "recast statement" because it usually reveals a much lower profit, which in turn, will produce a much lower value of the enterprise. Not only is this a critical number for you to understand before you sign on the dotted line, it's a great negotiating tool to bring the seller "down-to-earth" on price. And, now you're prepared to calculate value.

Step 2: Business Valuation

This next tidbit will save you thousands of soft cost dollars and will help you better understand any business and its worth. James Howard prepared a step-by-step guide to establishing an accurate value for a business. I've attached an example to depict how any company can be valued giving weight to its tangible assets and excess earnings. Mr. Howard, once affiliated with Country Business Services, Inc. in Brattleboro, Vermont, developed this simple valuation method that will be respected by all parties in a transaction and will address both the financial and subjective aspects of a business. Using his format, you do not need an accountant and you will be able to explain the price tag. You calculate the value of assets, cost of money, devise a multiple, and then apply it to excess earnings*. There are many factors to be considered when developing your multiple*.

Understanding and valuing a business requires not only some financial expertise but also the ability to assess risk, competition, industries, growth, and the desirability of the company. Accountants and lawyers simply do not possess the tools that someone familiar with business will be better able to grasp. Make this your job because once you complete the analysis, it will be an invaluable skill for you to purchase companies in the future. While this should be the job of the seller, more often than not, buyers are faced with the challenge.

The Famous "Rule of Thumb"

Many buyers seeking a value reach for the Glen Desmond Rule of Thumb® book. The appraisal of a privately held business is not an exact science, but the Rule of Thumb may provide a reference range. This is not a determination that should establish a selling price but it may be helpful in "quick-and-dirty" estimates for divorce, estate planning, or tax issues. It's an informal method of approximating the value of an entity based on an analysis of hundreds of completed transactions reported to various data collection agencies. For example, a shoe store may typically sell at three times its discounted cash flow. Some people estimate value by multiplying total sales by a percentage. Physicians frequently sell their practice based on 1.5 times annual revenue. This is my disclaimer whenever referring to a value based on the Rule of Thumb method:

> Many inexperienced sellers and buyers have fallen victim to simplistic "rules of thumb" or formulas that simply do not work. These "rule of thumb" data is provided because it is often discussed by parties as a way to ascertain value. It may produce a value range – if the information is clean and the comparison is meticulously analyzed. We never invest abundant time in this exercise because it gives no consideration whatsoever to many variables that exist in a typical enterprise.

The Accurate Value

There are nine approved methods to value a business. One first major methodology is the Discounted Cash Flow approach, which assumes an annual cash flow to the owners including an amount to be received upon disposition of the organization. The second assumes the owner will hold the organization indefinitely. In essence, this calculation places a value on future cash flow into today's dollars; it calculates the present value of the cash flow at a specific percentage*.

At times it may be appropriate to calculate value based on both the multiple of excess earnings and discounted cash flow approach and then weight-average them for a more specific conclusion*. The remaining methodologies are best left to professional valuators.

Buyers Should Guarantee Cash Flow

Just as there could be tenants that will not renew their lease, there could be people who owe the company money in the form of accounts receivable. Provide for a remedy in the event of post-sale negative cash flow. For example, add a condition that if more than 10% of the receivables are not collected within 90 days, the selling price and/or obligation due under the Seller's Note is reduced 10% percent. Often both receivables and inventory are only valued at a percentage of the current amounts. Without a discount, it's often best to leave receivables with the seller.

Zombie Debt

After you purchase your new business, beware of scam artists trying to collect debt that you aren't legally obligated to pay. First, you should demand an Affidavit of No Creditors and include a mechanism to reduce payments due to your seller if legitimate claims are made. But perhaps some debts have already been settled in bankruptcy, or the statue of limitations on the debt has expired. Other claims could be the result of identity theft or brazen fraud.

Closing Documents

The smart and frugal businessperson will visit the law library and pull a document set to close a transaction. West's Legal Forms or American Jurisprudence Legal Forms® will provide comprehensive Stock Purchase or Asset Purchase Agreements along with ancillary documents. Prepare a draft for your attorney so he begins to realize you can't be bamboozled with legal jargon and so he doesn't bill you an additional $5,000. However, do not close the transaction without a lawyer by your side.

Expanding Through Strategic Alliances

Now, let's look at other entrepreneurial strategies. As a music-store owner who wanted to expand, I pursued the dominance of modest-sized markets, to become the "big fish in a small pond." So, I targeted trade areas with 75,000 residents, a mall, and weak competition. I correctly foresaw that within 12 months, we could own each market. And we did so by locating in high-traffic areas, gobbling up recognized brand products and implementing intense sales training programs.

But, true entrepreneurs are never satisfied. They want to be the biggest and the best. They migrate to bigger cities, more states and even international markets. My business expansion took me to Pennsylvania's capital of Harrisburg. There I discovered a music store that had been in business for a century. It was nearly dead. Government-forced downtown redevelopment had pushed the company out of a charming four-story historic building and onto a highway location in the suburbs, where revenue sank 70%.

Smelling blood in the swamp, I began a dialogue with the owner and made a proposal: my company would rejuvenate his by bringing in our salespeople, revising the marketing program and filling the floor with more inventories. We shared in the profit on each item sold. You, too, could set up this arrangement with a Sub Dealer Agreement*.

Benefits to my company:

- 100-year reputation achieved overnight by playing off an established trade name.
- No rent or overhead with instant presence in a larger market
- Access to brand name products we could not acquire.
- Increased sales volume and purchasing power.
- New "dumping ground" for used or excess inventory.
- Provide platform to "test the market" and determine if we wanted to purchase the company.

Benefits to their company:

- Learned new ways to sell merchandise.
- Cost them nothing because they had excess floor space.
- Provided more work for their service department.
- Gave them access to brands they could not acquire.
- Reduced their cost of inventory.
- Offered their demoralized employees new hope and enthusiasm.
- Doubled sales and saved them from closing the doors.

Another version of this growth concept is to locate within a larger store. Suppose you operate a custom drapery and blind business out of your home, and nearby is a local hardware store. Negotiate for 500 square feet of space and pay a percentage of sales. If everything works the way it should, you play off their store traffic and they make more profit per foot than selling brooms. If you wait for others to think up and come to you with these ideas, you'll be dead before it happens. You must be the creator of "win-win" opportunities. This stuff ain't luck, baby.

Franchising Opportunities

Howard Johnson struggled to maintain the operation of a small cigar store inherited from his father. Unable to make a profit, Johnson, along with Reginald Sprague, went on to create the first national restaurant franchise in 1935. Johnson, known as "Host of the Highways," decided it was time to lure traveling consumers off the nation's roadways. The actual concept is old by centuries, yet it had a special rebirth in the United States after World War II, when the nation's interstate highway system branched out.

More than 900,000 franchised businesses in this country offer everything from tax return preparation to doggy daycare, provide more than 18 million jobs and have an annual economic impact of $1.5 trillion according to PricewaterhouseCoopers.

Franchising is a system of marketing products or services. The franchiser, who has developed a special product, service or system, grants franchise rights. The franchiser grants a right or license to independent business owners to merchandise this service or product under a specified trademark and in accordance with a proven, successful format. The franchise agreements typically contain common provisions that address these questions:

- Term: How long does the franchise last? Will you have the option to renew, and under what terms?

- Territory: What geographic area does your franchise cover? Do you have exclusive selling rights?

- Fees: What initial fee will you pay? What percentage of sales revenue will you pay? Will you pay a regular management fee and if so, what does it include? Will you be required to pay other costs? How are costs determined?

- Support: How much initial and ongoing help will you receive?
- Restrictions: What restrictions are there on what you are permitted to do and how you must run the business?
- Exit: What are your options if you can no longer operate, or want to sell, the business?

Traditional types of franchising, otherwise known as product and trade name franchising, consist primarily of product distribution arrangements in which the franchisee is, to some degree, identified with a manufacturer's supplies. The term "franchising" can describe some very different business arrangements. It is important to understand exactly what opportunity you're being offered.

Want to start your own business with a much greater chance of survival than similar ventures? Evidence supports the claim that franchising does just that. Compared with independent business owners, franchisees do seem to have a greater chance of surviving during the first three years of exposure to swamp danger. However, the model can be expensive. You may have to pay an initial lump sum in addition to a percentage of sales or profits. Less obvious costs stem from deals to purchase products from the franchiser, preventing you from seeking supplies at the lowest price.

The Pluses

- It is your own business
- Your risk is reduced as the U.S. franchise failure rate is only 5% while one-third of independent start-ups fail within the first year.

The Opportunity

- If the business format has been proven, many start-up problems are eliminated and risk is reduced.

- You receive ongoing advice and support.

- Your brand is already built, assuming the franchiser provides regional or national marketing programs. To create a brand image by you involves considerable resources. The franchiser should promote for you by using management service fees, royalties or an advertising levy which all franchisees pay.

- Many employees are more comfortable with the solid image of a franchise over a "mom and pop" operation.

- It may be easier to expand because lenders and landlords may be more apt to do business with a known entity.

- Given franchiser training, you may require little knowledge of the industry.

- Franchisers often have greater negotiating power with suppliers than smaller operators. Theoretically your purchasing power should be enhanced with volume discounts.

- You may obtain exclusive sales rights in your territory or a first right of refusal to expand.

- You may be able to assess the potential for success or failure of a concept by contacting other franchisees.

- Operation manuals, policy manuals, media and marketing kits, training and ongoing support can be extremely beneficial.

- Franchise prices are coming down.

Franchises may require more initial capital than an independent start-up. Up-front franchising costs fees vary. You could pay $35,000 for a Dairy Queen or $95,000 for a Hampton Inn. An initial franchise fee may be an unavoidable price. In some industries, operating a franchise is almost a necessity. It may be ill advised, for example, to operate a hotel without a franchise affiliation to sustain a stream of reservations.

Franchisers benefit from selling a franchise because they can expand with less capital and make more money than by owning a company store. Some franchisers boast earnings from franchisee-owned operations that are eight times greater than from their company-owned operations.

Attending the annual convention of the International Franchise Association (IFA) is an excellent way to compare programs and attend educational seminars. And, you may be able to apply up to $10,000 research tax credits against the cost of such a business trip. The IRS allows you to deduct for such exploration. No taxes due? No worry. Those credits are like cash in the bank and can be carried forward into the future.

The Minuses

- Your creativity can be severely stifled.

- You incur the cost of actually starting and operating the store, including legal fees.

- You are expected to act in the best interest of other franchisees and the franchiser who owns the product, service and system.

- Some franchises will lease space on behalf of franchisees so if they fail, the company can take control of the location to operate it themselves, or perhaps sublease the space to another operator.

- Some food franchisers will actually grant two franchises to different franchisees at one highway intersection to service travelers headed in opposite directions, shrinking your piece of the pie.

- Acquiring valuable franchises may require significant make-ready conditions or upgrades. For example, pizza delivery chain Domino's has forced franchisees to remodel store interiors no matter how functional or attractive they already were.

- Sometimes franchiser fees are based on sales rather than net profit. This could lead to cash flow problems if operating costs are high.

- Your franchiser may insist on being your supplier, too. Buying from someone else on the side could be futile because the franchiser has the right to demand that you open your books and records for inspection.

- Should the franchiser fail to promote the business or offer support, you may have little recourse. You are often at their mercy and if they fail, you may fail too.

- If your performance is acceptable, you will be able to renew but you may have to commit to spending more money on refurbishment and modern equipment.

- Many franchises are owned in groups. For example, Popeye's might require that you purchase six markets even if you are prepared to only open one store.

- Your local market may exhibit preferences that the franchiser fails to address.

- Other franchisees could create bad will, reflecting poorly on you.

- Your franchiser may prevent you from purchasing another franchise, even out of the industry.

- You cannot sell your business without franchiser approval.

Franchise Format, Dealerships & Licensing

There are other variations of a franchise, such as:

- Dealership: You sell the product but don't usually trade under the franchise name. You have more control over your operations, much like an automobile dealership.

- Agency: You sell goods or services on behalf of another, much like the real-estate model.

- Licensee: You hold a license giving you the right to make and sell the licenser's product much like a retail store selling sports memorabilia.

Some firms offer franchises that are multi-level marketing schemes in which self-employed distributors sell goods on a manufacturer's behalf. You receive a commission on any sales you make and on sales by other distributors you recruit. Some of these ventures are illegal pyramid schemes. Only a few participants seem to get rich while the rest end up with 100 bottles of furniture polish.

With that warning in mind, here is a checklist of things to do before investing in a franchise:

- Be extremely skeptical.
- Examine sales projections and undertake your own analysis.
- Determine the number of other franchisees near your target market.
- Require a clearly defined protected territory. Ask for a first right of refusal or an option to expand into surrounding markets and acquire franchises for sale.
- Visit other franchisees, and not necessarily those referred by the franchiser.
- A high initial fee and low percentage of sales suggests the franchiser knows the long-term return is low.
- Ascertain the effectiveness of the franchiser in marketing and purchasing.
- Be certain the cost of supplies is more competitive than on the open market.
- Avoid arrangements allowing the franchiser to increase the mark-up on products sold to you or determine if you can purchase from alternative sources.
- Negotiate terms that provide flexibility in the event of a sale, retirement or death.
- Ask the franchiser for financial evidence of the chain's budget for advertising and promotion.
- Meet the franchiser's training and support staff to learn the frequency and detail of what they purport to provide.
- Sign no contract without a legal review.

There are other ways to capitalize on today's market opportunities, but start-ups, acquisitions and franchising are the most popular canoes to carry entrepreneurs across the business swamp. As you can see, all have pros and cons, so think carefully about your choice.

Tips To Keep You Afloat

> More difficulty in entering your target industry may produce a higher return on investment.

> Carefully and methodically test your business name and logo.

> Implore extreme due-diligence before selecting a location.

> Attempt to purchase an existing business before you start one.

> Dazzle sellers with your professionalism.

> Save thousands of dollars by utilizing the downloadable documents referenced in this book.

> Don't become emotionally attached to any deal.

> Consider a strategic alliance to grow faster and lessen risk.

> Carve out a few years of your life for due-diligence, read "how to" franchise books and proceed with caution if you decide to take that route.

> Grow your own company using out-of-the-box strategies.

> From beginning to end, finding, buying, owning and operating a business is no less complex than performing surgery, but the successful businessperson can earn far more than a surgeon.

4. THE FINANCING

If you want to start a business, you'll need money. There are six ways of obtaining capital: you can inherit it, you can steal it, you can win it, you can marry it, you can earn it, or you can borrow it.

But unless you have rich parents, hold a winning lottery ticket, or have gotten away with a bank robbery, you should plan on financing your new venture through personal savings, funds provided by family or friends, or lenders in exchange for an equity stake in your business.

According to the Annual Survey of Entrepreneurs, conducted by the United States Census Bureau, entrepreneurs use a variety of sources for startup capital:

63.9%	Personal and Family Savings
17.9%	Banks
10.3%	Personal Credit Cards

Equity or Debt?

There are two basic types of money to start your new business or to acquire another company. The first is equity – investing your own savings or selling a share of the company to investors who will give you the funds you need to get going. The stock market provides a great illustration of this concept. Every day, millions of investors buy shares in publicly traded companies that allow them to become owners of the business. Of course, many sell those shares almost as quickly, making the U.S. and global stock markets an endless source of fascination for anyone in business.

The second type is debt financing, which also involves using someone else's money. You might get a loan from family and friends by signing an "IOU," or obtain a loan, line of credit, or some other type of financing from an institutional lender. In most cases, this means going to a bank, getting down on your hands and knees, and begging for some type of loan.

Most banks only make loans to businesses with a track record because they want to be repaid for placing their money at risk. If you miss a bank payment, you're in the marshlands. Therefore, you may need to start your new business with equity capital before you can go to a lender. If you can't pay an equity partner, they have little recourse. In fact, you could even go back, and ask for more money. But that approach is much more difficult with a lender!

There are pros and cons to both types of financing, and many entrepreneurs must tap both sources of capital in order to enter the swamp and make a successful crossing. So let's take a closer look at some of your options.

Family and Friends

Many young entrepreneurs first turn to family members for financial assistance with a new business venture. Others turn to their friends or try a crowdfunding service to generate those startup dollars from more casual acquaintances or total strangers. But think carefully about whether you want to bring money issues into your current relationships, and ask yourself some important questions:

- Can my friend or family member afford to give me money? There is a big difference between asking a rich uncle and asking your brother or sister who might be able to scrape up a few thousand for you.

- What will my relative or friend want in return? It might be a financial profit, or something intangible like spending more time with your parents. You should also think about whether or not you want this person to be an active participant in your business or simply a passive investor.

- How much money do I need to launch? Remember that many businesses fail because they are undercapitalized.

- Should I ask for an equity investment or a loan? In either case, use your Business Plan to explain the nature of the business, your timeline, your exit strategy and how you intend to pay back the funds. Also, be prepared to provide regular reports on how your business is performing.

Remember that money from family and friends usually comes with emotional strings attached. You might be better off seeking money from other sources, such as affluent professionals, retirees, or current business owners.

Doctors and Money

Some use the acronym "DDD" to describe doctors who make poor business decisions. It stands for "dumb doctor deals." Many doctors are brilliant in practicing their specialty. Investing is not their specialty.

Many of my clients are physicians. I wondered why and how they frequently managed to lose money and even file for bankruptcy. After some research, I learned that physicians usually have little business training and are disinclined to manage anyway. A physician routinely sees a patient for eight minutes, diagnoses the problem, and prescribes a treatment. The disease is managed, and the physician moves on to the next patient. Too many physicians believe that same succinct protocol works in the business world, not realizing that it could take years for their investments to mature. They are compassionate, trusting people with little time to monitor investments, leaving them prey to gators in the swamp.

Why do you need to know this? Because these physicians are going to become one of your major alternate funding sources. They can write a check to fund your project and quickly eliminate your need to beg for credit at the First National Bank of Noloans. So learn how to attract their interest and treat them with the respect they deserve so they become a never-ending funding source.

Venture Capital and "Business Angels"

While representing clients in bankruptcy, I've searched for "business angels." They're typically wealthy individuals who provide start-up capital in exchange for convertible debt or equity. I've only used them in bankruptcy because small business owners often lose control of their entire company when dealing with this predator. They will often make a secured loan and then if you're not able to crawl out of the wetlands, they convert that loan to a percentage of your company . . . most often more than half. They can be helpful if the bankruptcy judge has given you 90 days to meet your Plan of Reorganization or to emerge from bankruptcy. Otherwise, angels and "white knights" are swampland scavengers.

I've never found one venture capitalist who was of any help whatsoever to my clients. They may have a place in larger companies, but for the small guy, put them back on the raft they floated in on and try another strategy.

Getting a Loan

The first point to keep in mind is that you are choosing a banker, not a bank. Only when you have drafted your business plan and projected your cash flow and profits will you know how much money you need to raise. Optimistic entrepreneurs naturally believe their new company will meet projected sales. I suggest you ask your lender for twice your projected amount the first time around. Going back to your lender and asking for more money after a short period of time will likely not boost your lender's confidence, often resulting in a rejection.

Most banks lend money only to people who can show that they don't need it. Your personal financial history will come under scrutiny, along with the all-important "Five Cs", which are:

1. Character. What is your history of repaying college loans, car loans, and home loans?

2. Capacity. Will your start-up generate revenue and ample cash flow?

3. Capital. Can you invest at least 20 percent of your own money in the business?

4. Conditions. What is the big picture for the local and national economy, the competition, and trends?

5. Collateral. What do you have to offer the bank as security?

Many banks also require a personal guarantee of the loan. That means you promise to repay the loan from your own money, even if the business fails. The personal guarantee may be a non-negotiable condition. When they make that request, respond that you'll sign it, but when the loan balance decreases by 50%, it is no longer effective. Or, you might ask that it not be effective unless there are two events of default in one year, or that you will have 30 days to cure any default before it becomes effective. Never sign for loans where the legal fees are 15% or 20% of the amount of your loan in the event of a default. Make sure you add, "not to exceed $X", or you may be buried in legal fees if you get into deep water.

Loan Brokers Are Sharks

If you're having a hard time getting a loan, don't go out and pay a brokers fee to borrow money, often called an "application or processing fee." These animals will actually send desperate borrower's commitment letters in order to steal money. If you place an advertisement in the *Wall Street Journal* to borrow money, these buzzards will fly at you in droves, and they rarely do anything but deposit your processing check.

SBA Borrowing

The U.S. Small Business Administration (SBA) helps entrepreneurs launch new ventures by lessening the risk for a bank. If you qualify, your loan should be lower than the current market rate — one reason why these loans are becoming more popular. (A complete explanation is available online.) These loans typically require a personal guarantee. However, if you don't pay them back, the bank will seldom jack up your house and pull it into the swamp. This is more government money at waste — a giveaway arrangement funded by taxpayers. It may be in your best interest to have a management consultant or accountant prepare your application so that it meets the necessary criteria.

While I characterized the SBA as a lender that may not repossess your house, the legitimate business person never intentionally borrows money with no intention of servicing the debt. These business people do exist, so keep in mind they are stealing taxpayer dollars and, therefore, stealing from you. I've had unscrupulous business owners ask my firm to prepare muddy financial projections in order to secure a loan. If the government is good enough to support small business with fair lending terms, then borrowers should perform as promised.

Grants

All levels of government offer a large number of grants, and I've seen the funds used for startup companies, building improvements, and a host of other business related needs. A grant is usually established under a contract between the federal, state, or local government specifying the purpose and conditions of the award. Many grants call for matching funds. These are a great way to double your investment power.

Sale of Your Debt

In the fine print of your loan agreement, there's most likely a provision that allows the lender to sell the loan. During the last decade, this practice has exploded. Unfortunately, you can borrow money from a sweetheart lender and wind up doing business with an alligator.

In one of my cases, an investor bought a loan, not because he wanted the $8 million of debt, but because he wanted the company. This company was posting losses, and I was retained to assume control. On a cold, winter day my phone rang. The message was short. "Mr. Poorman, I want to meet you in Chicago in the morning, or I'm going to shut the plant down. My staff will call with instructions. Click." I left my home without packing a suitcase and grabbed a 6 a.m. flight to O'Hare.

Upon arrival, I was greeted by a chauffeur who put me in a Rolls-Royce limo, and drove me to the suburbs. We pulled up in front of a home that resembled a hotel. The staff took me into a library where I sat for nearly two hours. Down the long corridor came this small-featured man who introduced himself. We talked for two hours about nothing. He noted that all of his mahogany bookcases were manufactured by a furniture company he purchased (or stole in a leveraged buyout) in North Carolina. Next, he showed me his "netsuke" collection. He bragged about paying up to $20,000 a piece for these little pieces of ivory.

Lunch was ready. We entered a dining room with granite floors and walls and one brilliant chandelier over the table. The butler announced the lunch options and read the nutritional ingredients of each dish. By the end of lunch, the company had still not become a topic. Next we went to his office and, of course, he told me how much his desk cost and which president owned it before him. He placed me in a low, round stuffed seat, so that he could look down at me. And with no warning, he said, "Mr. Poorman, you are in my way. You may think your client owns the company, but I own it. And I want it. Sooner or later, I am going to gain control of that business, and it might be better for all of the employees if you cooperate now before more damage is done."

There was little debate. That was it. He stood up, walked me to the door, I got back into the limo and returned to the plant that same day. Fortunately, I had already retained bankruptcy counsel and called them from the airport with this directive: "File the petition." We sought the protection of the court, had success in the case and kept the company in the founding family. It's still in business today.

Floor Plans

In the retail world, floor plans are a necessary tool to stock your sales floor with high-ticket items. Under this form of leverage, a lender will purchase the inventory from a manufacturer, and as it's sold, the borrower will repay the debt. Floor plan companies will buy paper from your supplier and oftentimes the supplier will pay for several months of interest. Used properly, floor planning your inventory will avoid "selling from an empty wagon."

Floor plans can also be expensive and dangerous. Problems arise when the borrower/dealer needs cash; they forget the money in their account belongs to the floor plan company, and spend it themselves. Periodically, the floor planner will dispatch an agent to conduct a "floor check" to determine if you are "sold out of trust."

We once had a floor plan check where my company was missing 75 pianos and organs in a period of 30 days. Some were stolen, some lost, some on trial in customers' homes and some we hadn't paid for. We were faced with a $100,000 obligation, and because it was given in trust, we could have been held criminally responsible. Each month we "sweated" the floor plan check and hoped that our inventory control system and accounting department had properly paid for each item as it was sold. If you default on floor planning contract terms, the company may arrive with a tractor-trailer and unload your store without notice. Therefore, if you're going to make floor planning a part of your leverage strategy, verify that each item is paid when it goes out your door.

To show how unscrupulous one can be when financially desperate: I represented a car dealer throughout his bankruptcy (before he served 22 months in federal prison). He was caught for having customers bring their cars back for free detailing so the vehicles would be physically present on the sales lot during floor-plan checks — even though he had sold them without remitting funds to the consignor. He tried to avoid detection by removing the license plates and fooled the floor checkers, most of whom had become lackadaisical and more interested in where they were going for lunch. An appliance dealer sold off new appliances and then refilled and re-banded the shipping boxes with trade-ins. When floor checkers pushed and counted the boxes, they appeared to be full.

Have you ever read any of this stuff in a textbook?

Distributor Support or IPOs

Suppose you adopted the push strategy marketing approach to sell your product as will be described in Chapter 8. You've already secured patents for a new product or your products have been sold through successful distributors. You're broke. Out of desperation, you placed your name, and perhaps the name of your spouse, on a personal guarantee or pledged your home under a mortgage as explained earlier in this chapter. Perhaps you've borrowed from a Manhattan lender at 15 percent with daily payments and a requirement to pay all of the interest even if the loan is fully paid early. Your lawyer begins to mention the topic of bankruptcy. But your distributors need your product and they have cash in the bank. So, be creative here. Prepare a Proposal where under your distributors prepay for the next year's purchases. You give them, say, 20 percent as an additional discount, and say, 5 percent of your stock. You get the cash you need now, they were only going to purchase your product anyway, they made 20 percent more profit on those purchases and if they didn't believe in your product, they wouldn't be selling it in the first place.

You'll show them how that 5 percent equity could be worth a million dollars in the future and if they don't participate, their source for your product may disappear resulting in future lost profits. Win. Win. Win.

These strategies aren't found in textbooks. Make them up as you go along. Another solution for a desperate company with patents or products that will eventually sell is to contact a New York law firm that specializes in launching IPOs (Initial Public Offering) where your company can go public by the sale of its stock.

Often a company will raise capital by issuing new shares to the public. These strategies should be explored before any bankruptcy petition is filed.

The Financing

Alignment through Consignment

Consignment is similar to a strategic alliance affiliation that can make a startup less expensive. Think of it as the Danny DeVito movie title and use "Other People's Money."

This is one of my all-time favorite leverage tools for both a lender and borrower. Yet, many people think it's restricted to a used clothing store. Consignment is a wonderful profit-generating strategy with little risk. Suppose you have a base store in a large market, and Littleville is a small market 50 miles away that you want to capture. Perhaps you're a furniture dealer, and there could be an appliance retailer in Littleville. Meet the owner and offer to stock their floor with merchandise; you provide the goods at cost plus a profit. The owner may have minimal inventory with available square footage, but now they can enjoy an opportunity to make additional profit if a refrigerator shopper happens to trip over a sofa set that you placed on their floor.

As a 21-year-old college student, I opened a full-line musical instrument store and discovered the consignment concept. Having accumulated a savings account from working in my teens, I reflexively decided not to risk it all. When you work and save for years, you're naturally more frugal than if your funds are borrowed, or you're the recipient of Aunt Emma's trust fund. Therefore, I was drawn to the consignment concept as a way to grow a company with virtually no cash.

Under a consignment contract, a well-regarded dealer of keyboard instruments agreed to place inventory on my showroom floor and charge 15% over cost for each piece sold. We had specific geographical selling areas so there was a minimal risk of customer crossover. Given this dealer's buying power, he was able to purchase for less, so the 15% markup could have realistically been only 5% to me. I found a small retail space to serve as my first store and infused

$4,000 of my savings to pay rent and turn on the lights. I convinced a few musical instrument and accessory companies to grant small credit limits (while namedropping a bit, letting them know about my affiliation with the well-respected dealer). I began to write small accounts payable checks every week (not monthly). This pattern of frequent payments convinced credit managers to increase my "open to buy."

Five months after the grand opening, a major flood destroyed most of the instruments, and the consignor absorbed the entire loss. But I successfully used the same consignment technique to restock the store with new instruments. Within one year of the startup date, we were generating several hundred thousand dollars in annual sales with a low overhead. Eventually, I opened more stores and obtained my own product lines, and within eight years, annual sales broke $4 million. This all began with $4,000 and some ingenuity in the form of an out-of-the-box business model. This same model will work in many industries.

If you're the consignor, you must require a Consignment Agreement* to deal with insurance, payment requirements, and restrictions so the small dealer won't buy your products elsewhere. Also be aware that you could "grow a monster." Once that dealer finds there is a healthy market for furniture in their appliance store, they may simply obtain his own direct dealership and toss you back out on the street.

If you're a retailer and want to broaden your product mix or add some new lines without having to meet the volume purchase requirements of distributors, make that same offer to a larger company. Perhaps they have excess sofas in the warehouse and allowing you to sell some of them helps to pay their floor plan costs while increasing their purchasing power. While rarely used, consignment is a wonderful "win-win" leverage tool.

The Financing

Consignee's benefits:

- Pay as sold to increase cash flow
- Return unsold goods to increase turnover and eliminate stale inventory
- Avoid insurance expenses
- Eliminate freight expense
- Avoid interest costs on inventory
- Obtain access to broader inventory
- Contain risk

Consignor's benefits:

- Gain a 15% net profit on each sale
- Make sales not otherwise achievable
- Incur a minimal cost to insure the inventory
- Increase purchasing power and collect more co-op advertising dollars
- Enjoy more consumer exposure to sell specialized inventory

In my first consignment arrangement, for example, we couldn't accommodate sales of large church organs, so they were referred to our business partner for a referral fee. Often we might have a buyer for a piece of their slow-moving inventory that was "growing hair," as we called it. Everyone was happy. But again, you need to sell the deal by presenting a mutually synergistic "win-win" package. As with all business arrangements, you must be fair and produce. If my consignor needed anything, including a favor, I was right there, with bells on, because I was grateful for the opportunity and support.

Suppose you want to grow your existing company; reverse this arrangement and find perimeter market outlets where you can place some of your inventory and generate incremental revenue and ancillary benefits. Why not place your lawn and garden equipment at a nursery?

The primary risk to the consignor is a consignee who sold your merchandise without paying for it. Beware: when faced with a cash crunch or unmet payroll, the consignee may "steal" money they owe for sold property. And it is theft because title has not passed. So, the key to this program is to conduct a periodic "floor plan check" and to file a UCC-1 Financing Statement supported by a Security Agreement *.

Remember, consignment and other forms of business alliances are universally applicable across industries. Suppose you are an orthodontist. You could develop a similar arrangement with a dentist and work from his office in a perimeter market. Think "win-win."

Tips To Keep You Afloat

> Know your obligations to investors and lenders.

> Understand the different types of loans.

> Avoid signing personal guarantees whenever possible.

> Consider applying for an SBA loan.

> Document loan transactions thoroughly.

> Use floor stocking plans and consignment arrangements to meet inventory costs.

> Seek out government grants.

> Defend aggressively against finance companies.

> Negotiate modifications and abatements to outstanding debts.

5. THE ENTITY

"I wasn't lucky. I deserved it."
Margaret Thatcher

Finding, acquiring, building, and maintaining a business empire is not an accident. You must earn it. It's not a matter of luck. The freedom to be your own boss comes from stamina and a well-designed, properly executed plan. Owning a business means you'll never be fired or outsourced at the whim of another. Of course, nothing this exciting ever comes without risk. There are many things that could go wrong in your endeavor! One crucial component is the ownership and governance structure you select.

When starting a new entity, you must define its legal structure: a sole proprietorship, partnership, limited liability company or a corporation. You may want to incorporate a company in Delaware for lower taxes, form a corporation in Nevada for anonymity and no taxes, or form an Employee Stock Ownership Plan (ESOP) in another state because there are different benefits in different jurisdictions. But never make your business about YOU, make it about IT. Separate yourself from the company. It should not be a "shadow of yourself" but instead take on its own life. Always isolate yourself from the rest of the financial world. Protect your home from litigation.

Asset protection

Selecting the appropriate structure for your business is critical from both an asset protection and tax perspective. The U.S. Bureau of Labor Statistics says about half of all new establishments survive five years or more and about one-third survive ten years or more. So, don't swim too fast here.

One reason for creating a separate business entity is to protect your personal assets in the event of the worst possible outcome. Tax liabilities and business debts can arise early in the game, so don't embark on any venture until you're protected. If you attempt to transfer assets after they're at risk, creditors could claim a fraudulent conveyance.

At one time, I owned 17 stores and formed separate corporations to sign leases and do business. While operating those entities resulted in more time and expense, the autonomy was invaluable when I wanted to sell off or close one outlet in the chain. It was helpful with selling stock to store managers, making them logical buyers and becoming a key component of an exit strategy.

Be sure to get advice from your attorney before selecting a legal structure, and keep tax consequences in mind.

Here are some options to consider for your new entity.

Sole Proprietorship

The owner and business are one in the same, and a fictitious name filing may be required. This is the most basic form of ownership, but you are bare naked and personally liable for many risks, unless you're married in a state that has the benefit of tenants of the entirety where the ownership of property is vested in the marital estate. That may work fine unless you divorce. Plan for every possible event. Otherwise, this form should only be considered if you have virtually no assets and minimal exposure.

General Partnership

This is the same entity as a sole proprietorship but may have multiple owners. Partners' ownership interests need not be equal; liability is not necessarily proportionate to the percentage of interest. For example, as a partner you may face personal liability similar to that of the owner of a sole proprietorship. Your personal assets are at risk in addition to all assets of the partnership. If one partner signs a contract on behalf of the partnership, it may be fully enforceable against the partnership and each individual partner, even if those partners were not consulted or aware of the contract. Partnerships may work for real estate provided there is adequate liability and/or "first-to-die" life insurance.

Limited Partnership

This entity can combine the best features of a partnership and a corporation. There must be a "general partner" and one or more "limited partners." The general partner (or another entity) is liable for partnership obligations, but the most the limited partners can lose by funding this entity is the amount of their original investment.

Many use this vehicle for real estate given its tax advantages for passive investors. The passive investor is often able to personally write off depreciation and other real estate deductions. However, unscrupulous general partners often take advantage of limited partners who have no voice in management.

Corporation

A "C" (closed) corporation pays taxes based on net profit while "S" (subchapter) corporations pass some income and losses to the shareholders to be reported on their personal tax returns. Be sure to talk with a good accountant who can help reduce your overall tax liabilities.

This entity is separate from its stakeholders, who cannot be personally liable for acts or debts of the entity unless a third party is successful in "piercing the corporate veil." That can occur by showing that the officers or shareholders failed to do business in accordance with corporate law, or in a case of fraud. The stock may be privately held or publicly traded on a stock exchange.

A corporation is required to form a board of directors to govern the company at a strategic rather than day-to-day level. An effective board might be comprised of insurance agents, bankers, accountants, lawyers and other private individuals with experience in the industry. The board should meet regularly and give advice to the owners. Oftentimes people are hesitant to serve on a board of directors unless the business owner provides D&O (directors and officers) insurance, which is typically expensive.

Limited Liability Company (LLC)

The "LLC" is the newest form of business entity and has risen in popularity among both entrepreneurs and lawyers. Its members risk only the share of capital paid into the business.

Every state allows an LLC to be formed by only one person, but some states may prohibit certain professions from forming an LLC. For the majority of small businesses, the relative simplicity and flexibility of the LLC makes it a better choice. This is especially true if the business will hold property such as real estate that may increase in value. The LLC itself does not pay tax on its income.

You can form your own LLC by going to www.nolo.com and clicking Legal Forms. You will need to determine whether or not someone else has already utilized your intended name. The LLC does business under an Operating Agreement *.

Review books such as *Understanding Business Entities for Entrepreneurs and Managers* by Jason M. Gordon and obtain actual sample documents from Form Finder on West Law. This research will allow you to fully understand the entity that you select.

Strategic Alliance and Joint Venture

Depending on the nature of your business and your target market, you may want to team up with a larger company or investment partner. In this case, your relationship may take the form of a strategic alliance or a joint venture.

In a joint venture, two businesses sign a legal agreement, usually for a specific period of time, to create a new entity with a clear date to end the venture. This agreement allows the parties to share information, knowledge, markets, and profits. Oftentimes, a small company can benefit from a larger firm's position in the market using the larger partner's brand recognition, resources, and market reach. If a small company suddenly finds itself with a hot product or service, it might benefit from a joint venture with a company that has a larger sales force and stronger distribution channels.

Tips To Keep You Afloat

> Go to a business lawyer to properly register your new entity or do it yourself.
> Unless your name is extremely recognizable within your market, keep your name out of the business.
> Build a wall around your personal assets.
> Don't place a spouse on the board of directors or issue stock in that person's name.
> Create an appropriate Board and invite experienced businesspeople to serve. Learn from them, keep shareholders apprised of business affairs, and stay within the legal requirements of your chosen entity.
> The new enterprise mortality rate lends credence to purchasing an existing business or forming a strategic alliance.

6. THE REAL ESTATE

> *"Be fearful when others are greedy.*
> *Be greedy when others are fearful."*
> *Warren Buffett*

To get your business off to the best possible start, you should ask yourself, "Where should I open my doors?" The answer depends on the nature of your business, your finances, and your goals. For example, if you're starting a small online sales business, you could turn one of the bedrooms in your home into an office and avoid paying rent until your sales grow to the point where you need to hire people.

If you and a friend or two are teaming up in a technology or R&D startup, you might want to consider one of the new business incubators of "co-working" spaces that are popping up in cities throughout the country. Like the more traditional "executive office" concept, these facilities give you a business address, as well as support services like a receptionist and a conference room for meeting clients. There can also be synergies from getting to know other entrepreneurs and potential sources of investment capital.

However, many businesses need a certain type of commercial space in order to get off the ground and succeed. If you are launching a retail, restaurant or entertainment business, you should search for the right regional mall, neighborhood center, or mixed-use development. That might mean analyzing pedestrian or vehicular traffic and the location of competitive establishments, as well as the rental rates to find the best fit.

Other types of startups are best situated in a facility designed for office, warehouse, manufacturing or healthcare users. Again, you want to study the local market and compare your options before making a commitment. Of course, if you are acquiring an existing business, it undoubtedly already has a physical presence somewhere. Even an online retailer needs office space for its staff or warehouse space for its inventory. If you think you can find a better, less expensive location for that business without disrupting current operations, then that would be a strong reason to move ahead with a planned acquisition.

Consider your location

Many businesses fail because the owners did not spend enough time determining the best location. To avoid that mistake, ask yourself these questions:

- Is the location near your customers, suppliers, or major highways?

- Is the curb appeal and immediate neighborhood conducive to your business? What is the diversity and appearance of complementary businesses? A handbag shop may benefit from being near ladies-wear stores, an eyewear store near an ophthalmologist's office, and an ophthalmologist near a hospital.

- Are there nearby coffee shops, post offices, professional offices, restaurants, health clubs, and other facilities that may ease the workday for your employees and you?

- Is the area safe for your customers and employees?

- Does the location support your image? When people see the entrance, will it offer a positive perception?

- Is there planned highway construction that will block or reduce access to your entranceway for any extended period of time?

- Is your floor level even with the sidewalk or do visitors need to step up or down?

- Have you searched for a corner location with oncoming traffic?

- What does your state Department of Highways report as the daily vehicular count in front of the location?

- Are there available rental spaces on other nearby arteries?

- How does the square footage rent compare with other nearby spaces in similar buildings?

- Is the access convenient with ample controlled and uncontrolled parking? Is there adequate handicapped, employee and assigned tenant parking? Does the landlord possess a parking study? Are there parking lot water runoff problems visible when it rains?

- How attractive is the landscaping? Do you notice trash around the premises? Are the parking lot and common area well-lit and do they operate some lights during the night?

- Is there a "help button" in the elevator and a current inspection certificate in the frame? Will you be given a key code to the elevator and stair doors? If the landlord is annoyed with these questions, then you are about to deal with someone who will be annoyed when you call to explain the roof is leaking.

- Will your clients need to contend with parking meters? How much are the fines? Can you buy tokens?

- Can you avoid nuisance taxes such as mercantile or business privilege taxes assessed on your revenue by simply locating within a different taxing body?

- Is an adjacent neighborhood more business friendly with less restrictions? Some do compete for economic growth. Because of their population and class, are they able to offer more grants and low-interest loans to small business owners.

- Is the existing signage uniform and adequate? Are internally illuminated letters allowed and will your landlord allow you to sign the top of the building if you are leasing significant square footage? Are there zoning restrictions for your proposed signage? Do trees interfere with your signage visibility?

- How convenient and adequate is the storage and receiving area?

- Is there adequate space for current needs and a potential to expand in the same area or building if the need should arise?

- Are public facilities adequate? Are there any sewer odors?

- Is broadband wireless available? Can you place a dish on the roof?

- Is there an existing fire and security alarm system in your space? Are you near a fire and police department? Is there an automatic fire protection system within your space; is it dry powder or water? Are all entrances and glazed areas protected and storm-proofed?

- Do you notice stains on ceiling tiles from prior roof leaks?

- Who services the HVAC system and who is responsible to pay for maintenance? How old is the equipment? Will the existing system adequately cool if you increase the load? How is the space ventilated? Have you tested for radon or mold? Does a "sick building syndrome" exist?

- Is there insulated break metal around thermopane glass? Is there an awning, sunscreen or exterior soffit to protect glass that receives direct sunlight and rain to protect the show window and clientele?

- Is there insulation on the ceiling and ductwork? Do the walls contain Decoban or other sound deadening material or will you hear your neighboring tenants? Is there a two-hour firewall protecting your premises from adjoining spaces? Has your insurance carrier's inspector walked the property in order to list defects that you may be required to correct after the lease is signed?

Cities have "pockets of enterprise" and depending on your product or service, you may need to locate within them. The size of the market you intend to cover should affect your decision. I "shuffled off to Buffalo" with one store, but failed to realize we would ultimately require three locations to saturate the entire market. Oops! A half-million dollar mistake. It was expensive for me to learn that consumers shopped within their own commercial pocket with accessible services and the majority didn't travel 10 or 15 miles to make a purchase.

Starbucks is an example of a successful brand that has made a science of selecting its locations. Many national retailers develop location prerequisites, such as the distance to the nearest main intersection or red light. There can never be too much due-diligence relating to your location.

Dealing with "Lizard Landlords"

Just as your two types of business financing break down to equity or debt, your basic choices in real estate are leasing your space or owning it.

Dozens of factors will dictate buy-or-lease decisions. For example, if you require a high-foot traffic location, you may have no choice but to rent. By renting, your liquidity financial ratios will be more desirable, making you more bankable. You will be using funds to invest in your company, instead of bricks and mortar, with long-term rewards. Conversely, if you made the right purchase, your equity-to-debt ratio may be more attractive to asset-based lenders. But when you have equity in the property, the lender will still want to evaluate your cash flow. At least that is the cheap excuse they may give to reject your loan application.

Because most new businesses — and even Fortune 500 giants — prefer to lease space, we will look at that option first. The best way to avoid problems with a "lizard landlord" is to negotiate a good contract up front. But be forewarned. You will need all your negotiation skills with a commercial landlord. You are about to meet the king of deal making. Here are some of the issues:

- Landlords typically hand you their "boilerplate" lease as they matter-of-factly say, "This is what all our tenants sign." Listen up. This will be their first lie. The lease is written to fully protect them and strip you of everything from your store fixtures to your day in court. There will be nothing in that document to protect your best interest and only the naive sign it without significant modification. If a Confession of Judgment is allowed in your state – that is the first condition you will strike for the reasons I offer in Chapter 10.

- You have another swamp critter to fend off if a real estate broker represents the landlord because they're working for the lizard. While they may be more interested in compromise in order to get some commission rather than none, they are not on your side of the desk.

- The best tactic is to not sign their "boiler plate" lease at all; it is full of subtleties such as "shall" versus "may" that could create significant problems in the future. It is more economical for you to pay a lawyer to draft your own lease than toil over all of the modifications you will need to make in their boiler-plate lease. Smaller landlords will normally accept your lease.

- While best not to reveal initially, you will want to protect yourself (as suggested in the next chapter), and become a corporate tenant. The landlord may say they do not rent to corporations, but that isn't the case at all. They probably read Robert Ringer's shrewd books, *Winning Through Intimidation or Looking Out For #1*, and they make concentrated attempts to convince dummies to sign personally on the dotted line. And, you are a really big dummy if you fall for this.

Wait until the deal is 90 percent completed before springing your corporate entity on them. They are more apt to accept your corporation after expending a good amount of time and effort in securing the lease. And know this: if they are the type of landlord to demand a personal guarantee, spousal signature or guarantor, they are the type to sell furniture out of your living room to pay not only rent, but all future rent due under the lease, even after you have moved out.

- Discuss basic lease terms such as the security deposit, monthly rent, term, and renewal options. You are going to masterfully negotiate these terms in your favor.

- Tell them you must infuse money into the space so you want them to waive the security deposit entirely. If that fails, offer to pay it throughout 12 equal monthly installments, and then ask that it be returned if, after two years, your payments are timely made.

- Learn how long the space has been vacant and find how many other locations/centers the landlord owns. If there are significant vacancies, they should be more flexible with your demands.

- You do not want a five-year lease; you want a one, two, or three-year lease with two renewal terms. Often your company will require larger, smaller or more economical spaces over time. Keep the term short with options in your favor. Agree to an increase in the rent for the renewal term based upon the U.S. government consumer price index, but strike the word "cumulative" if they sneak it in. If the third year increase was 1.8%, that is the increase you want for the renewal term and not the cumulative total of the first three years.

- If the landlord refuses to discuss a shorter term, agree only if you have the right to terminate the lease with a 90-day notice. And make your renewal automatic unless you provide notice to the contrary. If necessary, agree to pay an early termination penalty equal to several months' rent, but do not make long-term lease commitments.

- Try this saga on the landlord: "If I lose my distributor, suppliers or dealership (make something up — you're the actor), I can no longer continue to operate and in that situation, I must have the right to terminate." How can they not sympathize with that plight? And when they tell you they can't assign your lease to their bank if it isn't a three-year term, know it's not true. They lie to you. You lie to them. Oh, I'm sorry — we call it "puffing."

- Learn to speak and think in terms of square footage. If you pay $2,000 per month for 1,400 square feet, you are paying $17.14 per foot per year. Mentally envision one-foot square floor tiles with $17.14 in cash laying on each one of them in order to occupy the space. That visualization might incentivize you to obtain a lower rent. Explain that you know what you can afford based upon the industry and that you want to be certain you are able to honor the terms of the lease.

- Tell them you have another location that is more suitable. Tell them anything – but do not agree to pay rental rates more than you've budgeted in your business plan.

- When they tell you they have someone else who wants the space, just say "I understand" and call their bluff. Two real estate agents tried that silly little game with me in Florida. One entered the closing room to announce that she had another buyer holding on the telephone for the same property and needed my decision. I said, "Well then, today is their lucky day," as I walked out of the room. She was probably talking to a Dial-a-Prayer recording. When she came back the next day to salvage the deal, I deducted $10,000 from my former offer as a punishment. Make business a fun game. You hold the gun . . . I mean the checkbook.

- Landlords and brokers love to throw confusing terms around like gross, double-net, and triple net. Although each extra "net" requires the tenant to assume more operating costs, the specific terms vary widely. Basically, this means that you're going to pay some of the landlord's expenses, or all of them.

- Play stupid and tell them you don't know what net means. Landlords with premium space can pass through all expenses to the tenant, but most pay taxes and insurance. Ask for a list of the expenses from the prior year and how much these expenses would be, per foot, for your space.

- Request a copy of former utility bills for your space so you can estimate your total occupancy costs. When they say they don't have that data because the former tenant paid the bill, say, "Okay, I'll just call the tenant directly." This is the last thing in the world they want to occur because when you compare leases and gather information, it will typically open your eyes to many problems you are about to encounter.

- The lizards may demand "CAM" or common area maintenance. This is where they charge you for a lot of things that you never understand or audit. It is another negotiable term, but more difficult to adjust than rent. Push them, and demand a "cap" and accounting.

- Request "phased-in rent." Explain that you will incur significant initial expenses and you will require time to become established. Moan about all the costs until they are sick of your whining. Say you want zero rent for the first few months of occupancy, 25 percent for a few more months, 50 percent for few more, and finally, the full rent to become effective. Make it up as you go along; this is your job.

- Because commercial space will often sit vacant for six months they have a lot of room to give you early reductions. There are no rules. Fake disappointment when they tell you "no way" and then walk. Do a little show where you are the hardliner as your spouse weakens. Have your accountant write a letter saying the most you can afford is $X. Drop the names of other locations you are considering.

- Dangle the deal in front of them. You must make demands. Push hard, suck up their time and only bring in your lawyer at the tail-end to sweeten the deal and protect your assets.

- Some landlords will seek to levy a percentage rent calculated on your anticipated sales. Most will deal it away if you're persistent. But if not, payment should only be triggered after your base rent equals the percentage of sales they seek. If they insist on, say 5% of revenue, tell them your break-even point is $X and make it high. If you reach that pinnacle of sales, you shouldn't mind sharing the profit. But it isn't your job to protect a landlord. He isn't going to pay you a percentage of his gain if he sells the center because generous tenants like you keep it full at premium rates.

When they ask for percentage rent, I may agree but counter this with demand: "If the shopping center storefront vacancy should exceed 30%, the monthly rent shall be reduced by 20%." The landlord's lack of tenants and traffic will negatively impact your business. Fair, isn't it? If you do well, you pay them. If they do poorly, they pay you! Nothing is set in stone; ask for it.

- If the space requires make-ready improvements, allow ample time so you are not paying rent during the construction period. If those improvements will ultimately inure to the benefit of the landlord, ask him to pay for all or part of the cost. For example, if you install a new suspended ceiling, it is routine for the landlord to pay that entire expense, or perhaps credit your rent for a "construction allowance" equal to a percentage of the cost. While they may not agree to subsidize cosmetic improvements, they should agree to participate in the cost of structural work or permanent improvements.

- Make certain you retain the right to remove all store fixtures even if they are attached to the freehold, and demand the landlord execute a Landlord's Waiver* so you can legally remove merchandise and fixtures at the end of the lease term, even if you are in default. Tell them your lenders and equipment lessors require the waiver.

As a tenant, I've encountered helpful and reasonable landlords and others who behaved like vampires and tried to squeeze the life out of my business. I once had six mall stores with the same hungry developer and paid my rent like clockwork for seven years. I came to understand that allowing staff to sign my name to checks is rarely an acceptable practice; assuming the rent was being paid, it actually became three weeks delinquent during my stay in the hospital. The store managers called in a panic: "There are chains around our gates!"

There was no notice. My office staff offered to overnight payment. The developer said, "Drive the cash to our corporate office and only then will the chains come off." We made the 12-hour trip. For these kinds of reasons, a lease written in your favor will have a notice of default with a right to cure. Your perceived personality of a landlord is not as vital as a comprehensive lease.

You should never, ever sign any commercial lease without review by a lawyer unless you know your corporation is worthless or unless you hold a unilateral right to terminate. While you may, or may not, have an attorney negotiate for you, it is always best to obtain a review and ask them to modify the legalese to afford you a reasonable level of protection.

If you've already signed a lease, renegotiate it! Landlords want uninterrupted cash flow, not vacant space. Empty rooms are embarrassing to a landlord, and it reflects poorly on their entire center and makes their lenders nervous. Don't hesitate to meet with them and prepare a case as to why you can no longer afford the rent. You will be shocked to find many smart landlords will modify the lease in order to avoid dark rooms.

After you've occupied the space for six months, new types of issues may surface and some could become critical. If there is a high turnover of either owners or tenants, you need to discover the reason. The best source of information is from adjoining tenants who will delight in talking about the landlord and property defects.

Having been both a landlord and tenant 1,000 times, I conclude that most landlords are jerks and most tenants are scumbags. While I've had some truly wonderful tenants, many will destroy the property and leave the premises in the middle of the night. It is difficult for a landlord to be a nice guy because when financial pressures arise, tenants quickly attempt to breach the lease. Their lawyers scour the document seeking ways to "get their client out." Worse, tenants blame the landlord for their demise because of outrageous reasons.

Owning your own property

While there are times to rent space, overall it is preferable to divert rental payments to mortgage payments, thereby creating principal build-up. Each time you mail your landlord a check, envision yourself tossing your hard earned dollars into the swamp, because you truly are throwing money away.

When purchasing a commercial property, doing your homework is as, or more, important than when you lease. After all, you are making a significant investment of your own or your partners' money. Not only do you want a location that is suitable for your business, you need to determine the market value of the property so you don't overpay.

You also need assess at the condition of the building, the parking lot, the landscaping and any other factors to reduce the risk of an unpleasant and unexpected surprise. If there was an oil leak years ago that contaminated the soil or ground water, for example, you could be liable for a costly clean-up. If the HVAC system is at the end of its lifespan, you may need to pour significant dollars into a modern, energy-efficient replacement. And if there is limited broadband service, you might have to pay for a high-speed fiber optic cable or a wireless system with multiple access points.

On the other hand, real estate can be a very positive long-term investment, increasing in value through the years. You can also use leverage in the form of a commercial mortgage in order to purchase your business site with "other people's money." Finally, there are a number of tax incentives and financial benefits that come along with owning property, making it a good stepping stone for the accumulation of wealth.

While still in college and against the strong advice of my father, I purchased my first apartment building for $24,000 — and then sold it when I needed cash for $155,000! Dad isn't always right! Learn to trust yourself. If time is on your side, you can afford to make some blunders.

When first in business, I spent my time scraping up a few thousand dollars as a down payment and didn't understand the power of leverage. One day a friend, who was also on the board of our local bank, said, "Do you know what the bankers in town call you? The Leverage King." I unwittingly used one dollar and turned it into a hundred. Borrowing to purchase good real estate is part of becoming successful.

Occasionally a client will boast that they have no debt. When I'm finished with my "leverage lecture," they're out trying to borrow to buy or invest. So, don't be afraid to apply for a loan when you see a good deal, especially if you can do it under one of the entities described in Chapter 5 – without a personal guarantee. Make the lender your partner in risk. They have cash and they need to put it on the street!

Before graduation from college, I also signed a lease for my first retail location. After using this location as a stepping stone, I later purchased a larger showroom that included apartments — the least risky real estate investment. Today, my office is still in that same building, which has paid for itself a dozen times. As you search for a business location, look for buildings with several other rental units and you may be able to operate your company "rent-free." Just remember that the good buys normally need improvements, or you may need to design the space for your own use. But when you make improvements in your own properties, you build equity for yourself, not your landlord.

How much is the property worth?

As you search for a promising property, here are three things that you should do:

1. Retain a buyer's agent from a commercial real estate agency in your local market. They will scour the market and come back with a list of suitable properties and buildings along with pricing per square foot. You may need to make some adjustments because of the condition, location or age of the properties. Be sure to get information on comparable sales as this will become your first estimate of value.

2. Ask your buyer's agent to obtain a copy of the last appraisal, no matter how dated it might be; adjust it for inflation.

3. Ask your buyer's agent to obtain the current income statement for the property and make adjustments to reflect your anticipated costs, remove their non-business expenses and compute your debt service.

If you're comfortable the property will meet your business needs or generate revenue adequate to pay expenses and service debt, or if the owner or the investment group you've created will finance all or part of the sale, buy it. If you're still unsure, pay for an appraisal. Do not share the conclusion with the seller, unless it is much less than you offered to pay.

If you must apply for a conventional loan, you will need an appraisal. However, don't order one directly because most banks are required to select the appraiser to be assured you're not hiring your best friend and paying him with a few cases of beer. Go to a local architect, and ask how much it costs per foot to construct a building with similar specifications in your region. Add the value of the land to that cost. Then, estimate the replacement cost value based on the total square footage.

Congratulations! By considering comparable sales, the replacement cost and the income, you've done your own appraisal. Weight-average the results for your own Estimate of Value*.

The cost for an appraisal may be anywhere from $300 to $5,000, especially if your appraiser has a lot of letters behind their name — but you can prepare your initial appraisal yourself. Tell the bank you want to place a limit on the cost, because it will select the most expensive appraiser in the county; it will also select conservative appraisers, so its conclusion may help you negotiate a lower acquisition price and support an upcoming appeal to lower real estate taxes. The appraisal isn't as difficult as it reads with all of the subjective gumblygook.

Now you know what it is worth — but is it a good investment? Several important rate-of-return measures are critical for evaluating the debt and equity structure of a project. The first is the rate of return on total capital (ROR):

Return on Capital Employed

$$\text{Return on Capital Employed} = \frac{\text{Net Operating Profit}}{\text{Employed Capital}}$$

You can calculate Capital Employed by subtracting current liabilities from total assets:

Return on Equity Ratio

$$\text{Return on Equity Ratio} = \frac{\text{Net Income}}{\text{Shareholder's Equity}}$$

The second important rate-of-return measurement is the return on the investor's initial equity investment (ROE), sometimes referred to as the cash-on-cash return or the equity dividend rate:

Return on Capital Employed

$$\text{Return on Capital Employed} = \frac{\text{Net Operating Profit}}{\text{Total Assets - Current Liabilities}}$$

Comparable sales can be obtained through a broker or agent, the replacement cost through an architect and the value by the income approach by simply applying a capitalization rate to the net income:

$$\textbf{market value} = \frac{\textbf{net operating income}}{\textbf{capitalization rate}}$$

Adjust the alleged annual gross income by reducing it to an actual, effective gross income by adding a 5 or 6 percent management expense, plus an appropriate vacancy allowance. Do not use a rule of thumb percentage for vacancy; apply the historical vacancy of the particular building.

Many people allow the process, professionals, formulas and terminology to bog them down, if not discourage them forever. Instead, focus more on finding deep pocket investors and negotiate hard with anxious sellers. You may not need the bank or the appraiser to cut a deal. Your second and third deals will be much easier and by the end of a decade, you'll be making more money and building more wealth than all of your loan officers and appraisers combined. Pull the trigger.

The Real Estate

It is almost impossible to lose money in a real estate investment if you purchase at a good price (which is where the real profit is made), take care of the property and cultivate happy tenants who pay their rent timely. This is because other factors are operating in the background, such as a continual demand for real estate and inflation. If your loan is fixed for a period of time, your rental income can be increased. If you borrowed money, inflation allows you to repay your loan with cheaper money.

Strive to play the game with integrity

A real estate investor should be as gentle as a lamb but as shrewd as a fox. A dear friend became one of the largest developers in our region. He was very soft spoken and avoided disputes and situations where contractors would lose. He structured deals that met the needs of the adversary's as well as his own. He understood that it is best to build an atmosphere of trust, honesty, and cooperation to succeed long term. This is always the best approach. But if it doesn't work, be prepared to trample on anyone who gets in your way or you'll never reach the end zone.

Hurry up and close a deal

Ask yourself a few questions to determine whether you buy a property:

- Does it look good?

- Do I care if it's junk?
- How much will it cost to fix it up?
- Is it worth the asking price?
- Will the owner accept a small down payment?
- Can I secure some investors?
- Can I pay the mortgage, improvements and expenses from the income?
- Does the owner have clear title?
- Am I willing to work?
- Do I wait to buy it or just buy it now and wait to get rich?

If you have more time and inclination to study the science of real estate, then the book you may want in your library is *Real Estate Investment* by Stephen A. Phyrr and James R. Cooper. Otherwise, go cut a deal.

Tips To Keep You Afloat

> As the sign on the cemetery fence says,
> "Get a lot while you're young."
> Buying versus leasing will be one of your most important
> business decisions; make it carefully.
> Study landlordism from the perspective of a tenant and
> property owner.
> As a tenant, consider all of the property and location issues
> the landlord considered when he made his purchase,
> and then some.
> Taxes and tax credits are as important as income
> and expenses.
> Your real estate agent can sell you a two-story property -
> one story before the sale and one story after.
> In the game of real estate, as in all business transactions,
> be fair and develop trust in long-term relationships.

CROSSING THE SWAMP

Operating Your Business

Perseverance and resiliency are crucial traits for a successful entrepreneur. You will also need to cultivate your people skills, such as listening to your customers, motivating your employees, and negotiating with your suppliers. Stay focused on your goal as you paddle across the swamp.

7. THE PEOPLE

> "When dealing with people, remember you are not dealing with creatures of logic, but creatures of emotion."
>
> Dale Carnegie

I t may sound crass, but people are a necessary evil in business. As German economist E. F. Schumacher said, "It is the ideal of the employer to have production without employees, and the ideal of the employee is to have income without work."

However, success as an entrepreneur depends on people. That includes managers, production teams and sales people, as well as the support staff needed to keep your venture cruising across the swamp. I've employed some pretty crazy people who were also good producers alongside the "normal" people who kept our companies going. Consider your people your biggest asset — as well as the biggest source of potential problems.

Know Yourself

You are the most important person in your business. Like everyone else, you have an individual combination of strengths and weaknesses or, as the politically correct HR folks would say, "potential areas of improvement." Your drive and determination to succeed as an entrepreneur may be based on your knowledge of technology or finance, your sales skills or your understanding of the marketplace. But there will undoubtedly be areas where your knowledge, skills and interests are, shall we say, less than perfect. That's fine if you are aware of those gaps and find good people to plug those holes in your canoe.

Business writer Michael Gerber identified two different types of business owners in his series of books on what he calls the E-Myth. Some have an entrepreneurial perspective that work on the business, setting goals and objectives and seeking out new opportunities and directions. Others have the technician perspective, working in the business, refining existing systems and procedures and fixing operational problems. Ideally, you should strive to be both types so you can become your most productive employee.

Another part of knowing yourself is understanding your own personality. A number of tools are available for this purpose, such as the Personality Compass, a book by Diane Turner and Thelma Greco that divides personality traits into north, south, east, and west with these attributes:

NORTH:

A leader, goal centered, fast paced, task oriented, assertive, decisive, determined, confident and independent

SOUTH:

A team player, process centered, slow paced, good listener, non-confrontational, sensitive, patient, understanding, generous and helpful

EAST:

A planner, quality centered, analytical, organized, logical, focused, exact, perfectionist, industrious and structured

WEST:

A risk taker, idea centered, creative, innovative, flexible, visionary, spontaneous, enthusiastic, free-spirited and energetic

Understanding the various personality types is also very helpful when hiring new employees, managing their activities and building a sense of collaboration and teamwork. So pay attention to personalities and strive to include all four types in your organization because they bring different strengths to your business.

Be mindful of which personality type is more fitted for specific assignments. For instance, it is important to give North a project that will motivate them and hold their interest, rather than make them bored. Some personalities may complement each other, and having those employees team up on a project could be a positive thing for each individual and the company.

Selecting and Hiring People

Building an effective and efficient staff is crucial to the success of your operation. Traditionally the primary recruitment medium was "help wanted" advertising in newspapers, magazines, posters and fliers. Crafting copy, reading and sifting resumes and preparing a short list of candidates is time-consuming, and these tasks were frequently delegated to an expensive recruitment agency in large organizations.

The Internet and social media have made it much easier to identify and attract prospective employees. Most entrepreneurs can do the work themselves, rather than hire a search firm or employment agency. But the automation of the process has numerous pitfalls.

Search engines can screen resumes far faster than humans, but their efficiency is based on searching for keywords. Applicants know this and tailor their resume accordingly; as a result, the talents and attitudes of the applicants can be lost.

After you have sorted through the emails, you can schedule some preliminary interviews over the phone, messaging apps or Skype, and then follow up with at least one face-to-face interview before hiring. As a general rule, do not quote an hourly rate or salary range until you have this face-to-face interview and verify past performance history.

Depending on the position, you may want to consult with an attorney before extending an offer to a new hire. In any case, try to be as specific as possible in terms of the job description, probation period, salary, and benefits, so everything is clear at the start.

Always ensure that potential recruits complete a standard company application form with sufficient detail to permit a criminal background check and seek past employment verification. The form should contain language that warns the candidate that untruthful information would constitute future termination of employment, and grants permission to investigate their credit history. Desperate, financially, strapped employees will rank higher on the internal theft meter.

Here are some things to consider when hiring new people, assessing their performance, or determining if they are ready for a promotion:

- They're driven.
- They accept responsibility.
- They know that success is never an accident.
- They know the customer is their real "boss."
- They look, listen, and learn.
- They find out if they're not sure.

- They set an example for others.
- They know the next field only looks greener.
- They welcome new ideas.
- They profit by their mistakes.
- They speak clearly and convincingly.
- They do not expect all the credit.
- They cooperate.
- They realize their future is their own responsibility.
- They believe that good manners are good business.
- They know the world does not owe them a living.
- They are willing to go that "extra mile."
- They are careful about their finances.
- They set goals for themselves.
- They realize that everything worth having has a price tag.
- They know the value of enthusiasm.
- They try to help their employer.
- They never "pass the buck."
- They control their temper.
- They work to cut expenses.
- They never use drugs.

Onboarding New Employees

This is an excerpt from a message to my employees in 1976 — and it is timeless:

This is plain talk about you, your job, and your future. You'll either believe it and do something about it — or you won't. Your decision may mark a turning point in your future.

The People

Whatever your work happens to be, your own progress, and that of the company, are tightly bound together. Each is dependent upon the other for success.

Our company will continue to progress only as long as it continues to provide a better product or service to satisfied customers.

You and your team members will continue to progress only as long as you place more and more intelligent thought, effort, interest and enthusiasm into the everyday operation of your career. This is the only way our company can provide better products and service.

This is easy to understand when we realize that every business is simply a group of people working together for the purpose of providing goods or services to another group of people to make a profit for our company and provide a livelihood for our employees.

The primary reason not all companies in the same industry progress equally is usually because not all of the people working in those companies place the same degree of thought, effort, interest and enthusiasm into the everyday operation of their career.

Unfortunately, the attitude of many people is "I guess that's good enough," "What difference does it make?" or "What's in it for me?"

History shows that people who advance are people who derive genuine satisfaction in doing a better job. Remember: someone will make a success of your job and use it as a stepping stone to bigger things. Why can't that someone be you?

I would suggest you consider including these ideas and concepts in your "welcome aboard" talks with new employees. After all, you want to set the stage for the future and remind them from the start that they are working for the company — not for you. It's important for employees to feel they are part of the big picture rather than just working for an individual.

In your onboarding communication, you can emphasize the values of your business, your corporate culture or the ways your company is contributing to society. Talented people today like to feel they are part of a "worthy" organization, and it's up to you to establish that ambiance. But don't worry about having to create a "fun" work environment or letting your assistant bring Fido to the office. Some Silicon Valley firms encourage employees to play games at work, but that will be a distraction from focusing on the key issues: getting new business and serving your customers. Otherwise, they may start thinking about your lifestyle, family, hobbies, and other non-business issues. Do everything possible to keep your people focused on the business.

Motivating People

Extrinsic motivation derives from anticipation of external reactions, including praise, recognition and money. Intrinsic motivation comes from a worker's internal sense of purpose and personal satisfaction of work. You will need to tap into both types of motivation to keep employees paddling your canoe across the swamp. Earlier in this chapter we talked about finding employees who are motivated to contribute to your business. Now, we will turn our attention to extrinsic motivators.

For example, I have always been a proponent of non-monetary demonstrations of appreciation such as flowers to a spouse, dinner coupons, theater tickets and providing daily lunches to my staff. Do this because you truly care about your good people – and because it may be less costly than raises. Along with manufacturers, I co-funded trips around the world for a hundred people. We devised programs for clients to send productive employees on paid vacations. Few competitors make this effort and sometimes it's seen for what it is – the boss rewarding his allies.

Other suggestions include weekly, monthly or quarterly recognition programs – a nice luncheon, an email with an "atta-boy" message or an article in the organization's newsletter. Recognize top performers and let them enjoy their moment in the spotlight.

Along the same lines, set aside funds to invest in training. Too often entrepreneurs are so consumed with creativity and cash flow demands that they do not design training programs. It's vital to the success of an organization that staffers understand and meet your expectations. Selecting someone for a training program is also a great motivator, since it shows you care about that person's future and trust their ability to mentor others in your company. It's often said that the pace of change in business practices is so great that few people will remain in the same job, or even career, for their working lives. Training staff is critical to retention and a dollar of training is worth three dollars of recruitment. If you fail to provide some level of internal or external training program in each department every three months, revenue tends to decline.

Perform and Prosper

Money motivates when tied to performance, and demotivates if it is thought that rewards are not distributed fairly. Ensure that the award of merit increases and performance bonuses are clearly and openly tied to superior levels of output. It's often said, "If you pay peanuts, you get monkeys."

Conversely, your company is not a social welfare program. What

was originally seen as a way of avoiding escalating wage growth by providing non-monetary benefits has transformed itself into a major cost burden on employment. In today's economy, with a higher demand than supply, benefits are almost a necessity. Remember that most employees will "jump ship" as soon as your canoe takes on water; benefits will help keep them in your boat. No longer do employees care about long-term employment relationships; some actually prefer change.

The successful entrepreneur must harden his heart to these considerations and focus solely on ensuring that his workforce is productive. Carrying a less effective employee is not only unfair to the owner, but also unfair to more productive workers. By offering compensation plans with bonuses and educating and indoctrinating people, the loyal and successful people will help you "weed out" poor performers because they will adopt a healthier interest in the company. That's important because in many small companies, a large majority of employees can be somewhat inept.

With 17 outlet stores, I invented my own approach to this dilemma. In order to corral and manage ineptness, I rewarded one person in each building, store or office to supervise the rest. This allows you to scream at one person as opposed to a hundred. Pay this person very well so he or she won't quit if reprimanded. Move payroll dollars from marginal employees to producers. How's that for a departure from all the motivational business books written by shrinks?

Employees must have financial incentives for superior performance. When employees receive only a salary, big producers are scarce. While there are many sales compensation programs, the thread of consistency is the need for rewards. Entrepreneurs want to live beyond the norm and so do good employees. If an employee can generate an additional $100,000 of profit a year, there's no reason he shouldn't receive a $10,000 bonus. However, sales department compensation is entirely different than other professions. If you want to grow, you must share. You can't eat the whole pie: "A pig gets fat; a hog gets slaughtered."

Always remember that people are your most important asset, especially those who are incentivized and are loyal and proud of their company. They are your true competitive advantage; other assets can be copied by others. If you want to develop a new mobile app, give your coders a bonus. If your service technician refers a customer to your sales department, give them a split of the revenue. Incentivize everyone!

Phantom Stock Program

A non-traditional, seldom used mechanism to attract and retain key people, especially salespeople, is to offer a "Phantom Stock Program." This creative, long-term incentive plan allows you to reward employees without stock dilution. In effect, it is a type of deferred bonus – the value of which will ultimately be tied to appreciation in the equity or market value of the sponsoring company. You will need a lawyer to create this effective, but seldom used incentive vehicle.

Leading People

If you are the owner of a business, you're in the position to lead. You possess these skills and qualities at a higher level than the average person. Whether because of intentional reasoning or a lack of ability, your employees will rarely outperform you. Therefore, the myth that employees should be in control of your company is a farce. If you're not constantly providing oversight, trouble is on the horizon. Few will ever negotiate as strongly as you or generate the same level of profit; few will love your customers or act in your best interest. Everything your employees do, you will be able to improve. Every time they think something has been resolved, you'll find a way to make a further improvement. If you don't believe that about yourself, then step aside, promote people you respect, and pray.

John Maxwell says, "Most people who want to get ahead do it backwards. They think, I'll get a bigger job and then I'll learn how to be a leader. But showing leadership skill is how you get the bigger job in the first place. Leadership is not a position, it's a process. Before you're a leader, success is all about growing yourself. When you become a leader, success is about growing others."

As a leader, you must realize that many employees do not understand profitability and how much business the company must capture in order to survive. Many owners believe professionals pocket $275 out of every $300 per hour they charge; that's as untrue as believing a retailer making a 50 percent mark-up is keeping 40 percent of the sales price. Thus, it's important to constantly remind employees of the cost of doing business so they understand that most of the revenue dollars coming in the front door are going out the back as costs. By explaining these realities, you can ensure that people will harbor less resentment of your success.

Be Truthful with Your People

When assuming control of a troubled company, I gathered all of the employees in the factory and stood on a crate to announce that we filed bankruptcy that morning. I knew from company appraisal forms that the workers harbored resentment against the founder's son who flaunted his lavish lifestyle with airplanes and vacation homes.

It was the Board's practice to keep sensitive information from employees. I dropped a copy of the 100-page financial analysis on the crate. I wanted the employees to know that we were approaching difficult times, needed their support, needed them to understand why they would temporarily lose health insurance benefits and that we had a plan to recover. I explained that, without their cooperation, the company would be forced to close its doors. If they had any questions or doubts, they were welcome to peruse the financial documents at my feet.

These wonderful people, many of whom had family that worked in the firm, came to our rescue with increased production. Tell employees the truth, because they know the truth anyway, and they deserve to know it.

Managing People

The management of employees will prove to be one of your major challenges. Poor levels of ability will threaten the survival of your business. But you have the power to overcome this obstacle by hiring good managers and establishing and enforcing solid policies and procedures. The three R's of managing people are:

R = Require

R = Review

R = Reward

Determine what you expect from employees and communicate those expectations. Then determine whether those expectations were met and fairly distribute raises and benefits accordingly.

There are some big differences between leaders and managers. Professional managers can repeat the same task over and over, but most successful entrepreneurs can't handle boredom. The difference in these two familiar types runs so deeply that, if you're a manager, it's unlikely you'll succeed in the role of entrepreneur – just as entrepreneurs tend to make poor managers.

Leaders are proactive; managers are reactive. Managers seek compromise; leaders challenge the norm. Managers meet expectations; leaders create them. Leaders not only possess high energy, they can energize their followers. The smart entrepreneur recognizes that he or she is not the best listener and may not have the personality to enjoy mundane tasks.

While good managers focus intently on the details of programs and policies, good leaders are less consumed by operational minutia. Instead, leaders inspire people with their clear vision of the big picture. Therefore, the wise entrepreneur will appoint someone to keep track of the mess he or she is making. Entrepreneurs often require a small army of helpers with brooms to clean up after them. People who are both creative and organized are rare.

Great leaders who groom others for greatness are rare, too. Jack Welch, the hardnosed former leader of industrial giant General Electric, demanded what he called the "Three Es" from GE's senior management. His focus on training and leadership succession helped GE retain its keen competitive edge.

E = Energy

E = Energize others

E = Execute plans

The People

Jack Welch also had some keen insights into the different types of people that can be very helpful when managing others. He came up with the following four types:

Type I: As Welch said, "This is everybody's star." This person will deliver on commitments and share our values. He or she possesses attributes like the love of speed, a hatred of bureaucracy, is not paralyzed by change, and respects everyone engaged in the cause of winning.

Type II: They are just the opposite. They do not meet commitments or share company values, so get them out of the organization.

Type III: They are a bit more complicated. They try hard but miss commitments and do not always make the numbers. But they share company values and work well with other employees, so work with them.

Type IV: This employee reaches company goals but disregards values rather than building production upon them. This is your big shot and a tyrant you would prefer to eliminate, but can't afford to fire. Although this person will deliver performance in the short-term, he or she will likely be poison in the long-term.

As for payroll compliance, the Department of Labor says managers should meet the following criteria:

- Regularly supervise two or more other employees
- Have management as the primary duty of the position
- Have some genuine input into the job status of other employees

The importance of this criteria will be explained later in this book. The supervision must be a regular part of the employee's job. They should perform typical management duties which, as defined by the Fair Labor Standards Act, include:

- Interviewing, selecting and training employees,
- Setting rates of pay and hours of work,
- Maintaining production or sales records,
- Appraising productivity, handling employee grievances or complaints, or disciplining employees,
- Determining work techniques,
- Planning work,
- Apportioning work among employees,
- Determining the types of equipment to be used or materials needed to perform work,
- Planning budgets for work,
- Monitoring work for legal or regulatory compliance,
- Providing safety and security of the workplace.

Look for Diamonds in the Rough

After assuming control of another manufacturing company facing bankruptcy, I bumped into one of the 400 employees in the parking lot and said, "Brian, let's grab a sandwich and a beer." We landed in a bar and began to talk about the plight of the organization where he had been employed for 25 years. I began to hear intriguing opinions surrounding the production lines. I turned over a placemat and asked that he list the opinions. The next day I presented his ideas at a management meeting and most drew skepticism. Next, I contracted with a consulting firm that identifies waste, and they concluded the ideas were viable and we could save hundreds of thousands of dollars each year!

In his blue shirt and jeans, Brian accompanied me to the next

Board meeting. He was terrified. "What's he doing here?" the fat, cigar-smoking dinosaurs asked. I announced: "Meet your new Director of Operations." Stunned, they challenged my decision. I conveyed the placemat notes and consultant's report. "Brian", they asked, "why didn't you ever give us these solutions?" "Well, you never asked me," he said. Off he went to buy a white shirt and tie for his new position.

If a current management team has not been able to fix financial debacles, their opinions carry little weight. But be cautious, because advancing line and staff employees who excel is dangerous; management requires a learned skill set. Many people with a mouth and desk believe they're management material.

Before fully appreciating the complexities of management, one of my regional sales managers came to me with a suggestion. "Steve, I want to make Larry Lizard manager of our New York store. Larry's been with us for six years and he sells more pianos in a week than the rest sell in a month! I think he'd make one hell of a good manager." I said okay, and we gave him a copy of the One Minute Manager, a desk and the job. But Larry had no training or aptitude for management. During the next 30 days, he sold virtually nothing and two of our good salespeople quit. It was an expensive lesson. As Lawrence Peter purports in his Peter Principle, "Anything that works will be used in progressively more challenging applications until it fails."

Management Tools

As a proponent of staying in touch with employees, customers, and clients, I utilized the old suggestion box and online opinions to gather their ideas and opinions. It's extremely important to learn if your people are satisfied with their jobs, and it gives your employees an outlet to gripe, as well as offer their suggestions.

It may not be possible for your managers to monitor progress of their subordinates and track their to-do lists. The Weekly Activity Report* will not only solve this dilemma but will keep the staff focused. You'll know what they were charged to do and what they did or did not accomplish. The use of this Report will lessen your interaction, and it is indispensable when your staff is working off-site.

Another good tool is "PERT" (Project Evaluation & Review Technique)* a method of managing projects, monitoring productivity and meeting "drop dead dates." Your managers can use this approach in conjunction with the Critical Path Analysis, which charts all the processes and activities involved in accomplishing a task and quantifies each of them in terms of time. The Critical Path identifies all the elements in the sequence that cannot be accomplished until certain prior tasks are complete. Thus the total time needed to complete the project is the sum of the time needed for each of the critical elements.

Put it in Writing

From the time you extend a job offer to the exit interview, you must constantly document your actions with employees. As a general rule, verbal employee communication is worthless and dangerous. Here are some documents to consider.

- **Employment Agreement**. Many owners avoid employee

contracts even though the new hire is entering into a business relationship. The Employment Agreement* should set forth expectations and include a Schedule of Compensation to avert disagreements. Remember that you can give some employees a Winnebago as a bonus, but when you ask them to pay for the gas, they'll feel cheated.

- **A Non-Compete Covenant.** Whether you hire a doctor, carpenter or retailer, an employee may decide to steal your business secrets and use them as ammunition to destroy your firm. If they leave your employment, they typically head to the comfort zone of your competitors. Having developed disdain for you and your company over the years, or being disgruntled by a termination, they may take joy in machine-gunning you by stealing your customers. An employee who does not anticipate acting in this fashion should not be hesitant in signing a non-compete covenant*. Otherwise, do not place them on your payroll. Someone will eventually raid your company and influence other employees to join them in the exodus.

- **Company Policies.** No firm should do business without a comprehensive Policy Manual*. It minimizes valuable time wasted on gripes and problems because communication can be lessened with a simple reference to your manual. An indispensable manual also eliminates confusion and misunderstandings. It will solidify the organization, set direction, protect you in the event of litigation, and offer employees a sense of security. I've represented business owners without written procedures who were accused of sexual harassment. Since most insurance policies do not protect against that peril, a sleazy lawyer could squeeze a $10,000 nuisance settlement from you along with your defense costs.

- **Operations Manuals.** Develop an Operations Manual so the company is run in a manner you designed; system mandates should be in writing. For example, a major reason for fast food success is that guests know what to expect. If you're a restaurant, you may benefit from an ingredients manual so your staff will not test their culinary skills on your customers.

- **Employee Evaluations.** Evaluate your people and allow them to evaluate management as well. While often overlooked in the rush of the fast-paced business world, the benefits are an absolute necessity. Have your employees write their own evaluations to describe their progress and plans to develop business in the future. Monitor their productivity with an Employee Appraisal* that will provide a guideline to their abilities.

- **Corrective Action Interviews.** Infractions should be reduced to writing and signed by the parties involved. The Corrective Action Interview Form* will allow your employees to understand how they made an error. It will explain the problem and how it should be corrected. It allows your people to acknowledge that if they continue to ignore policies or use poor judgment, their actions will not be tolerated. The warnings will be a matter of record, and eventually they could cause a termination. This form is essential when attending a hearing where an employee is attempting to force you to pay for their incompetence or a "voluntary quit" due to alleged "compelling reasons." This may negatively affect your unemployment account if those claims should be approved. If you do not attend hearings to defend your position, you are damaging yourself financially and allowing employees to fuel abuse.

- **Personnel Files.** Employee arrangements, whether with managers or laborers, should be formal understandings retained in the employee's personnel file. The state and federal government will accept the word of an employee over an employer. If you have any delusions the government is working on your behalf in this arena, put them to rest. As Henry Ford once said, "Any man who thinks he can become happy and prosperous by letting the government take care of him . . . better take a closer look at the American Indian period."

The agencies established to process employee claims can only survive with many cases; hearing referees are often extremely biased against the employer. However, if you present information to explain incidences in violation of your policy manual and demonstrate that you gave the employee an opportunity to correct the problem, there is some hope of success. Without that written evidence, you will lose.

Labor-Related Issues

One of my long-term technical employees requested to have his salary increased because he was working nights and weekends. We needed the production, and he was anxious to fulfill the demand as opposed to hiring more people. His salary went up and up and up and when he finally retired, he filed a claim with the Department of Labor stating that he was working 80 hours each week without overtime or double pay. Remember, overtime wage rates are a penalty levied to pressure business owners to hire more people.

The Labor Department levied a $15,000 penalty against my company and we were required to pay him time and a half-calculated on his increased salary. Therefore, the higher base rate became the yardstick and it cost dramatically more than it would have cost to retain additional technicians. Thus, a $100,000 judgment was entered against my company due to a retired employee who was smarter than our personnel department. Some owners would hide in a swamp and pay the assessment. I drove to Philadelphia and appealed. After presenting my case, the hearing officer abated the penalty and compromised the claim. The only reason for some relief was because

I had written documentation in his personnel file.

To avoid unemployment claims, overtime and the like, hire someone as an "independent contractor" rather than an employee. But be mindful of IRS tests. The degree of importance of each factor varies depending on the occupation and the factual context in which services are performed. These 20 factors are offered only as guides for determining whether or not an individual qualifies as an independent contractor:

- Are they given instructions?
- Do they receive training?
- Are they integrated into business operations?
- Is there a requirement services be rendered personally?
- Does the employer hire and pay assistants?
- Is there a continuity of the relationship?
- Do you establish the hours of work?
- Are there requirements of full-time work?
- Are they working on your premises?
- Are you setting the order or sequence of work?
- Do you pay the worker by the hour, week or month?
- Do you pay business or travel expenses?
- Are you furnishing tools and materials?
- Is there a significant investment by the worker?
- Is there a realization of profit or loss by the worker?
- Are they working for more than one business at a time?
- Are they available to the general public?
- Did they sign an Independent Contractor Agreement?
- Do you have the right to discharge the worker?
- Does the worker have the right to terminate the relationship?

You may never meet most tests, so sign an Independent Contractor Agreement* and hope you're not audited.

People Problems

At 21, when deciding whether to open my own business or continue working with an established company, I learned an invaluable lesson. After giving notice that I decided to start a company, my employer said, "Steve, you won't have problems with your vendors, landlords or customers . . . your employees will be your real problem." No truer statement was ever spoken.

Certainly sincere, dedicated, and honest employees are abundant. But this is a book about real business life so let's be blunt. The primary reason people are motivated to work is money. Many do not want to be there, but they have no choice. Many will develop disdain for "the rich boss" and envy sets in. Few will thank you for providing the means to feed their family.

While still in college, I hired a key employee to operate my first retail store. We planned our vacation to Rome, leaving him in command. When I arrived at the hotel front desk, I was handed a note that said, "Steve, I quit. Jack." Be prepared for this type of incident, learn to ignore it, keep forging ahead with your plan, and don't allow it to spoil your vacation.

Imposing Discipline

When your people start to pose problems on the job, there is an art to imposing discipline without generating resentment. My preferred style is one labeled by Douglas McGregor as the Hot-Stove Rule. This approach draws an analogy between touching a hot stove and undergoing discipline.

When you touch a hot stove your discipline is immediate, consistent, and impersonal. Your employee will learn their lesson quickly because:

1. The burn is immediate. There's no question of cause and effect.

2. They had a warning, knowing the stove is red hot and what may happen if they touch it.

3. The discipline is consistent; everyone who touches the stove is burned.

4. The discipline is impersonal; a person is burned not because of who he is but because he touched the stove.

The act and the discipline seem almost one. Employees are disciplined not because they are bad, but because they committed a particular act. The discipline is directed against the act, not against the person. The purpose of discipline should be to obtain compliance with established rules of conduct; it should not be punitive in nature. Strong discipline is also necessary to dissuade employees from stealing.

Let's put all of the soft management styles aside, especially one from some nut who wrote, "I'm more interested in serving my employees than having them serve me." This mindset may be effective for sweet mom-and-pop operators and perhaps a preacher, but if you're going to grow your revenue, people, and profits, you simply will not have time to coddle the masses.

It's important to temper the Hot Stove Rule. You can't allow the Hot Stove Rule to cause you to become the "Napoleon Leader" who surrounds himself with "yes-men." Otherwise, you'll never create a loyal organization or learn what employees need. You'll shut strong, independent, and original minds down. Discipline is a balancing act.

When firing people, avoid being your own hatchet man; assign someone to make unpopular decisions who can "take the fall" when they get too harsh. However, if you're determined to be tough, you must have the mindset of a drill sergeant. As Al Capone said, "You can get much further with a kind word and a gun than with a kind word alone." Your troops are not going to love you, but they'll respect you – as long as you can show them you're tougher than they are, and you're willing to drive yourself even harder than you're driving them.

Protect Against Internal Threats

Strong monitoring and enforcement programs are critical to safeguarding your assets. For example, when in the music business, I sat alone one night on a fire escape until early morning to observe two of my salespeople exit the warehouse to retrieve half a dozen guitars they had placed in the Dumpster during business hours.

As an entrepreneur, you should never allow "sweethearting," which is when employees perform an unauthorized give-away of service and merchandise to "sweetheart customers" like their friends, family, and even fellow employees.

They'll give free drinks to their friends at your bar, toss in freebies in a sale, and take supplies home simply because they think it's their right. Ask your accountant to assist you in developing an internal audit and financial management system. Ask yourself:

- Does someone other than the cashier or bookkeeper open all mail and prepare a record of receipts?

- Is the person who keeps the books the same person who keeps the money?

- Is one person preparing accounts receivable and another preparing accounts payable?

- Are all receipts deposited daily without delay?

- Are 941 payroll and sales taxes deposited and timely paid?

- Is postage either purchased online or metered?

- Are sales invoices pre-numbered in all instances?

- Are pre-numbered receiving documents used for incoming goods?

- Are all credit memos and gift certificates pre-numbered and recorded?

- Are checks pre-numbered and is the back-up supply locked in a safe place?

- Do you require two signatures on all checks?

- Are signature stamps only allowed for petty cash payments, C.O.D., freight and miscellaneous charges under $300.00 per check?

- Do you have money escrowed from employee deductions?

- Do you restrict the use of petty cash to funds for the payment of small expenditures?

- Are petty cash disbursements signed by an employee and the individual who receives the money?

- Is the computer system backed up on-site and off-site?

- Are fireproof filing cabinets utilized for important documents?

- Do you have a video monitoring and security system accessible on your cell phone?

- Do you manage and utilize a locked key cabinet?

- Has employee bonding been considered?

- Do you require employees to take annual vacations to allow for spot checks on their work while out of the office?

- Are time clocks or computers utilized for hourly employees?

- Are personal credit checks run on your employees?

- Have you created an Equipment List and assigned an ID number to fixed assets?

- Is there an annual inspection of the fixed assets?

- Are inter-company sales or transfers accompanied with the generation of an invoice from the transferor entity to transferee entity?

- Do you monitor dual endorsements and payments to unfamiliar vendors?

- Are inventory records maintained by someone other than receiving or shipping departments?

Failing to adhere to all of these precautions cost my company hundreds of thousands of dollars together with an IRS audit and criminal investigation. Forgive my cynicism, but you must recognize that some employees would steal the Last Supper.

Theft Tolerance Level

At age 20 while managing a music store, I noticed a drop in the instruction book inventory. Each night before locking the doors, I counted the books and recounted them in the morning. We gave access to music instructors who taught customers in the evening and sold instruments in the daytime. Sure enough, books were disappearing overnight! I caught the thief and fired him on the spot. Word got to the corporate office, and I received a phone call to meet with the company president. Expecting an "atta-boy," I made the four-hour trip, and the conversation went somewhat like this:

Steve, I hear you caught Mr. Butt stealing music books.

Yep, that thief was selling our instruction manuals at night!

How many did he steal?

At least 40 a month.

How much do they cost us?

About $3.00 a piece.

So Butts is stealing about $120 a month?

Yep.

What were his keyboard sales last month?

I'm not sure.

$15,800.

Really, wow!

What's our profit margin?

40%

So we made $6,320 profit?

I guess so.

And you fired him?

Yeah.

Well son, put your big fat ass back in that Caddy, go to Mr. Butt's home, get him back on my sales floor by tomorrow morning and gently let him know that we inventory the books.

Yes sir.

When my firm undertakes a forensic audit, we typically find thieves in all kinds of businesses. In my first music store, a well-to-do, motherly-type accountant stole $37,000 within six months! I caught her, prosecuted her and recovered about half the money. I still have her photograph today to remind me to keep my guard up. By the time we had a dozen stores, 5 percent of our merchandise went missing each year. I closed the stores and administered unannounced polygraph examinations to determine that most of the loss was due to internal shrinkage. We offered amnesty and employees returned pianos, organs, and stereo equipment! Among the thieves were some of our most trusted people.

But don't utilize the polygraph today as it may invite litigation or be a violation of the Employee Polygraph Protection Act.

Employees also steal time and intangibles. They might put their personal needs first or have the misguided belief they're being exploited. Consider a waste of anything theft. When you have an employee being paid $10.00/hour to browse Facebook or post photos to Instagram, you're losing money. If you have two people in the break room talking for 20 minutes about their weekends, they're stealing your time. That's one reason office cubicles were invented.

Prosecute Thieves

Think before you call the police, who may do little with theft claims, as lazy prosecutors who often deem them to be a civil matter. Instead, confront the thief. You can often evoke an admission by indicating there were cameras, and that you have evidence – the same strategy used by police. If they admit to taking $2,000, double it because they probably stole more.

Insist on financial restitution. Tell them to finance the repayment over a few years with interest. Turn problems into profits. Adopt a zero tolerance policy for theft. While I'd rather they not steal, the additional recovery compensates you for your time, which is also money. Require thieves to sign an admission statement and if they do not pay, threaten an arrest. You will see the sense of this policy after you've encountered a few thieves.

Be Wary of Disgruntled Employees

As assistant to the chairman of the board of a large, publicly traded corporation in the medical field, it was my responsibility to monitor operations of the organization. A complaint call came into my office from an angry physician. I approached the president and made a request to meet the doctor for dinner and learn of his grievances. The response was: "No. These guys are a dime a dozen. Screw him. He earns $250,000 a year and that's all I need to know."

I pleaded for a mandate reversal but was unsuccessful. Months later the doctor filed a "whistleblower complaint" against the corporation alleging Medicare fraud and abuse for over-billing certain procedures. At the time, company stock had risen to $16 per share. The Wall Street Journal printed a front page article revealing the company was being audited for fraud. Overnight, stock plunged to $3 per share and subsequently, a bankruptcy was filed.

Another client who was embroiled in a divorce had his spouse involved in the business, and he filed a "snitch complaint" with the IRS. It's a little known fact that the IRS will pay a recovery fee of 10 percent for the name of someone believed to be defrauding the government. This retaliation destroyed the business for the family, and the filing spouse never did receive the recovery fee.

Oh No, Here Comes the Union

If you're not following along with the concepts in this book, you just might infuriate a large segment of your employees. If so, you had better become familiar with the Labor Management Relations Act. The Bureau of Labor Statistics reported a total union membership of 14.8 million in 2015 – out of a 133.7 million workforce.

In your business, a core group of disgruntled employees can cause the "tail to wag the dog." Some employers simply accept unionization, believing it's inevitable. However, that's not the case. Many union members do not join out of desire but because of existing contracts or give-away government lawmakers

A carefully crafted Policy Manual may counter unionization by promoting goodwill. Attitude surveys, scheduled appraisals, "open door" access to management, scheduled company meetings and the effort to communicate vertically will dramatically lessen the desire for a group to unionize.

In larger organizations, union interest oftentimes begins with a "Trojan Horse" who becomes an employee and then quietly talks to workers about terrible working conditions and the need to organize. Given that risk, you're permitted to adopt a non-solicitation policy to state that "no employee may solicit another employee on working time." This policy should be adopted before any organization drive, not after. In order to be effective, it must be a general "no solicitation" policy and not simply one that targets unionization. There are more liberal rules for retail store policies.

If employees are attempting to form a union in your company, you need to do two things, in this order:

1. Immediately retain an experienced labor relations attorney.
2. Develop a program to defeat the organization effort in its infancy.

When my electronic service department raised the desire to unionize, I first called a lawyer and then an independent service company to request a proposal to outsource all of our work. That ended the discussion. This is one more time the government has its nose so far up your sawgrass that there is no light. And, as with all government labor-related agencies, they are "pro-employee."

There are dozens of important things you can and cannot do during an organizational effort and you should never attempt to manage the problem without good legal counsel. One lawyer warned,

"You can't fire them for considering a union, and you can't threaten them. That would be an unfair labor practice. But you can call them into the office, one at a time, and tell them of the great progress they'll make if only we can all strive for a common goal, without outside interference telling us how to run our company."

Some unions have destroyed companies. My birthplace was the home of Piper Aircraft. Its founder, William T. Piper, Sr., known as the "Henry Ford of Aviation," struggled with the union throughout his career. A union formed in 1939 and went on strike in 1941. In the next 15 years it idled the production line a half dozen times. In 1954, the union struck for three weeks after a two-week vacation. This disruption contributed to its downfall, production slowed and operations were eventually moved to Florida. When Mr. Piper was asked, "How many people have you got working here?," he said, "About half."

You should treat your employees fairly to avoid a unionizing campaign. Your job is to give voice and dignity to people. You don't have to do exactly what they want, but you do have to listen. Do the right thing first and prevent the desire of your people to unionize. While I've generalized some employees as being thieves, enemies and scoundrels, they're also your most important asset and you should treat them as such.

Tips To Keep You Afloat

> People are your number one asset and your number one problem.

> Employees may rob you blind.

> Pay key people well to monitor the others.

> Make key people owners.

> Discipline and communicate with employees in writing.

> Rely on Policy and Operation Manuals.

> Determine which management style is best for you and your people.

> Do not promote people to positions they cannot handle.

> Require written reports from employees.

> Formally evaluate employees and allow them to evaluate the company.

> Request evaluations from your customers.

> Defend against unemployment claims.

> Hire people as independent contractors whenever possible.

> Incentivize everyone.

> Respond quickly to the threat of unionization.

> Train your people so they have the tools to succeed.

> Communicate with your people regularly.

> Be fair and reward the winners.

8. THE MARKETING

> "Good marketing makes the company look smart.
> Great marketing makes the customer feel smart."
>
> Joe Chernov

Marketing is not advertising. Marketing involves promoting your company's products and brands to your intended markets and ensures they are offered at the right prices in the right places. As you might expect, this is not an easy task. You must do your homework and think through every step of the process. You should also gather opinions from family, friends, colleagues and potential customers themselves, regarding:

- What needs will my products or services fulfill?
- What are the key benefits they offer prospective buyers?

- Are there any innovative or distinctive features that offer promotion advantages?

- How do my products or services differ from the competition?

- What pricing strategy do I want to follow: low, competitive or high?

- Where should I locate my business — online, in a bricks-and-mortar location, or both?

- If I plan a physical store, where should it be situated?

- How much money do I have available to market my products/services?

A well-crafted marketing plan will start you in the right direction. It's much better to have a road map than to take a "shotgun approach" and try to sell to everyone. But be prepared to make adjustments once you start rolling out your products or services. Your customers are likely to surprise you at some point, so you need to be flexible as you move forward.

Another important point to consider: While everyone today seems to talk about innovation and being "unique," it's much easier to sell a product that meets an already perceived need rather than to try to educate a market to buy a new, perhaps revolutionary, product or service.

Market Research

Marketing research is the process of gathering, analyzing, and interpreting information about past, present, and potential customers for your products or services. You must research the characteristics, spending habits, location, and needs of your customers, your industry, and your current competitors.

To do so, you can take advantage of online sources of information and services. Today, it's easier than ever to gather facts about your market, but it's often more challenging to decide what to do with those facts. Familiarize yourself with both online and traditional marketing tools, from search engine optimization (SEO) strategies to print advertising to live event planning.

You should also study the financial ratio statistics for your industry. For example, if the typical advertising and marketing cost is 5 percent of revenue, budget at least that amount in your spending plan*.

Branding

Branding is a popular topic; research and articles on branding are available from many sources. That's because it provides the foundation for your marketing, as well as your advertising, public relations, and sales programs. An excellent brand will generate customer interest and engagement, helping you carve out a strong market share.

If you purchase a franchise, you will be paying many thousands of dollars to be part of an established brand which can certainly accelerate the process of bringing in customers and generating revenue. The alternative would be to open your own business, and spend your money trying to make consumers aware of your personal brand.

If acquiring a company, you should consider the value of that brand when making your offer. Then, you must evaluate the brand again after the sale is closed. If the brand has negative connotations, for instance, you might want to rebrand the entire operation or simply merge it into your current business.

Creating a strong brand is essential when starting a new venture. It's like being an artist with a blank canvas, where you can paint anything you want. Maybe you want a brand with a logo that is easily recognizable, or perhaps you want to appeal to technical or industrial markets that respond to certain buzzwords.

Branding is the start of your marketing plan. The image that your business presents to the public is critical. Your website, social media pages, publicity, signs, logos, stationary, business cards, brochures, and even your phone number contribute to your brand. Here are some things to consider:

- Who are your customers?
- What "first impression" do you want to make?
- What are your company's values?
- What are your company's products and services?
- What are your competitors doing?

Branding goes hand-in-hand with naming your company. You want something that will stand out in a noisy marketplace, and cause prospective customers to take a look. Your brand should also be authentic, reflecting your business values and mission. As Tony Hsieh, CEO of Zappos, once said, "Your culture is your brand."

Pricing

Pricing your products and services appropriately is one of the basics of a successful marketing program. It will impact how buyers perceive your brand and the competition. For instance, there is the designer fashion market, where a high price is often perceived as a competitive advantage. "Notice my designer purse?" a shopper might be thinking about their Hermes purse. At the other end of the spectrum are dollar store chains, whose customers want to pay as little as possible for their products. It's two different worlds and two different pricing strategies.

When evaluating price, it's vital to know the costs of bringing a product or service to the customer and also what the competition is charging. But that's just the starting point. Do not use cost as the basis for setting your prices, at least not without first trying to price the product according to what customers will pay.

Conversely, one ultra-successful national retail chain never advertises. Instead, every item is marked up only 28 percent and if that price is substantially lower than competition, consumers reap the benefit. That's an effective strategy for building a loyal base of customers. But small business owners will lose by marketing only price; they simply can't compete with the big chains.

The Sherman Anti-Trust Act (1890) outlawed practices considered harmful to consumers such as monopolies. The Clayton Antitrust Act (1914) sought to prevent anti-competitive practices. The Robinson-Patman Act (1936) arose to stop chain stores from purchasing goods at lower prices than other retailers and imposed treble damages and criminal penalties for a violation. During the 1980s, lawmakers determined that consumers are better off, and will pay less for goods and services, if they allow larger firms to retail products for less than the small operator's wholesale price. For this reason, smaller companies can no longer compete on price alone. Instead, emphasize the non-price benefits such as quality, reliability, local service, and delivery. Direct your advertising to consumer benefits, not pricing.

Back in the 1970s, my music company was purchasing a significant number of pianos and organs, but much less than our largest competitor. We noticed that new models arrived at their stores long before they were available to us, and we wondered how they could afford to offer such low-margin retail prices. But after growing too fast, our competitor filed bankruptcy, and one of their senior executives told me about their unfair pricing practices. I engaged one of the premier antitrust law firms, went into the bankruptcy court, purchased the defunct company and gained access to their books and records. They were cutting deals with suppliers and violating antitrust laws. Sadly, there are many predator suppliers and unscrupulous competitors in the swamp.

Be Responsible in Your Marketing

Don't ever try to cheat your customers. During my time as CEO of a snack food company, the director of marketing said, "Mr. Poorman, I have a great idea for our barbecue chips. By making the label larger, frosting the bag, and making the weight less, shoppers will think they're getting more for less and we'll save hundreds of thousands on product costs each year!" He was proud of his ingenuity, but I fired him on the spot.

To me, responsible marketing includes:

- Exceeding customer expectations
- Being consistent and dependable
- Meeting the goals of your customers
- Communicating regularly with customers
- Constantly improving your products and services

Having an integrated overall marketing strategy that includes customer service is the foundation for a successful journey across the swamp. It is your job to be sure that all the strategic elements merge to form a clear and consistent brand for customers, employees and the community.

Advertising Tricks

If you place a fair amount of advertising, form your own agency and receive a 20 percent discount on your invoice! That's what a typical agency charges. If you can't bluff your way through this trick, advise your sales representative that you want the 20 percent discount anyway or you'll place the ads through a competitor — and you may get it. After repeatedly being told this tactic wouldn't work, I did it successfully and named my bogus agency "Brain Sells." The branding was so effective that I filed a trademark.

Along those lines, talk with your suppliers about sharing the cost of advertising in return for a mention of the supplier's trade name. In fact, one of your first questions when selecting a source of goods is whether that supplier offers co-op advertising. If they do, explore the program. If not, immediately ask for an additional discount on your purchases. If opening a new store, ask suppliers to pay for some advertising, signage or a searchlight. You're a creative actor and negotiator.

Fringe perks may be available from business suppliers if you negotiate for them. For instance, manufacturers often sent my family and employees on fully paid vacations around the world. Demand they convince suppliers to pay your expenses to attend national trade shows.

While in the music business, I created a weekly radio program called "Organ Melodies" and gave charitable organizations a platform to promote their services. We also played music and interviewed nationally known entertainers who came through my home state. The station began to sell enough advertising that I eventually paid nothing for the show. I was able to promote my business at no cost, and the show was syndicated to other markets we served.

Put Your Marketing Plan into Action

Now, let's look at the way you can launch your marketing plan, starting with the all-important online channels: website, social media, and mobile applications. To connect with your audience in today's inter-connected world, you need a strategy that encompasses all three aspects of online communication. Here is a quick look at the issues to consider as you develop a comprehensive marketing plan.

Website

Shopping and consumer research begin online, so you need to have a robust website that reflects your brand and values, while offering an engaging experience for prospective buyers. That's true for both consumer and business markets, as Marketing Sherpa reports that 98% of business-to-business buyers use Google to search for products and services.

The home page should be visually arresting, with easy navigation to pages that describe your product or service and contact information for prospects. It's important to ensure that web content remains fresh and is regularly updated.

You should also build your site with keywords that improve your search engine optimization (SEO) results so prospects don't have to go through page after page of search results to find your company. Unlike fishing for trout in a trout stream, where you know the habits of your target and the right bait to use, online marketing is like fishing for minnows in the ocean. An SEO strategy can help to bring the big fish onboard.

Social Media

Social media allows you to engage with customers, employees and the community in a personal and professional setting in real-time. With the appropriate company culture, social media can unite a brand's marketing strategy and lead to increased trust, loyalty, and sales.

Social media hotspots like Facebook, Instagram, and Twitter provide an extension of the online or in-store experience and customer service. In fact, that's the biggest opportunity for businesses: building relationships through positive brand experiences. As consumers invite brands into their living rooms, they are also sharing valuable insights into their daily lives, which can help you shape your overall marketing program.

Brands that use social media effectively will reap the rewards of customer loyalty, unforgettable experiences, employee retention, and ultimately increased revenue.

Mobile Applications

Unlike your website and social media presence, a mobile application may not be essential to your venture's success. However, the steadily rising tide of smartphones, tablets and laptops means that you should pay close attention to how your prospects access information. Even if you don't build a mobile app, you may want to optimize your website so the content is easy to read on smaller screens.

If your new business is focused on a particular geographic market, as is the case with many retail, restaurant, entertainment, and service businesses, then a mobile app can help you attract, engage, and retain customers. For example, this can be a natural fit for a customer loyalty program. However, you will need to have funding in place both to do the technical design and development and to promote your app with your target audience.

Advertising Media

While businesses must pay attention to online channels, there are plenty of effective ways to promote your venture using traditional advertising media. Here are some suggestions:

• Mailers/Fliers. Readers refer to your ad and it can be reread. Pass-along media may give you a fighting chance to reach the prospects, especially if you utilize coupons or design impactful copy.

• Newspapers. Newspapers reach many people, particularly older adults, at a relatively low cost. If you're holding a one-time event, there is no better medium. Strive for weekday placement when grocery stores advertise, request a news or editorial page and the right-hand page. These tips will help you optimize your impact.

• Magazines. Magazines allow you to reach your market with a more specific message than newspapers. Readers generally pay for the publications, so they're more likely to take note of the message. Magazines also offer better quality paper than newspapers, so illustrations and photographs look better. Always request placement in the first third of the publication.

• Radio. Ninety-three percent of Americans listen to local AM/ FM radio, despite streaming and online radio services. Radio allows you to concentrate your advertising dollars on the most promising markets. Each radio station is formatted to appeal to a distinct market segment. Ask the radio salesperson for their station's Nielson Ratings and other data that will reveal the average age of their listeners, the geographic area they cover, and other valuable demographic information. Radio works best when you saturate the airwaves and create a reason to act now, like a live "3-day only" carpet sale in a carpet showroom with you live on the microphone.

• Television. Television is still the primary at-home entertainment for most families. The average American watches five hours of TV per day. Television is the way most people keep in touch with world events. Prospects and customers change their view about your business when they see a TV advertisement as it adds momentum to your message and builds credibility for your brand.

• Direct Mail. Direct mail aligns your advertising dollars with your target consumer market. Direct mail can be "hot" or "cold." "Hot prospecting" means sending your message to past customers or prospects you have contacted previously without success. "Cold" prospecting targets an entirely new audience. Blanket mailings to every address within a given zip code or everyone on the voter registration list can be an expensive way of filling people's trashcans. If you cannot buy mailing lists for special interest groups, spend some time defining who you want to reach and compile your own list.

View your mailer as your opportunity to have a one-on-one conversation with your prospect. Use it to emphasize the benefits of your product or service. If your mailing is in narrative form, get to the point early and then build on it. No one has the time or patience to read through an elaborate lead-in. Most direct mailers are read between the mailbox and trash can, so make it short and sweet or that's where yours will end up.

• Outdoor. Billboards work, but don't tell your life story. Keep it short and memorable, like a Florida ad advertising an air conditioning service that reads: "Your Wife is Hot." If you're going to use billboards, they need to grab attention. I've even posted the advertisement upside down to cause intrigue.

Here's a personal example of the power of outdoor advertising. I assumed control of a financially troubled private golf course where most members were male. As part of the turnaround effort, I focused on the bar, restaurant and banquet center to offset weather sensitive golf income, proposing that women should golf free, and then launched a promotion directed to female golfers. I purchased space on 20 junior poster boards, measuring 6 foot by 12 foot, and in bright copy printed: "Women Golf Free at Greenway Country Club."

With that one strategy, we pulled business from the competitors and quadrupled income overnight. After the first free year, new female golfers were comfortable in the facility and became regular members. Low-cost outdoor advertising saved the company. When launching a new cosmetic surgery center in South Carolina, we were one of nine facilities with few patients. After advertising on billboards using butterflies and clocks that read, "Turn Back the Hands of Time," the practice became number four.

- Vehicle Wraps. If your company's rolling stock is not plastered with your name or image, you are wasting free exposure for your business. Mary Kay, with her pink Cadillacs, founded the craze and now you can make a major impact with a minimal expense. The Truly Nolen pest control company wrapped yellow VW bugs with mouse ears on the roof. The genius who devised this cheap gimmick grew the company overnight.

Be aware that some municipalities have enacted ordinances to stop you from parking wrapped cars along the highway. Whenever you try to promote your business in order to pay more taxes and hire more people, the government will devise a way to drown you. Become resourceful or you'll get steamrolled at every corner. This was my most recent response to the new anti-business code: First, I moved the car to another location. Then I told them to go to hell. Then I placed a sign in the window reading, "Impeach the mayor." Finally, I accepted the fine and then appealed it. Bureaucrats go away if you make them go to work.

- Yellow Pages. While Yellow Pages have become as antiquated as roadmaps, they're still effective for some industries and in markets with more than 50,000 people. Yellow Page advertising does not need to be large and extravagant. Instead, being placed in primary books with a bold line and five-word message is often adequate.

Assuming you advertise through traditional media, you're normally visible in your regional market and people will think of you quickly. You can insert a single line ad in every Yellow Page directory within 75 miles of your base location with a toll-free number. Your byline might read "We Will Not Be Undersold!" Note that a name like AAA Discount Furniture makes your ad first in the category; those who appear first get called first. Or try one of my favorite creations: "Customers Love Us – Competitors Don't" or "Best Possible Price – Call for Bid." Superlatives, if allowed, such as the biggest and the best, will generate calls. Cover your perimeter market while stealing business from those secondary markets.

• Brochures. The tri-fold brochure is a tried and tested method for getting the message out. As with all forms of promotion, it's important to present the content to the customer in a way that emphasizes benefits more than features – not many companies have the luxury of telling someone how their product works and being believed. The front of the brochure should be almost totally devoted to your logo and other symbols. A "picture is worth a thousand words" and an immediate and positive impact will encourage the recipient to read on. The last page should summarize the content of the brochure, or better yet, be a "call to action;" the customer can request a free sample, schedule an appointment or register for a mailing list. The reverse panel can be used as a mailing label.

The main thrust of your message should appear in the large section seen when the brochure is opened up. This gives lots of space for visuals and good graphics, and will reduce the temptation to write excessive copy justifying your existence.

The brochure is a golden opportunity to capture the undivided attention of your customer. You don't have to compete with other advertisements or the football game. It gives you more space than other advertising methods for a modest unit cost (which decreases as the print volume increases) and can be made available for free — or for the cost of a plastic brochure holder — in many establishments across your service area. Most non-competing businesses will agree to give you some counter space.

• Kiosk Advertising. It's believed that 80% of sales come from 20% of inventory. The most economical and effective way to market almost anything is to rent "carpet space" in an enclosed mall. Although I opened a dozen stores under the traditional mall concept, I developed a portable 10 foot by 20 foot kiosk for my Brain Sells company. This metal and glass enclosure allowed us to display 20 pianos and organs in the middle of the shopping center. Your monthly rent for an in-line store could be $3,000 plus utilities compared to $1,000 for a weekend kiosk. You will do more business in the kiosk, preserve your time, move from mall to mall and interact with more consumers passing by than in a permanent store.

Public Relations

For many businesses, public relations can be a very economical approach to connecting with prospects, without the heavy spending that an advertising campaign often requires. Many publications, both online and print, are looking for fresh content and often run news articles and feature stories from contributors.

You could write a blog for your website and then turn those posts into announcements or articles to be distributed to the media. You can also look for other opportunities to promote your product or services through social media channels, live events, and community activities.

Remember that publicity is free exposure for your business, so take advantage of media opportunities. Sponsor a golf tournament to raise money. Make charitable contributions and announce promotions. But don't get carried away; if you sponsor a tournament for $1,000, you may reach 100 people. In your newspaper, you might reach 50,000 for the same investment.

Advertising Basics

Advertising is not marketing. Whether you plan an online, broadcast or print advertising campaign, your first decision is whether to employ a "push" or a "pull" strategy. A push strategy concentrates on the middlemen between you and your customers, such as convincing retailers and distributors to stock a product and promote it to customers and end-users. A pull strategy targets end-users. You create a demand for your product or service that the middlemen must satisfy, whether they want to or not. For example, if you're a dealer for a piece of medical equipment, radio advertising will not be as cost-effective as aiming your advertising at medical-related trade publications.

When revenue is down, companies tend to slow advertising until cash flow improves — and then they advertise more frequently. This "places the cart before the horse." The purpose of advertising is to stimulate demand, not respond to it; soft sales may indicate the need for more advertising, not less.

Unless you want to pay an advertising agency exorbitant rates, look for a company far away from your own market and "borrow" their advertising ideas. There are unlimited free ideas out there that you can review in order to charge your own creative imagination.

No invoice is more painful to pay than one for advertising that has already run. While sales agents may want to sell you a quarter page print ad, it's often less effective than a one column by two inch "teaser" ad that appears every night of the week. Frequent exposure is one of the keys to changing beliefs about products and services. It is said that consumers must see an ad seven times before they take action. I'd rather spend $500 on advertising over 30 days than $500 for one chance to be seen.

Another inexpensive and effective approach is the advertorial, an ad that resembles a news article. Some publications require a different type style and/or the word "advertisement" at the bottom of the copy for this kind of advertisement. This disguised ad could be one column under your photograph about a relevant business topic. For example, a real estate professional could write an article on "How to Find the Right Home."

One of the most unscientific and wasteful areas of a small business is how advertising dollars are spent. This occurs because they didn't create a Marketing Plan before advertising. Whether you own a gift shop or dental practice, it's critical to monitor both advertising costs and effectiveness.

Advertising is Making Noise

My turnaround consulting firm recently assumed control of a 30,000-square-foot automobile collision center that was losing money. The building was located "off the beaten path." We sent a few college students out to survey people on the street; most locals had never heard of the company and had no idea of its location. I knew advertising would be among the many financial demands.

Our city had an antiquated outdoor advertising ordinance that effectively barred "billboards." However, I found a glitch in the ordinance, so we purchased eight high-impact junior panels and erected them all over town, with no permit.

The city's code enforcement office reacted as the signs went up and immediately issued notices. It became front page news. So we covered a few with black plastic and put up small signs, "Is this still a billboard?" That drew even more attention and the illegal billboards became the talk of the town.

Insane, you say? Because I had a client in foreclosure that was facing bankruptcy, I had little concern over the government restriction. Also, the future of 15 employees rested on our ability to reverse the trend.

Within six weeks, everyone in the region knew of the company. Revenue began to soar and not one employee lost their job. We could afford the fines. It was free overnight success. You must learn to swim around government regulations or you'll croak. Remember, you can either pay a commercial outdoor advertising company or buy your own metal signs and pay a property owner to lease space. This approach could save 90 percent of your expense and keep your message up year round. And if people believe you're a lunatic, you just may be an entrepreneur!

Advertise Against Competitors

Your competitors are constantly devising ways to sink your canoe, so never let your guard down. I once had a competitor who was pulling customers away from our company by using concocted stories purporting that we had tax problems and sold drugs. I placed the owner on notice but the practice continued. My lawyer sent him a threatening letter. Next, I obtained the wholesale price list for his primary merchandise brand, changed the list title from wholesale to retail, framed it and placed it on the wall in our stores. When his customers came in to shop, they saw the price list and in shock said, "I paid twice that price." Back to my competitor they went, fuming mad and demanding refunds. My phone rang, the competitor met with me at Perkins and we made a verbal truce: "You stop the slander and I take the price list down."

Competition is generally unhealthy. You should be stealing ideas, suppliers, employees and customers from your competition. I would often approve a sale at my cost because it crippled my competitor's ability to market and sustain their business. But go ahead and believe this is a warm and fuzzy playing field. Those who do not grasp the consequences of knowing their enemy shall sink. Who coined the phrase, "friendly competitor?" Were they on drugs? Save that jive talk for your speech to the Rotary Club. Your competitor is your enemy and competition is unhealthy. Seek them out, learn everything about them, and then stab them in the chest before they jeopardize the future of your business, your family, and your employees. This is war, my friends.

Know Your Competitors

To build an effective marketing program, you need to understand your competitors. This will help you craft an appealing message that distinguishes your venture from other businesses. For instance, "We stock the largest number of widgets in Anytown," or "Fast service, top salespeople, and free parking," or "Bet you can't guess how many types of pizza we serve."

Take the time to do your homework, so you can stand out from the crowd. Pay attention to your competitor's issues:

- Competitive websites, social media pages and mobile apps
- Product and service selections
- Pricing strategies
- Reputation
- Years established
- Changes in ownership
- Whether they own, rent or mortgage their facilities
- Space capacities

- Average sale or service amounts
- Estimated sales volume
- Sales efforts
- Franchise affiliations
- Competitors up for sale
- Styles of service
- Hours of operation
- Distance from your business
- Numbers of employees
- Quality of the facilities
- Types of management styles
- Convenience of access
- Number of parking spaces
- Visibility of facility

Tips To Keep You Afloat

> Build an integrated marketing plan.
> Construct an appealing brand.
> Develop your pricing strategy.
> Know the competition.
> Advertise frequently.
> Keep your messages short.
> Know the pros and cons of different marketing media.
> Measure the return on your advertising dollars.
> Remember that your competitor is not your friend.
> Be a responsible marketer.

9. THE SALES ORGANIZATION

> *"If you want to become good at something, do it as often as possible. If you want to become an expert at it, do it every day."*
>
> Robert Ringer

You can't operate a successful business and write your own paycheck until you learn the art and science of selling. In fact, building your sales skills will help with your first job interview, marriage proposal, car purchase . . .the whole world is selling everything to everybody every day.

Whether you live in L.A. or Louisiana, and whether you're 20 or 60, these techniques set forth in my first sales manual, "Techniques of Successful Selling®" will work for you. Before you decide this chapter is "chintzy" or dated, understand that becoming a good salesperson will open the door to one opportunity after another throughout your life.

Let's start off with a simple concept: When selling a product or service, never take "no" for an answer. The vast majority of salespeople give up before reaching that "yes." In fact, 44 percent quit after the first "no," another 22 percent after the second, 14 percent after the third, and 12 percent after the fourth. That's a total of 92 percent who never get to a successful "yes."

It didn't surprise me that a survey of salespeople with annual earnings over six figures found that they averaged a close on their fifth attempt. In other words, the prospect had said "no" four times already and still they persisted. That paid off big-time for that 8 percent of salespeople who were able to keep asking for the close, long after their opponents gave up.

In this chapter, we'll also address the art of negotiating. In some ways, it's a variation of the sales process, since you want to "close" on a favorable agreement. But while the sales process generally proceeds on a clear step-by-step basis, negotiations advance in many different directions. There might be a quick initial agreement and then months of discussion over the details. Or it might require significant concessions to convince the other party to agree to a deal. In any case, there are effective techniques to consider when engaging with others in the business world.

The best barometer to determine if you have the propensity to be a real negotiator, or the stomach to be a successful entrepreneur, is to read the following quotes from Robert Ringer's best seller, *Looking Out for No. 1.* If you find them to be disgusting, you may not want to be a negotiator. Sadly, some are reality.

- "Reality isn't the way you wish things to be, nor the way they appear to be, but the way they actually are."
- "With a written agreement you have a prayer; with a verbal agreement you have nothing but air."
- "Theory is good for the intellect, but action is good for the soul. It's also good for your mental health, your physical health, and

your pocketbook."

- "Surround yourself with problem solvers, not problem creators."
- "The best way to let others know what you're going to do is to actually do it."
- "The desire to impress others is one of the worst forms of mental imprisonment."
- "It's not stress that kills people, but how they react to it."
- "One of the biggest mistakes that most people make is clinging to the excuse that the time isn't quite right to take action. In my experience, conditions are never right at the right time. So if you're waiting for everything to be perfect before taking action, you have a foolproof excuse for never taking action."
- "Everything changes for the better when you take ownership of your own problems."
- "The cost of procrastination is generally far greater than the cost of making mistakes."

Marketing versus Selling

In the last chapter, we looked at marketing and advertising, which are designed to make customers aware of your brand, products, and services. A good marketing program will help identify the ideal customer for your company, and the communication channels to consider. But in my experience, sales is a much more personal process. You have drilled down from customers in general to a few specific customers with their own wants, needs and desires. It is your job as a salesperson to explain – in person, on the phone or online – how your product or service will meet those wants, needs, and desires.

At the same time, the personality and skills of the salesperson make all the difference between a customer saying "no thanks" and closing a sale. A good salesperson can close the deal, with or without a great marketing program. On the other hand, the best marketing in the world won't help if your sales staff can't close the deal.

Early in my life I achieved much success with cold calls — approaching someone without the slightest clue whether they might want or need my products and services. I remember taking one of my top employees to a prospect's home at midnight where I woke the family, unloaded a piano into their living room and consummated the sale. In sales, it's all about approaching someone to propose an opportunity.

However, as referenced in my Call Reluctance Manual®, there are nine types of salespeople who are hesitant to venture into the world of cold calling:

- Threat Sensitive – won't take social risks.
- Over Analytical – will over evaluate and under act.
- Persona Conscious – overly concerned about personal image.
- Glossophobic – fearful of group talks and interaction.
- Circumspective – fearful of loss of friends.
- Role Reluctant – ashamed of sales career.
- Disruption Sensitive – concerned over intruding.
- Class Conscious – intimidated by social standing.
- Endorsement Sensitive – fearful of lack of approval from others.

Fortunately, there are proven techniques to overcome these types of personal issues and find success in cold calling.

Never Prejudge People or Deals

I closed the doors to one of my music stores at 6 p.m. one Christmas Eve. As the owner, I was naturally the last one out the door while my employees were spending the entire day sucking up the yuletide. Circling the block, I noticed a raggedly dressed elderly man peering in the display window with his hands in his pockets. I got out of the car and asked if I could help. He said, "Could I hear one of those organs?"

With skepticism running through my veins, I re-opened the store and went through the full demonstration on a large instrument. He said, "Any chance you could deliver one tonight?" I would have pulled my grandmother out of a nursing home to make that sale, so I agreed. He said, "Well then, I'll take eight of 'em." By now I thought he must be both broke and intoxicated – until he began to pull rolls of cash from his pockets. He said, "Here's a list of all my kids. Just drop one off to each house." I called my drivers, roamed the streets handing out $100 bills for extra help and finished the deliveries at 2 a.m.. That was my most memorable lesson to never, ever prejudge anyone.

Excellent Salespeople are a Different Breed

While driving to one of my music stores, I heard this wild man screaming on the radio: "PIANOS AND ORGANS! ORGANS AND PIANOS! IT'S THE GIANT PIANO AND ORGAN LIQUIDATION SALE AT MILLER'S FURNITURE. 3 DAYS ONLY! BRING YOUR TRUCK!" I was mesmerized. Who was this guy? I turned the car around and headed directly to the furniture store to find Ron, a very big guy with a mustache. He had loaded 30 instruments into a local furniture store, and by using their good name and creating urgency, held a three-day "blow-out" sale for one of my competitors.

Ron was smart enough to always explore a potential deal, so we began to talk. My growing company needed a good salesperson just like him. We came to terms, and he brought along two fellow salespeople with their own customer lists.

Ron immediately began to grow my company and move into new markets. He was the rare breed who would work a fairground 12 hours a day for ten days and only care about how much merchandise was sold. Plus, he was a much better personnel manager than I. He selected employees for their talent, not their experience or intelligence. He focused on developing their strong points and didn't concentrate on their weaknesses. He didn't look for a person to fill a job, he looked for a job to suit the person. This brought a string of crazies, potheads, and weirdos into my company. . .people I never would have hired. Then, he put them on the street at fairs and home shows. They became friends with freak show personalities like the "lizard lady" and "gorilla man," and stuffed instruments in their campers. This was all business I never would have captured. . .and he made it fun!

Along with being a great salesperson, Ron was an exceptional leader of our sales organization. He garnered trust, respect, and loyalty. One day when we were both in our 20s, I quietly stepped down and made him president of my own company because I knew he was a better person for the job. I bought him a new diamond fire rose Lincoln Mark IV. I knew this man would grow my organization. It was a good fit. He would negotiate the best purchasing deals and we often played the "good guy, bad guy" roles. Ron ultimately went on to form his own company in another state, and we've remained best friends ever since.

Connecting the Dots

A great salesperson like Ron knew how to connect dots between your product or service and the customer, completing the sales process. So, how can you follow in his footsteps?

No matter how brilliant or capable a businessperson you are, or how thoroughly you know every benefit of your product, you'll struggle to close the prospect unless you are armed with a forceful and intelligent presentation; it's an absolute prerequisite. After all, the average salesperson spends only about 50 percent of his or her time with customers and clients. The remaining time is spent traveling, waiting for interviews, preparing reports, and delivering their wares. The "money time" is spent in front of the prospect, so be prepared.

A sales presentation is a series of short, snappy, logically connected talking points offering reasons why a prospect should buy your particular product or service. It must reflect the buyer's point of view, not yours. It must define customer benefits in their most effective order, giving proper emphasis to each important point. It can't be achieved on the spur of the moment but must be planned well in advance. There is only one best way to tell your benefit story, and it can only be found after painstaking study, analysis and field-testing. Once you've found this one best way, it's foolish to toss it aside in favor of some loosely connected, rambling discourse that you must concoct every time because you believe "no two prospects are alike."

Actually, all prospects are very much alike. They may differ outwardly in their personality makeup, but their buying reactions are alike most times. It is this similarity that makes selling possible and points the way to a standardized talk.

Successful salespeople have found that regardless of their industry, there is no substitute for a well-planned, standardized talk. As someone once said: "Give me anyone who will deliver a presentation exactly the way I write it and I'll show you someone who will sell rings around the most brilliant salesperson who insists on ad-libbing."

Some people are scornful of what they consider a "canned talk." They'll maintain that canned talks are for parrots. "Only dopes who can't think on their feet use them," they say, or "a prospect can always spot a canned talk because it doesn't sound natural." Well, anything will sound "canned" if it's delivered in a hum-drum, perfunctory fashion. You must practice your delivery until you acquire a "studied naturalness" that sounds spontaneous. You've got to make the talk live and breathe — make it sound sincere, convincing, and straight from the heart — every single time you deliver it. Otherwise, it will fail.

Civilization is built by what people before us have learned and passed on. And just about everything we do in life is really a canned sales talk. From the moment that you're born and first learn to walk, you learn by observing other people. You fall many times, but you get up again and try until you learn. Practicing a canned sales talk is no different. Through constant practice and effort, you learn to deliver a canned talk and close the deal.

Why then, do so many people sneer at preparing their presentations, preferring to make up their story and selling pitch as they go along, hoping to hit the prospect's "hot button"? The biggest reason is that we all crave variety.

But change for the sake of change can prove to be expensive, especially when it means a loss of sales, loss of earning power, lower income for you and lower profits for the company. And that's exactly what it means — the minute you start selling "off-the-cuff" instead of using a tried and tested formula.

New to the Prospect

It's true that a salesperson may tire of giving the same talk over and over again, month after month, using the same words, the same gestures and the same variations in tone. So what? All this may seem "old hat" to the agent, but it's all brand new to the prospect. He's never heard the presentation before. He's never seen your product or service demonstration or listened to your carefully prepared selling arguments.

There's no possible reason why the prospect should get bored listening to you tell the same story you've told a thousand other prospects – unless you are bored. And when you do feel that way, take a page from the actor's handbook. How long do you suppose a play would last if the actors grew tired of following "the same old script" word for word, gesture for gesture, and started improvising their parts? How long do you think people would buy tickets to see a group of actors ham it up and try to do the playwright one better?

Practice Makes Perfect

Regardless of how well you know your role or how much of an expert you may be in performing before a prospect, sooner or later you're going to develop a few rough edges or perhaps gloss over certain parts of your talk. Therefore, rehearsals and dry runs are necessary to be assured you're still giving your talk the most effective way.

In the 1800s, Chopin, the renowned classical pianist, said that if he practiced ten hours a day instead of twelve, he would at once notice a difference. If he cut it down to eight, the manager would notice it. If he cut it still further the audience would notice it and stop coming to hear him perform.

As Charles B. Roth, well-known sales consultant and author of *Secrets of Closing Sales* wrote: "Many a man owes his six-figure income to the fact, not that he has something special by way of a brain or voice, but that he has had sense enough to thoroughly learn a carefully prepared presentation and stick to it through thick and thin."

Canned Equals Confidence

Another advantage of a canned pitch is that it helps you say the right thing at the proper time. This is practically impossible to do spur of the moment.

A prepared presentation gives you confidence because you know what you are going to say in advance, and it allows you to make powerful points in the fewest words necessary.

Before you begin your journey into salesmanship, lay the groundwork:

- Understand the buyer's situation or problems
- Build rapport
- Be sincere
- Be enthusiastic, but not pushy
- Relate to people and talk with them, not at them
- Be confident and in control
- Ask questions
- Listen to what they say
- Convey an attitude of service
- Trial close and prod
- Avoid any type of debate
- Respect their opinion
- Crystallize their ideas

- Internalize how much they need your product or service
- Explain the benefits of your product or service
- Make them feel important
- Speak at their tempo

Remember people do things for their reasons, not yours. People are less interested in your products or services than in what you will do for them. You must be sincere and exhibit:

- A desire to be helpful
- A pleasant disposition
- An energetic personality
- Persistence
- Tolerance
- Sincerity
- Integrity
- Reliability
- Enthusiasm
- A sense of humor
- Some modesty
- Self-confidence
- Self-restraint
- Poise
- Courtesy
- Good manners
- Creativity
- Cheerfulness
- Knowledge

. . . because nothing happens until you make an impression.

Qualifying Customers

The science of selling demands that you be prepared to ask all these questions before you are too far along in your presentation. Don't interrogate. Ask, listen, relate and reinforce. Qualify your customer and understand the basics: who, where, when, why and how.

Qualifying is your GPS to direct where you should be going with the customer. Ask questions such as these:

- Do you use our product or service now?
- Who will be using it?
- How did you first become interested in it?
- What is your company's/employees'/family's background?
- Have you ever shopped for it before?
- What have you seen that meets your needs?
- Where is your place of business/home?
- Is there any particular room you would place the furniture in when you get it home?
- Who in the family will be making the final decision on which style of furniture to buy?
- What price category would you be interested in?
- Would you want to take advantage of our financing?

Features and Benefits

In your sales presentation and conversations with the customer, sell benefits over features. You're a salesperson, not a brochure. Mention your company's programs and focus on benefits your competitors don't offer. For example:

- Large selection
- All brands available
- Factory-trained technicians
- Service guarantees
- Educational seminars
- Customized payment plans

Be prepared to relate real benefits to all the features you sell. For example:

- Racquetball playing is a year-round hobby.
- Owning this classic car provides status and pride of ownership.
- It's easy to play and every family member can express themselves musically.
- Physicians endorse this equipment for your good health.
- Our art classes will enable you to satisfy a very basic need to be creative.
- This gemstone is a tremendous investment and is sure to become more valuable in the future.

Preparing for the Close

Throughout your presentation, your goal is to keep the sales process moving forward to a successful close. Asking engaging questions is one of the most valuable tools in the process. Questions move you closer to the close for several reasons:

- They help a prospect recognize what he wants and how to get it.

- They avoid arguments; it's very difficult for a prospect to argue if you keep asking questions that require positive answers.
- They help people participate and feel like they are part of the process.
- They help you find the best point with which to close the sale.
- They help to crystallize a prospect's thinking; in other words, the idea becomes their idea.
- They give prospects a feeling of importance; when you show respect for their opinion, they're more likely to respect yours.

You can also use questions to reinforce your sales presentation. Pay close attention to your prospect and watch when their face lights up after you make a certain point. Then, you can reinforce those benefits by asking questions like these:

- Isn't that a beautiful fabric?
- You're interested in having your children learn music, aren't you? Well, don't you think this would help you do just that?
- Don't you think this copier would make your office more efficient?
- Wouldn't it have been wonderful if we had this equipment in the home when we were growing up?
- You realize crime is up, and this security system would protect your family, right?
- This piece of art will surely look great in your home, won't it?

What About Objections?

At this stage of the sales process, the prospect might object to something. The first time, ignore it. If he repeats it, you know it's important. It will be a rare presentation in which there will be no "objections." This simply means one of three things:

1. You've not completed the job of convincing the prospect he can use your product or service.

2. You've not helped him see the benefits clearly enough to make him want to investigate further.

3. The prospect should be written off as a "dead end" because, for some legitimate reason, he doesn't need the item or service.

The professional salesperson welcomes objections as a sign of interest and as a tool in learning how the sale is progressing. By objecting, prospects are literally telling you what you must do to help them decide.

When the prospect raises an objection, he is either giving you an excuse, asking a question or setting a condition. You must make the objection clear in your mind. You must approach the objection by first restating what the prospect said to be sure you interpreted it correctly. You may want to turn the restatement into a question like, "Let me be quite clear on this . . .is what you are saying . . ?" Once you're clear on the objection, categorize it and deal with it.

Here are some lead-in statements to use when overcoming objections:

- "I see."
- "I understand what you mean."
- "I see your point, I'm glad you brought that up."
- "Isn't that what you mean?"
- "Yes, now I know what you mean."
- "Let's just suppose..."

Many objections can be cleared up by asking the customer "why?" But oftentimes, a direct "why?" will build resistance. So, reply with things like this:

- "Why do you feel that way?"
- "Why would that be the case?"

Remember, be friendly and sincere and always wait for a reply!

In overcoming objections, never get defensive or insult the prospect's opinion. My wife recently walked out of a Jaguar showroom the moment the salesperson said, "Lexus (her current vehicle) hasn't made a change to its design in over 14 years." She loves her Lexus, and he immediately lost a sale.

Be in control. Remember that most objections only mean you haven't yet sold the value of owning your product. Most salespeople stop before they discover the real objection. One way to find out if you have found the real objection is to say, "Is that your only problem?" Be silent. If they say "yes" then say, "Then if we could solve that problem, you would want it, right?"

If the customer says, "I want to think about it," he hasn't told you the objection. If you are going to have any chance of making a sale, you must learn what he needs to think about or if this is just a way of putting you off. For instance, you might reply, "I understand, but let me ask you this: do you like what you've seen so far?"

If the customer says yes, you might respond by saying, "You know my real job is to serve you! Unlike the car salesman or the person who sold you your refrigerator, my service to you will extend far beyond the sale. Unlike other businesses, our success depends on you being a satisfied customer. Obviously there must be a question in your mind or you would buy it now. Please, let me help you with it if I can."

Here's a good response if the customer says, "Well, I don't know, we just never make decisions like this without thinking it over," You could reply, "I understand; you should take all the time you need. But as you know, this is a very special situation. You're here, the motorcycle is here, and I'm here to answer any questions you may have. I'm in no hurry . . . let's look it over."

Or, you could lighten the encounter. If the customer at the car dealership says, "I'd like to sleep on it," you could say: "The hood is pretty hard. Why not buy the car and sleep on your mattress!"

While you may scoff at these chintzy comments on paper, they actually work with almost every prospect.

So, when the customer raises objections, here's how to respond:

- Reverse it. Show an idea for buying it now.

- Explain it. Show, by careful explanation, how the prospect has misunderstood some point.

- Admit it. If the objection is absolutely true and you know it, admit it; especially if it's a minor objection.

- Deny it. Flat denial is the only answer if the prospect makes a derogatory statement about your company.

- Ask why. Often an objection is a smokescreen for unstated negative feelings. It's necessary to ask questions of the prospect, but especially wise to do so in handling objections. "Why do you say that?" can often reveal hidden objections.

- Restate it. This is a powerful tool for getting at the heart of the matter and shifting the emphasis of an objection. By restating an objection in more favorable terms and showing there is no problem, you effectively answer the objection.

Here are some examples of how to address objections:

Customer: "I can't afford it."

Salesperson: "Yes, I know what you mean. I think everybody feels the same way when they first think about it. But the more we get into it, we realize all of us have trouble in turning loose money, don't we? Actually most of us spend more than this on miscellaneous things in a year and after it is all said and done, we don't have an awful lot to show for it. Yet, this is something that will be in your home for years to come." Other responses might be:

• "Let me ask you this. Is it the entire thing you feel you can't afford or is it the down payment or monthly payments you feel you can't afford?"

• "I understand. When do you feel you could afford it?"

• "I understand what you mean. It does seem like a lot of money when you first think about it. But I'm sure you would agree it's going to be very helpful for your husband to have a truck."

Customer: "I want to talk to my partner first."

Salesperson: "Yes, I certainly understand how you feel. I'm glad you brought them up. I surely wish they were here. Let me ask you this. If they were here and saw how much you wanted it, they would want you to have it, wouldn't they?" Or,

• "I can understand that. What do you think they will think about it?"

• "Why don't we write it up subject to your partner's approval?"

Customer: "We always pay cash."

Salesperson: "I understand, it is nice to be in a situation where you're able to pay cash. Let's write it up and we will clear the finance charge for you." Or you could say:

• "I understand that. But you know very few people ever pay cash for a new patio. As you might know, we often sell to professional people, some with a great deal of money. The reason these people don't pay cash is this: a home improvement is a great investment and interest rates are low, so you might want to take advantage of them. Or, just use our store account."

Customer: "Hey look, I don't like high pressure salesmen."

Salesperson: "Oh, I'm sorry I gave you that impression. Sometimes in my enthusiasm I get carried away. You know, I guess the problem is this: Of all the photocopiers I've sold, no one seems to be sorry they bought one. That's a fantastic feeling for a salesperson who really enjoys what they're doing. And when I talk to business owners like you, and see what this could do for your company, I get excited because I believe in the product.

Get a Commitment

As you work through the prospect's objections, you should try to get a preliminary commitment to your product, service or company. A good salesperson listens closely for comments that signal a commitment, even if the customer isn't yet ready to decide. For example:

- "I like your dishwasher, but I already have one."
- "What do your customers like best about your service?"
- "I've read the reviews about your company on Yelp. While most of them were very positive, I was concerned about one post that said you didn't stand behind your product."

These types of questions — which often seem to be objections — actually signal that the prospect is preparing mentally to make a purchase. You need to be able to turn that comment into a commitment.

Remember that whenever a person buys anything, there are four factors they must consider:

- Do they like the product?
- Do they feel it is a good value they can afford?
- Do they like the company they're dealing with?
- Do they want to do business with you?

Keep Quiet

One of the greatest negatives of salespeople and negotiators is that they talk too much. The most powerful sales technique is silence. Ask your customers one of the commitment questions, then keep quiet until they speak. Silence is profound. It causes tension and some degree of anxiety in the mind of your customer. Your silence demands they speak. The moment you open your mouth after a commitment or a closing question, you lose ALL ground! Silence IS pressure.

Trial Close

When a prospect has demonstrated a commitment, you should be prepared to move to a trial close, which may finalize the sale or expose another objection. This is the cycle:

1. Sell the idea (overcome objections).
2. Get commitment (through questions).
3. Begin a trial close.
4. Do A, B, C, again and again.

You need to be patient. You haven't lost the sale if the prospect raises more objections. You simply need to address those issues, regain the commitment and try to close the sale again.

More sales are lost with the following words: "I'll think it over." This statement means, "We're going to buy the item but we're not quite sure we'll buy it from you." Again, don't let this be the end of your conversation. You could reply, "Okay, that's fine. Obviously you wouldn't take your time to think it over if it weren't important to you. You're not telling me this to get rid of me, are you? Why not step in here and discuss it in private. If you have any questions, I'll be around the corner to answer them."

Ask the customer: "Just what is it that's not clear to you that you have to think it over?" Turn the conversation back to them in the form of a question.

You also have to keep your customer's personality in mind when answering objections and gaining commitment. Here are some people you'll get to know:

- Know-It-All: You can't tell him anything because he's read everything on the Internet, so switch him. "No problem. If you really want that one, I'll write it up now. I'm just surprised you'd choose a plastic case dishwasher over stainless steel."

- Gimmick Prone: Show him every button and feature on the product.
- Mr. Late: Talk fast when he shows up, because he's going to use his phantom appointment as an excuse not to buy today.
- The Thinker: With pipe in hand and a beard, wearing leather shoes, this professor-type is going to assess the deal to death. He's as interested in how it works as what it will do for him.
- The Disbeliever: They will say, "Yeah, sure. Are you serious? You're telling me this thing is actually going to give me 32 mpg?"
- The Super Star: Hidden behind her Rayban sunglasses and wearing Gucci loafers, she thinks you're lucky to sell her something.
- The Time Capsule: This is exactly what I want and I'm definitely going to buy it from you . . .as soon as Aunt Mary passes and the estate is probated."
- Mr. Ho-Hum: He will tell you, "Yeah, we had one of these before, but the family rarely used it. Maybe I should get it out and see if it leaks."

Closing the Sale

Making the sale is the culmination of the steps you go through from the time you first contact the prospect until he is satisfied with the purchase. Everything that you do during your sales interview is in preparation for the act of closing. Here are some suggestions for closing the sale:

Use the multiple choice close:
- "Would Tuesday or Thursday be the best delivery day?"
- "Do you want it in this style or this style?"

- "Do you want to pay cash or use our financing?"
- "Do you want the green or tan?"

Answer a question with a question:
- "If I could get you that, would you buy now?"
- "If I throw in a shirt, would you take the suit now?"
- "Why don't you go ahead and get the car today?"
- "Your wife seems to like the feature and you agreed it was a great value; well then, how would you like to handle the money part?"
- "Do you like this style or would this be better?"
- "This sure will look great in your home! How soon do you want it delivered?"
- "Yes, we do have financing. Come right this way; I'll work out some figures for you."

Confirm the prospect is making the right decision:
- "This is the right model for you."
- "This is going to be the greatest vehicle you ever bought."
- "I'm sure glad you can afford to get this one."
- "That's really going to look good in your home."

Sell what your company will do for them:
- Cut costs
- Improve productivity
- Be accessible when they need help

Sell what you will do for them:

- Offer support anytime they ask
- Make certain they are serviced properly
- Deal with them honestly and with integrity

Create a sense of urgency:

- "Tell you what! Buy it now and you can drive it off the lot tonight."
- "You seem to really like this unit, let's get the paperwork out of the way and see how soon we can get this in your home."

Now you're down to the finish line. If you're failing, your only hope is a successful "turnover" to someone else or a final, successful close. In sales, tomorrow never comes so arm yourself with these proven techniques:

1. Ron's "No Close, No Price." Developed by my best salesperson, the reality of this close is hard to grasp, but it works. It's the "price hold" commitment. "The price I'm about to give you will be SO LOW that I don't want you to know it unless you're ready to buy right now. I don't want this price out on the street." If they refuse to commit themselves, they don't get your lowball price. This amazing salesperson got the commitment first and only then did the customer know the price! You'll know you're a real pro when you master this one.

2. Order Blank Close. Start writing and making notes; show the total purchase with tax and details on a Sales Invoice. Write until they stop you.

3. Similar Situation Close. Tell a story about one of your other customers who put it off until it was too late. They knew they needed the insurance protection, but just put it off too long.

4. Sharp Angle Close. When the customer asks questions such as, "Does this plane have an auto parachute? "Do you want it if it does?"

5. Puppy Dog Close. Put the new piano in their home so they fall in love.

Cross-Selling

There's one more important step to take in the sales process: cross-selling. There's no better time to sell an add-on product or service than at the point of sale. That's why appliance sales people will ask if you want to buy a three-year warranty or a fast-food employee will say, "Would you like fries with your burger?" This principle applies in virtually every industry, from online stores to local service providers.

Now, it's time to congratulate yourself for bringing the sales process to a successful conclusion. And try not get too upset if one of your colleagues tell you that "sales is easy." You know the truth!

Building Your Sales Organization

In this era of keen competition, your business needs an effective sales organization. That means hiring a good sales manager, as well as salespeople who are energetic self-starters with the ability to connect with others and turn prospects into loyal customers. Training your sales people is a must and it fosters accountability. It's not just the immediate sale that matters — it's also the impression your salespeople make on their customers.

Every sale should be made in such a way as to create a new friend for your company and a source for new leads and prospects. When a salesperson misrepresents, you stand to lose that friend and resource.

Calling on satisfied customers after the sale is made and asking for leads and prospects is the most effective way of obtaining a live prospect list. You can actually train your customers to look for prospects, so your salespeople will not have to spend as much valuable time on cold canvassing.

Why is sales training so important? Just look at these estimates as to how repeat business is lost:

- 68 percent is lost because of sales staff ineptness
- 16 percent is lost to a lack of customer or client satisfaction
- 11 percent is lost to stronger competition
- 4 percent is lost because people move
- 1 percent is lost because people die

Just think about what your sales would look like if you could retain that 68 percent of lost repeat business. That's revenue that should belong to you as you propel your canoe across the swamp.

All successful sales organizations offer a continual hype meeting, incentives, awards, and recognition. It's a never-ending struggle to keep people motivated. If you do not re-train and motivate every 90 days, your revenue curve will typically start to decline.

After all, professional salespeople must be tested, trained and guided to their destination: prospects who are ready to buy your products and services. While writing this chapter in a dumpy diner at 6:15 p.m., a time when consumers are off work with time to consider big-ticket purchases, I peered out at a used car lot across the highway. Three potential buyers were milling around the vehicles, without a salesperson in sight. The owner had apparently gone home, leaving no one in charge of convincing the customers to buy a vehicle. Entrepreneurs with this lack of energy and organization typically sink.

So where do you find great sales managers and people who actually know how to sell? One way is to steal them, like an older guy named Bob, who sold pianos at county fairs.

When opening my second music store, I called Bob and asked if he would come to work for me because I still hadn't learned to say "with me." He laughed me off as a punk kid; his employer was well established. So, I went into my competitor's store where he worked and tried again. Undaunted, I visited him at his home. In his kitchen in front of his wife, I offered him a trip to Europe. That didn't work. But, I continued to court Bob and finally caught him on a day when he and his employer had a tiff. He took the job and produced sales of $200,000 annually for a decade. In this case, it took me more than five tries to convince Bob to come aboard, but I persevered until the deal was closed.

Another technique I've used is inviting someone into my home for a free product or service demonstration. I knew that only top producers would work in the home sales field. If they did a good job, I'd hand them a $100 bill, thank them for the pitch and discuss the sales opportunities in my own company. Go ahead and laugh. These tactics make the difference between success and real success.

A final thought on sales: Act as if you're happy, successful, and wealthy – and you will be!

Negotiating 101

If you succeed in selling, you're ready for the more complex world of negotiating. Negotiating is all about the process of achieving your goals – sometimes at the expense of the other party and sometimes to the benefit of the other party. There are two main approaches to consider:

• Distributive bargaining – an approach to negotiation that is used when the parties are trying to divide something up; in other words, they want to distribute something. Common tactics include trying to gain an advantage by insisting on negotiating on one's own home ground or having more negotiators than the other side, using tricks and deception to try to get the other side to concede more than you concede; making threats or issuing ultimatums and generally trying to force the other side to give in by overpowering them or outsmarting them.

• Integrative bargaining — when the parties are trying to make more of something or "growing the pie," rather than carving it into slices. In general, integrative bargaining tends to be more cooperative, with the parties collaborating to create a "win-win" situation.

You must learn both approaches and when to employ each.

Rehearse the Session

Never go into negotiations unprepared or without having thoroughly researched the topic under discussion, as well as the other people involved. Search online and seek out people who may have had dealings with your opponents in the past. Remember that you have been consciously or unconsciously negotiating your whole life and have probably lost more than you've gained. These lessons are going to save you from further losses.

Learn to present your case clearly and forcefully. Learn to gain control of the process and not leave yourself vulnerable. Don't be afraid to ask for the things you want. Always have a fall-back position or alternative plan. It's called BATNA — the Best Alternative to a Negotiated Agreement — and you must be able to switch to it without BATNA'n eye.

Navigating the Business Swamp

Here are some tips to success in negotiations:

- Be patient.
- Determine what you want.
- List all the goals you hope to achieve.
- Be prepared to be flexible.
- Exhibit resistance for every concession.
- For every concession you make, ask for one in return.
- Provide reasons for your concessions.
- Be prepared with other options.
- Never rush negotiations.
- Watch for the many nonverbal cues.

You will deal with an aggressive negotiator differently than one who is more passive. If the other person is demanding, self-centered, controlling, defensive, competitive, forceful, rude, intimidating, ambitious and/or impatient, you'll need to take control with an equal force. Tone it down if the other person is nice, friendly, considerate, insecure, uncomfortable with conflict, sensitive, shy, calm and/or reserved.

Your entire approach may change if the other negotiator is spontaneous, talkative and/or easily distracted.

Here are some other techniques to consider:

- Good Guy/Bad Guy. Probably the most easily recognizable trick is the good guy/bad guy tactic, an entertaining display of two people who are on the same team but act out completely opposite roles in an effort to control your emotions with their distortion of reality. If the good guy/bad guy act is successful, the victim of this mind game is rendered powerless.

• The Straw-Man Technique. Straw-man techniques involve making the other party believe something is valuable to you when it really isn't. Each concession made during the negotiations is made to seem like the negotiator is giving up a lot, even if that's not actually the case.

• "One-Time Only" Offers. Assuming you invested a good amount of time to prepare for a session, don't succumb to a phony take-it-or-leave-it tactic. It's a cheap bluff, and as soon as you say you'll leave it, they're now your prey.

• Delay Tactics. Delay tactics are used to stall and test your urgency. Allow people time to think about the issues and don't give the impression that you are desperate for their decision.

• Surprise Attack. In order to take you off guard and derail your strategy, be aware of negotiators who drop new issues or information on the table to weaken your case.

• Especially for You. Just for me? As phony as this "today and today only" phrase sounds, people will fall for it if they really want the deal.

• Nickel and Dime. I recently negotiated a $2 million transaction with a wealthy physician who pushed me for a reduction in fees. He asked me nine times to lower my fees between the time I closed my attaché case and the time I was in the corridor closing the door to his waiting room. Don't be shocked when people with the most wealth are those who will "nickel and dime" you to death. Even when they realize their deal is good, they'll seek more, so start high.

Tips To Keep You Afloat

> Everything in life is a sales job and negotiation process.
> Selling and negotiating is a learned behavior and they both require practice.
> Never give anything away unless you have a commitment.
> Remember the ABC's of selling: Always Be Closing.
> Nothing is sold until value exceeds price.
> Price is not the only component of value.
> Tell the stories of satisfied customers.
> Emphasize value – what you offer that your competition doesn't.
> Nothing happens in an organization until someone sells something.
> Watch for talented people, then steal them and train the ones you have.
> Know your competitors.
> Negotiations should be "win-win."
> Sales and negotiations are fun!

10. THE FINANCES

> *"Cash is king."*
> *Anonymous*

Cash flow is the lifeblood of any ongoing business. If more money is coming in than going out, you can consider your venture a success — at least on a modest level. Ideally, you will have a huge flow of cash — or credit card, debit card, PayPal or ApplePay payments — arriving each month with only minimal expenses to pay. That's how you get rich!

In this chapter, we'll cover the basics of finance, including ways to increase your revenue, cut your costs and use loans to your best advantage. We'll also cover how to offer financing to your customers and how to collect from "Danny Deadbeat." But let's start with the basics of accounting — the tools you use to measure your financial success.

Monitor Your Finances

In the accounting world, there is a big difference between revenue (what your business generates) and income (what your business keeps after costs are subtracted). Other important terms to know include "cash," which is money that comes into your businesses' bank account, and "receivables," which is money owed by your customers that has not yet arrived at your doorstep. If your customers are slow to pay ("the check is in the mail"), you might have a difficult time turning those accounts receivable into revenue. But if your receivables are falling, you might need to push your sales team to hustle a bit more and pick up the pace.

Business owners and their accountants use several tools to monitor the financial health of your business, including:

• Profit and Loss Statement (also known as an Income Statement). This shows your net profit or loss when expenses are subtracted from revenue – hence the term "bottom line."

• Statement of Cash Flows. This indicates where money came from and where it went. Usually, payments from buyers are received 30, 60 or 90 days after a sale, while the costs related to that sale, such as materials, labor, commissions, and overhead, are borne up front.

• Balance Sheet. Unlike dynamic reports such as revenue, expenses and income, the balance sheet provides a snapshot of the company's financial position at a specific point in time. It shows what a company owns (assets) as well as what it owes (liabilities). The difference between assets and liabilities is called the "owners' equity," or "net worth" – the amounts invested by shareholders plus profits and losses kept within the company.

There are other accounting terms that you should also know, particularly when planning for the future of your business:

• Pro-Forma. This projects the revenue, expenses, and profit that you expect at the end of a future period. If you are applying for a loan, for example, the lender will likely ask for a pro-forma statement for the next few years.

• Cash Flow Forecast. This is a valuable tool for business owners, because it estimates when you expect to receive cash and when you need to pay it out. This allows you to anticipate potential cash problems in advance or show a potential jump in revenue. It's not unusual for your accounting firm to provide financial statements without a Statement of Cash Flow, so require that report at no additional charge when negotiating your fee agreement.

Finally, many new businesses are operated on a "cash accounting" basis. This depicts the income and expenses at the time cash is actually received or paid out. It works best in small organizations. The alternative, "accrual accounting," is more complex, but provides a more accurate snapshot of a company's status at any given time. This method recognizes income and expenses at the time they are incurred rather than when cash actually changes hands. Talk with your accountant about which method will be best for your venture.

Owners often confuse Profit and Loss Statements with Cash Flow Statements or cash accounting with accrual accounting. You must become familiar with these different concepts as they form the basis for making intelligent business and financial decisions.

In any case, you need to understand and address those cash-flow demands and refuse to succumb to the "ostrich syndrome," where you avoid scrutinizing financial statements. You can delegate many tasks when creating a new business, but monitoring and forecasting cash flow is not one of them. It's your responsibility.

Cutting Costs

Let's start by examining your expenses. You have a great deal of control over your outgoing payments — and every dollar you save drops right to your bottom line. Show me a profitable company; it will be once that minimizes expenses.

In most cases, your employees' paychecks and benefits will be your biggest monthly expense. In Chapter 7, we talked about how to keep your workforce motivated and productive so they add to your company's profitability. But you should review your labor-related expenses on a regular basis and consult with an accountant to determine if there are any new ways to reduce those costs. For example, the federal rules regarding health insurance premiums for employees may be changing in a way that could reduce your benefits payments.

Here are some other cost-cutting tips and frugal habits to cultivate if you want to get rich:

- Never indulge in fancy office or reception furniture unless your particular business demands that you impress clients.
- Never buy a business meal if the other side offers; show off later.
- Pay yourself just enough for your basic expenses.
- Step-up collection activity personally.
- Monitor all staff travel and entertainment claims closely.
- Sparingly issue credit cards, company cell phones or vehicles to staff.

- Turn off lights and equipment overnight; be frugal with everything.
- Contract with a firm to reduce utility bills or taxes for a percentage of the savings.
- Consider "going green" whenever possible.
- Negotiate hard, utilize my 92 Percent Rule and let lawyers, vendors and others know that you're always comparing costs.

Many business owners, executives and sales people travel frequently. Here are some unconventional tips you can apply on the job and also in your personal life:

• When registering at a hotel, tell them you "get the government rate;" it could save half the price of your stay. Do not misrepresent yourself as an agent of the government but only ask for the government rate. Most times you'll receive a major discount without any request to see your ID, which you left in the car.

• Carry every AAA, AARP, or hotel discount card for the lowest rates. Check Internet sites like hotels.com or Expedia. Some hotel agents will negotiate directly. If you pay the rack rate, you're foolish. There is a minimal cost to make up a room and most hotels would rather have some revenue rather than none.

One extremely frugal businessman painted "For Official Business" on his vehicle and parked free. Successful businesspeople treat cash with respect and aren't shy about cutting costs.

Make Fixed Costs Variable

Any operation has certain fixed costs that are constant regardless of the level of business activity, such as payroll and rent. There are also variable costs that are dependent on the level of business activity, such as sales commissions that can go up or down depending on your team's success. If you run a hotel, you might hire more desk clerks and maids during the busy season when the number of guests goes up — another example of a variable cost.

You may be able to improve your bottom line by converting some of those fixed costs into variable expenses. For instance, if you're paying $2,000 a month in rent, you may want to negotiate for a $1,000 base rent plus 2 percent of your sales revenue each month. If you're paying salaried employees to work in a manufacturing setting, you may want to lower base wage rates and incentivize them by paying a production bonus.

If you plan to apply for a loan, your lender will scrutinize your fixed (overhead) costs to be sure you have the ability to pay your debt on time. The lower your fixed costs, the better your business will appear to a lender!

Increasing Revenue

The flip side of cutting costs is increasing revenue. The wider the margin between your operational revenue and costs, the greater your pre-tax income. We'll cover taxes in the next chapter.

The first step toward growing your revenue is seeking out new sales opportunities. For instance, you might market your current products or services to a new set of customers. You could train your sales team in cross-selling to increase the size of each customer's "shopping basket." You could also launch a new product or acquire a competitor (although either of these strategies will likely require a financial investment).

Because we covered marketing and sales in the last two chapters, this discussion will focus on other ways you can boost revenue. Consider these actions to grow cash:

- Sell off underutilized assets.

- Barter with products and services.

- Sell assets to yourself individually and lease them back to your company, which may also isolate them from creditors.

- Seek out new distribution channels.

- Require sufficient deposits for special orders.

- If your credit card processing fee is 3 percent, offer a 2 percent discount for cash.

- Automatically deduct 2 percent from an invoice if you pay it within ten days, even if the creditor does not offer it. This is a negotiation issue and you have the checkbook.

Higher Turnover Means More Cash Flow

If your inventory is a major investment, examine the turnover of each product. If it sells infrequently or not at all, dump it! Sell off excess, obsolete and damaged inventory. The higher the turnover of your inventory, the more cash you will have in the bank. Of course, you can't "sell from an empty wagon," so maintain enough inventory to fill customer orders. Divide the total number of units sold in one year by the average number of units in stock at one time to develop a ratio – and then compare it with the norm in your industry.

A decrease in turnover rates is an early warning signal that something is out of control. Poor turnover is an indicator that inventory is increasing in relationship to sales volume. The inventory ratio may also reveal that your purchasing is excessive, you are purchasing the wrong items, or sales are dropping. You can also gift stale inventory to a non-profit organization in return for a charitable deduction.

Turn Receivables into Cash

If you can convince your customers to pay more quickly, then you can turn those receivables on your balance sheet into cash in your bank account. Depending on your business, you could offer a discount for quick payment or impose a service charge for customers who don't pay on time.

You could also create an in-house collection department to remind your customers that it's time to pay for their purchases. But your team needs to walk a fine line and accelerate that revenue without insulting or aggravating a customer who may return and make more purchases in the future. And never underestimate the power of personally reaching out to a top customer, thanking him or her for the business, and asking for a payment!

Collection Agencies

A side benefit of establishing your own credit department is the elimination of your friendly credit collection agent who will take 25 percent to 50 percent of your money. Plus, you're not restricted by the same credit collection laws, so you can do the same work providing you had proper documents executed at the time of the transaction.

You will always give the account more attention when it's your own money.

One advantage of collection agencies is that they typically have a large staff permanently glued to a telephone. Their pursuit of deadbeats is therefore relentless. They also have national coverage so that there is less chance of a debtor "skipping out" of his obligations by fleeing. Third, they also have sophisticated software programs to track and dun debtors. On the downside, they keep a high percentage of the debts they collect. Your priorities may not be their priorities, and time delays can ensue.

Factoring

Another way to collect your receivables is the practice of factoring. Basically, you transfer all or a portion of your outstanding invoices to a factoring company. The factor then pays you a percentage of those invoices, perhaps 50 to 75 percent of the face value. You get that cash immediately, and then the factor goes to work on those receivables hoping to collect the full amount and make money from the transaction.

For many owners, factoring is a "deal with the devil." Do not attempt this strategy unless it's an emergency. Someone once said, "factoring debt is like smoking cigarettes. You know that smoking leads to death – but that death is some way off and you need a cigarette now!" Smoking and factoring are both unhealthy and dangerous. And, this tactic is not a means to "dump" bad debts. These companies will only buy your paper if they have a reasonable expectation of getting their money back.

Offer Financing to Your Customers

A great way to make money and generate profits is to finance your customers' purchases or services. Often you can earn the same high rate of interest that your customers pay to credit card companies – an important consideration when interest rates are low on other types of investments. You can also reduce stiff merchant processing fees on credit card sales. Consumers often return to businesses that offer credit terms, so be sure you consider adding this exciting profit center.

However, it's unwise to extend credit until you develop a system for credit checks and collection procedures. Be sure to investigate the usury rules in your state, which could limit the interest rate charged on loans. Regardless of the rate though, you can improve your incoming revenue by offering in-house financing on purchases.

Become a Banker

After purchasing, amortizing, selling and depreciating real estate, I took off my landlord's hat and became a banker by diverting the proceeds from those sales to loans. The legal opinions on private lending restrictions fall into a "gray area," and there are no barriers to entry. Go to your bank, explain that you want to take out a commercial loan and ask for a copy of the standard loan documents. Voila! Replace names on the documents and you can launch your own lending institution: The First National Bank of Bullfrog.

Provided you accurately control and monitor your own cash flow, offering credit may generate new profits and allow you to sell at higher prices. Suppose you're selling a used car for $5,000 with "easy terms" for which you allowed $2,000 on trade. If the buyer pays $2,000 down, you're only financing profit. If the buyer's parents will co-sign for the vehicle, you have additional security. If you hold the title, the buyer cannot resell the vehicle. If you're named as a loss payee on the vehicle insurance policy, you'll be paid in the event of an accident. If you offer terms, your competitor may lose the sale while you make 18% on your "loan" and keep the buyer long-term. You simplify the transaction and eliminate the risk of the buyer shopping or talking to a lender. These third parties will only serve to jeopardize your deal.

My aggressive "zero sum" mentality has always been that stealing a deal from a competitor is an equally important gain: it cripples their ability to advertise and commensurately gives you a volume purchasing power edge. Your buyer will bring you more customers, and you'll know when they're shopping for a new car because you'll be asked for a payoff.

If the buyer signs a Promissory Note, you can charge an "origination fee." If the buyer defaults, you can file a lien against his or her assets for the full amount of the vehicle. If they pay you off early, you can assess a prepayment penalty. You can go as far as to install a "shut-down" service so if the payment isn't made, the car won't start! Postdated checks can also be accepted as a promise to make future payments. Turn risk into opportunity, Froggie! I've even taken precious metals, jewelry and other assets as additional security. For sensitive people, remember what Judge Judy says: "Danny Deadbeat," in his twisted mind, will get mad at the lender even though he's stiffing him. So, never grant credit to a family member.

When a buyer applies for a loan from your business, you can get a credit report from Equifax, Experian or TransUnion so you can investigate payment performance and learn if there are other judgments, charge-offs or delinquent obligations. This report will also reveal asset details.

Extending credit can be extremely profitable if you have well-written sales and financing agreements. While many business owners say they want "nothing to do" with offering terms, I'd much rather loan money than compete only on price. If you need cash and have too many "store accounts" or loans on the street, you can impose your "balloon" right to call the loan or factor your receivables to generate instant cash.

Without all of these repayment safeguards and before you lose a sale, suggest your customer approach other people to borrow the money. Bankers refer to these lenders as the "3 Fs": Friends, Family and Fools.

Use Promissory Notes

If you present a one-page Promissory Note to customers who want to make timely payments, they will sign it. Otherwise, the cost of obtaining a judgment through civil litigation may dwarf your recovery. Obtaining Notes is not optional. If people intend to pay you, they should willingly sign a Note. Otherwise, keep your merchandise or money.

A Note may provide for the acceleration of payments so that the entire balance will be due upon default and it typically allows you to recover attorney fees if the debt is referred for collection*. Sadly, Notes are seldom demanded by small businesses owners. So, have your borrower (i) sign a Note (ii) write six checks dated the same day or one for the first day of the following six months and (iii) swipe a credit card as backup security.

Despite popular belief, postdated checks may not be illegal; they reduce your collection activity and risk. They're a promise to pay an amount of money on a specific future date. Because the event is in the future, the maker of the check cannot know at the time of issuance that it will or will not be honored. But, it's better to hold a post-dated check than no check . . . even if it bounces.

Bounced Checks

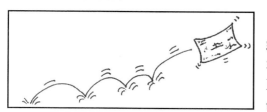

Not to worry! It's good news! Now there's real pressure on Danny Deadbeat to cough-up the money. He may face criminal charges if you can show an intent to defraud and if you have evidence. You may charge three or four times what your bank charges for a returned check, however maximum insufficient funds fees vary from state to state. Most law enforcement officials require you to send a 10-day payment letter to the debtor by certified mail before they will even consider filing "bad check" charges.

I encountered a crooked contractor who charged for work not completed, concealed the fact it was not completed, installed cheaper, substitute equipment and filed bankruptcy three times to avoid collection. I thought we lost all hope for justice until his wife wrote a slew of bad checks and went to jail.

Demand a "Confession of Judgment"

Insert a Confession of Judgment (COJ) in your documents. It's a provision that allows the lender to summarily enter judgment against the borrower if there is a material default under the terms of a loan. The borrower essentially waives his due process rights and the lender can proceed directly to a judgment without giving evidence, going to court, allowing the borrower to present a defense or even giving the borrower notice of the intention to enter the judgment. A COJ, implying "the borrower confesses he's guilty," gives the lender a quick, easy, and low-cost method to obtain a judgment and to preserve the priority of his lien. This is a major benefit if you're the lender, and a catastrophe if you're the borrower. "Get em . . . don't give em." The COJ is controversial and many states have barred it under the right to due process in their state constitutions. States that allow COJ clauses have strict requirements over the language used in those clauses.

Some states and courts have expanded the rights of debtors. Therefore, a debtor may have a confessed judgment opened or stricken with a meritorious defense if a petition to the court is timely filed. If a petition is granted, the case will proceed to trial like a traditional lawsuit. If you fail to invoke a COJ, Danny's lawyer could tie you up in court for a year or more. Do not loan money without this provision!

Require a Guarantor

Guaranties allow you to collect unpaid debts from someone other than the borrower. Generally, to be effective they must:

- Name the guarantor
- Name the party whose debts are being guaranteed
- Be in writing
- Be clear and specify exactly what is being guaranteed
- Contain terms and conditions of the guaranty
- State the consideration to be paid.

Personal Guaranty

Don't loan money without demanding a personal guarantee!* Most major banks won't do so, and neither should you. A typical guarantee will say, "The undersigned individual, to induce the granting of credit to the above-named applicant, hereby personally guarantees the applicant's obligation." Get em . . . don't give em.

The Statute of Limitations

This legal "stop sign" is the maximum time after an event that you can initiate legal proceedings. It varies from state to state, but most commonly it is four to six years for a written contract and either two or four years for an oral contract. But if your borrower is trying to hide under a lily pad, you need to file your complaint before the time has lapsed. You may get an extension if you filed a complaint or made a "good faith" effort to serve the debtor. Here are a few sneaky tips for the collector:

• Get any payment. If you find that you're approaching the "drop dead date" to sue, then convince Danny to send you $10. On the date you receive that payment, the clock starts ticking all over again and you bought more time. Of course if you owe someone money, don't fall for this trick. Never send a partial payment. And, if they don't sue you in time and you have a legitimate reason not to pay, send them a certified letter to announce the big hand hit 12, and, if they do sue, you'll counter sue for all of your legal costs.

• File a Writ of Summons, or other appropriate notice, which suspends the Statute of Limitations and preserves your right to sue in the future. It's just a few pages and the only downside is that you may be forced to file your complaint upon notice. However, most deadbeats aren't anxious to poke a swamp critter in the eye so they normally allow you to preserve your right.

Become Familiar with Basic Collection Procedures

Learn how to communicate with debtors. It's helpful to adhere to these general rules even if they do not seem to apply to the specific accounts or loans you need to collect.

Many debtors routinely lie, cheat and "work the system" to defraud creditors. However, they are still customers so if they've fallen on hard times, treat them with respect. After you've been stiffed often enough, you may develop the "collection mentality" as you wade in very infested waters. If you have a weak personality, don't be a lender.

My first electronics employer held a boatload of bad debt. As a 16-year-old, I had no compunction about collecting money or repossessing a TV. It was akin to making a sale. I'd always cooperate with a debtor but if they were intentionally taking advantage of my employer, then I became so aggressive they paid me to leave. A good screaming match at the front door is sometimes effective. But if you're not prepared for that type of confrontation, give the debt to a collector.

The Fair Debt Collection Practices Act
Limitations on Consumer Loans

This law, found at 15 U.S.C. §1692-1697, is important to understand. Whether or not legally required of you as a private lender, respect the provisions of the act:

- Don't communicate with third parties about the debt of the consumer.
- If you know a debtor's employer prohibits communication, don't communicate there.
- If the debtor advises, in writing, that they do not want to receive any further collection efforts, avoid them. However, you may give notice that you intend to take some specific collection action.
- Avoid contacting the debtor at unreasonable times or places.
- Do not use threats of violence or harm, publish a list of debtors who refuse to pay or use obscene or profane language.
- Do not falsely imply you are an attorney or government representative, imply the debtor committed a crime, represent that you work for a credit bureau, misrepresent the amount of the debt, give

false credit information about the debtor or send the debtor anything that looks like an official document from a court or government agency when it is not. Do not use a false company or organization name.

• Be cautious with answering machines, emails and text messages.

If Danny's spending your money on a Harley, it's time to get tough, and as litigators say, "sue the bastard." File a complaint in the right court, typically where Danny lives or where he, and hopefully his spouse or guarantor, signed the contract. Since you're not a lawyer, you can attempt to file it in your backyard and hope Danny doesn't appear and you'll be awarded a default judgment; then move the judgment to the county and state in which he resides. However, be aware that some states, notably New York and Connecticut, won't accept foreign judgment transfers obtained by default or by a COJ. The Uniform Enforcement of Foreign Judgments Act provides a simplified way of transferring foreign judgments in all states except California, Vermont and Massachusetts.

Garnishment

In the collection world, you may navigate the troubled water of garnishment. This is a way of collecting money from the debtor through a third party who has some control over part of the debtor's income, known as the garnishee. Unless you're the IRS, garnishment can be difficult to achieve since most states regulate and limit the types of debt for which it can be used. For example, your state may only allow garnishment for an unpaid residential 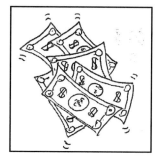 rent claim. You can apply to receive funds directly from the debtor's paycheck or bank account, but there could be limits to the percentage of the debtor's disposable income that can be attached.

You must first determine the venue and start the collection process by filing a Writ of Execution with the sheriff in that county; you will receive an employer's return form. The debtor can file a claim if he does not have adequate income to afford the garnishment and if the court denies that claim, the debtor's employer will be notified to begin the wage garnishment. The check will normally come from the garnishee directly to you.

Tenancy by the Entireties

This situation generally exists only in real property and only between a husband and wife. When a married couple takes title together, they are said to hold title as tenants by the entireties. The reason for this is the common-law concept that a husband and wife are one person. In some states, this asset protection arrangement is as good as being a corporation with no assets. When the sheriff attempts to levy on anything, unless the spouse was also foolish enough to extend a personal guarantee, spouse "A" owns 100% of the asset and spouse "B" owns 100%, thereby stopping the levy process in its tracks.

Leasing

In some types of businesses, you can offer your customers a choice between financing a purchase and leasing the product, such as a car, truck, boat, RV, or office equipment.

Under this arrangement you give an end user the right to use equipment that you own in return for a fee. You retain title to items to hold as security as you lease them. As the owner of the equipment, you enjoy all of the depreciation credits — a valuable tool to reduce tax obligations. Consult with your accountant to be certain that your lease contains language acceptable to the IRS. Your lease may offer the lessee a one dollar buy-out; a lease termination can be open-ended, so payments continue long term, or it may be close ended and the items revert to you. But remember, the lessee is often coming to you because they can't finance with traditional lenders.*

Leases can be better than loans as the higher interest rate is built into the payment. But once again, you may be in deeper swamp waters. I recently leased business equipment. The lessee took possession of the items and didn't pay a dime. I sued under the COJ provision contained in the lease*. Next, she sold my equipment and still didn't pay; this is a crime. The case went to court and a judgment was awarded in excess of the lease obligation. She appealed, and she is now into her second appeal. Then she went into hiding which resulted in the loss of my time, trouble, and money associated with collection. Be vigilant and make periodic inspections to eyeball your property before it disappears.

Working with Lenders

If you've paid attention to the points so far in this chapter, you might decide never to borrow money from a bank or other lender. However, there may be times when you might need a loan or line of credit to grow your inventory, develop a new product, open a new office or make it through a difficult financial period. In that case, re-read all the above material and remember what you should and shouldn't do as a borrower!

If you want to apply for a loan, think carefully about the amount you will need, how long you will need the money and how much of your cash flow will need to be diverted to making those payments. You should also think about what type of security the lender will want and whether you are prepared to accept the restrictions and covenants found in loan agreements.

Once you have those things clear in your mind, then shop around. Pretend you're going to the mall where you can shop in store after store for a new pair of shoes. There are plenty of banks and finance companies available, both locally and online. Contact several prospects and compare their offers, and consult your accountant or tax advisor for advice. In other words, treat this as a major purchase: You are buying someone else's money, and you want to get the best deal you can find.

Here are three types of loans you might find in today's financial marketplace:

• An asset-based loan. This is essentially any form of loan secured by tangible or intangible assets of the borrower, such as accounts receivable or equipment. If you're borrowing money to buy a new bulldozer, for instance, the lender might secure the loan by holding the title to the machine until you pay off your debt.

• Working capital loans or lines of credit. These are utilized by companies to provide the daily cash needed for operations. This loan may be unsecured if you pay your bills on time and have a good credit rating. However, they may not be available to a startup with no financial history. In some cases, the lender will require you to provide collateral to support the loan. That could mean securing the loan by accounts receivable and/or inventory.

• Cash flow lending. This is an unsecured loan that is based on the borrower's perceived ability to service the loan from regular income.

Why is security so important for creditors and debtors? A secured creditor holds a lien on, or interest in, the assets, which can then be sold to satisfy debts. If a borrower files bankruptcy, a lender most likely has a zero chance of being paid if the loan is not secured.

Conversely, an unsecured creditor, such as a credit card company, has no claim on real property. An unsecured creditor must first sue, then win, then get a judgment, then try to get sheriffs to levy on or seize whatever property they can find and eventually sell it off.

And remember, if a lender asks for your personal guarantee, don't give it. Use your negotiation skills. You're a company. Listen up. If you cave in, you'll regret it. If you're a partner in an entity, negotiate less punitive personal guarantees by making a strong case against joint and several guarantees. Under joint and several, each partner is liable personally for the full amount of the loan. If the loan is for $2 million and you and your three partners are each jointly and severally liable, then each of you is liable for the full $2 million. As that is clearly overkill, a good case can be made for several only — that is, the aggregate guarantees the total debt.

Remember that lenders build in a cushion for bad debt. They make profits on their loans. They extend credit to do more business at higher profit margins and they need to accept risk. Some will factor or sell your debt, so you must take a hardline refusal to grant a personal guarantee. Tell them your bank or spouse won't allow it. Tell them anything . . . but your personal signature is the kiss of death.

Tips To Keep You Afloat

> Put spare cash to work.
> Take a hard look at costs and expenditures.
> Learn and master basic accounting reporting tools.
> Strive to improve your inventory turns.
> Shift costs from fixed to variable.
> Turn receivables into cash.
> Offer a discount for early payments.
> Negotiate harder with creditors.
> Consider financing as a separate profit center.
> Build customer loyalty by offering credit.
> Demand customers sign a Promissory Note if you offer terms.
> Include a Confession of Judgment in your Note.
> Require loan guarantors, and a personal guaranty from borrowers.
> Avoid being caught by, or taken advantage of, the Statute of Limitations.
> Learn all the available collection procedures.
> Use collection agencies only as a last resort.

11. THE GOVERNMENT

> *"Thank God we don't get all the government we pay for."*
> *Will Rogers*

As an entrepreneur, you'll spend more time than you want dealing with local, state and federal government agencies. You'll probably have to abide by regulations that seem to make no sense, with zoning codes and state laws that restrict your ability to grow your company and with several types of federal taxes that must be subtracted from your operating profits.

Welcome to the topsy-turvy world of government, whose attitudes toward business hasn't changed much in the past few centuries. While cities, counties, states and Washington say they support business growth — because it adds to their tax revenue — in practice, they do very little to help. Instead, the agencies will take your money, slow you down and irritate you in the process. In terms of necessary evils, dim-witted government employees are high on the list of challenges you'll need to overcome to succeed in business.

On the Positive Side

But before we get into all the issues you're likely to face with government, let's start with some of the positives. Yes, there are a few!

First, the government compiles many types of useful statistics that can be helpful in developing your marketing programs and managing your company. For example, the U.S. Census Bureau can provide you with a wide range of consumer information: ages, household size, housing types, and population growth rates. These data can help you determine the potential for a new market you might want to enter. Be sure to include some census statistics in your next business plan or loan application if you want to show the "money men" that you've done your homework.

The U.S. Bureau of Labor Statistics has a wealth of data on specific industries and types of jobs. If you're wondering how much an accountant, a nurse or an engineer earns on average, you can find that information here. This can be a help when hiring a new employee, but be aware that there are vast differences in wage and salary levels around the country. A receptionist position in San Francisco will likely command a much higher pay rate than one in Detroit.

Another good source to explore is the North American Industry Classification System (NAICS), which was developed to provide industry-by-industry insight into economic behavior. Your business – and the competition – will fall into one of these categories. Also, the Small Business Administration (SBA) uses NAICS codes to classify small businesses by industry. They set size standards within each classification to determine whether an entity is eligible for government programs and preferences reserved for "small business" concerns.

Local, state and the federal government may also be customers for your products or services. In most cases, they require a bidding procedure and are fixated on price, rather than value. Personally, I have always preferred to sell to consumers or businesses, rather than the government. But you should be aware that this is a potential market that you could pursue. In a few cases, such as products with military applications, government might be your only prospective customer. Place your company on the General Services Administration bidding list. As an example: If you have a source for ink pens, submit a bid for $200,000 at a 5 percent margin and you might be awarded the bid and make $5,000 because no one else responded to the Invitation to Bid.

A Tangle of Regulations

As consumers, we may applaud the government's regulatory role in our society. Automobile safety features like airbags, anti-pollution laws and Food and Drug Administration (FDA) standards are among the many ways that federal and state regulations protect our interests and help us live better and healthier lives.

But as business owners, all too often we are faced with a confusing tangle of regulations that add significantly to our costs without necessarily benefiting anyone other than the bureaucrats whose jobs involve enforcing those rules.

How bad is the regulatory situation? In 2015, there were 115 new federal laws passed together with 3,378 new rules and regulations. It's hard to say just how many laws and statutes are on the books in your state, but no business owner has the time or desire to understand them all. Fortunately, you can ignore most of the laws because they won't affect your business. But if you do make a mistake, then the agencies will be ready to pounce. They'll tell you that "ignorance of the law is no excuse," as they try to part you from your hard-earned money. I recently had a client who moved some dirt on his property near a stream. We learned a DEP helicopter photo revealed the change, fined him $25,000, and he incurred another $90,000 in remediation expenses and professional fees. Government is everywhere, even overhead.

However, business-related laws and regulations vary throughout the country. If you have a choice in your business location, you might pick a city or state that welcomes your company, rather than a government that's ready to tax your business to death. A recent study by the Pacific Research Institute analyzed the impact of 14 regulatory measures on small businesses in all 50 states. Indiana emerged as the most business friendly and California was the least friendly.

In 2010, San Francisco banned McDonald's from giving out free toys with Happy Meals, claiming it was an incentive for children to make unhealthy choices. New York City's Board of Health sought to limit sugar-sweetened beverages to 16-ounce cups. While recently working on a project near Seattle, I came upon an ordinance to reject restaurant occupancy permits if the staff wore uniforms, obviously targeting franchises. Government regulations are completely out of control. Politicians pontificate about how they support small business, which studies have shown accounts for 60 to 80 percent of U.S. jobs, and then they enact ordinances such as these! Politicians, most of whom couldn't operate a lemonade stand, will surely travel to the top of your frustration meter.

Grow accustomed to losing encounters with government. You'll lose to big business with the near abolition of fair trade practices and lose with almost every parasitic branch of government that makes your life miserable at every turn. And, at the time of this writing, the payroll burden for every employee has risen over 2 percent in the last year and modern-day liberals want to double the minimum wage to $15 per hour.

I never begrudged it when people availed themselves of unemployment benefits to sustain their families in troubled times, or because we were unable to provide them with work. But, these types of social programs are severely abused by thieves who capitalize on government assistance without a real need. It's why businesspeople tend to register Republican.

Fighting City Hall

Whether you operate your business from an office, a warehouse, a store or some other location, at some point you'll have to deal with "City Hall." You will need some type of local permit to open and

operate your business. If you plan to build a new facility or remodel an existing building or office suite, you'll have to get more permits. That might mean hiring an architect, an engineer, a contractor, or a government relations attorney who can help guide you through the maze while adding to your start-up costs. If you're more ambitious with your plans, you could find yourself applying to the local zoning board for approval, passing a review by the architectural board and spending months waiting for a thumbs up or thumbs down from the city, township or county commission.

But don't worry – your local government will collect the higher property taxes you will pay for improving your place of business. It will also charge you an annual business license fee, which will probably go up as your company adds employees and becomes more successful. As you paddle your canoe through the swamp, imagine more and more "critters" trying to grab your paddles and hitch a ride. That's the experience of local government.

Personally, I became so disgusted with our local government when the council imposed onerous codes that I conducted a "moving-out sale." As Howard Beale screamed from the balcony in the 1976 movie, *Network*, I told them, "I'm mad as hell, and I'm not going to take this anymore." I plastered that slogan on the windows of my showroom, called for television coverage and hung posters explaining the inept actions of our local government. For the next three decades, they were totally cooperative with my business needs. So, there are times you need to speak up and protect your rights as well as the rights of others. As our third President Thomas Jefferson said, "When injustice becomes law, then resistance becomes duty."

State Government

State governments have their own rules and regulations, along with their fees and taxes. They license a wide range of occupations from doctors and lawyers to beauticians and massage therapists. They often require you to pay an annual fee for doing business, and they almost always impose a sales tax on your products and possibly services. Some states also levy high corporate and personal income taxes, while others do not.

Chances are you'll choose to incorporate your business in a state close to your home or family. But if you have options, shop around. Check online and compare taxes and fees on a state-by-state basis. Then, once you're up and running, and ready to expand, look first at other states with a similar business-friendly climate. Otherwise, you might find that big jump in sales revenue is eroded by state taxation.

I once had a bookkeeper who, for a reason we never understood, hid unpaid sales tax notices until the debt became six figures! Then it became my problem, we retained an accountant, suffered through a nine-month audit and made four trips to the state capital. I went, with "hat in hand," and pleaded with an assistant attorney general to accept 50 percent of the assessment over three years. And, he agreed. Everything is negotiable.

In general, government's greatest conjuring trick is to make your earnings disappear before your eyes, and it never runs out of new versions of the same game. Federal, state and local governments all want to feed at your trough. At the time of this writing, the combination of the federal marginal tax rate, my state's flat rate income tax, my local school district's earned income tax and state and federal employment taxes means that 51.82 percent of a person's annual income never makes it to the intended recipient. Assuming that one then devotes 70 percent of his disposable income to expenditures that require payment of sales tax, the effective tax rate could become 53.84 percent.

However, the bloodletting doesn't stop there. State and federal taxes on gasoline currently add 69.8 cents to the price of a gallon. Your electricity bill contains surcharges allowing the power company to recover certain of its own state tax liability at the expense of its customers. The phone bill includes a tithe for support of government emergency services operations and the 911 system.

Finally there are "sin taxes" levied by states on alcohol, tobacco and drugs – a favorite way for these governments to balance their budgets. However, these particular taxes have two different goals: increasing revenue from the sales of these products or reducing consumption by imposing high taxes. By the way, if you win the state lottery, the taxing bodies may take half of your earnings right off the top.

Federal Government

Meanwhile, federal workers' special benefits increase while entrepreneurs struggle. In 2001 Congress created a program to progressively pay down the student loans of employees of federal agencies. In 2015 a total of 32 agencies paid $69.5 million in aid to 9,610 employees. The program was designed to aid recruitment and retention of federal workers, presumably in response to Ronald Reagan's dry assertion that "The government does not have the best brains. If it did, private industry would buy them."

Since then, employees of the Senate and House of Representatives became eligible for similar programs. In 2009, these programs cost the House – or rather taxpayers – $12 million and the Senate $4.9 million. In 2007 the Department of Education instituted a program to pay down the student loans of workers in any qualifying branch of public service, once they had made 120 loan payments while employed in a public service field. The first such payments will be made in October 2017, so the cost of it remains to be seen.

Members of Congress and their staff may also have advance notice of company activities that can affect investment decisions, before this knowledge becomes public. To eliminate the possibility of using that information for personal gain, the STOCK Act (Stop Trading on Congressional Knowledge) was passed in 2012. It requires all members of Congress to file online any stock market transaction in which they were involved within 45 days. But a year later, the law was modified making it more difficult to track down this information. Being a member of government makes you special compared to ordinary citizens.

Understand the IRS and Your Responsibility

Now, we come to the not-so-fun stuff: the Internal Revenue Service (IRS) and its ability to tax your business, your personal income, your investments, your estate and more. The only difference between death and taxes is that death, on occasion, is allegedly painless. Government, by its very nature, is wasteful and you, my dear reader, are going to pay for the waste until you die. As soon as you start to make serious money, you will come to appreciate the enormity of high taxes. The IRS had become so aggressive that in 2002, Congress issued a directive to back-off small businesses.

Unfortunately, the IRS will come calling at some point in time. Dealing with them is like spending three weeks in a dentist's chair. It's also hard to predict what the outcome will be. In some cases, the IRS will come charging after you. An IRS agent once conducted a field audit in my office. He concluded that my company owed $15,000 and indicated that he would place the obligation on a 90-day payment program. I agreed. He then left the office, walked to the courthouse, filed a judgment against me and then walked to the bank and seized the $15,000 from our operating account.

The Government

On the other hand, I recently had a client who didn't file tax returns for 16 years and never heard from the government. This is because the IRS can be institutionally lazy. After all, they are not dealing with their own money, so they don't lose sleep if they don't collect everything. However, not filing or paying is foolish and potentially fatal for the taxpayer.

Whether you file your return with a tax preparer or use one of the online services — or even the IRS Free File — consider this a vital aspect of your business responsibilities. Plan your taxes, use your accountant if necessary, and maintain a detailed set of books in the event of an audit. Oftentimes clients have come into my office, sweat on their brow and a shoebox under their arm crammed with receipts, saying, "What the hell do I do now, the IRS is after me?"

Learning the Rules

To help you understand the Internal Revenue Code, the IRS provides online advice and suggestions on different topics. It also issues Publication 583, "Starting a Business and Keeping Records." It contains essential information along with references to other publications that contain the remaining things start-up entrepreneurs should understand. While trying to be helpful, the IRS nevertheless divides and compartmentalizes subject matter, leaving you to bounce from publication to publication. That's how the Code of Federal Regulations has grown to well over 200 volumes and 175,000 pages.

Nevertheless, Publication 583 gives a useful basic outline of the taxable structure of a new business, from obtaining a tax identification number to specifying your tax year and choosing an accounting system. It outlines the basic types of taxes and how to pay them and also the various deductions that are available.

Deduct, Deduct and Deduct

As a business owner, you may qualify for hundreds of possible deductions on your federal income tax returns. If you buy a new computer, lease a vehicle, pay your employees' healthcare premiums or improve your place of business, you probably can deduct those expenses. There are also tax credits or dollar-for-dollar reimbursements available from energy companies when you install energy-saving products. Just be sure you keep good records of everything you pur-chase during the year, and ask your accountant to find ways to cut your taxes as much as possible.

There are also important deductions that often go by the wayside. For example, you can depreciate the value of many types of assets, such as expensive office or manufacturing equipment. There are strict rules that must be followed, though, when preparing your annual corporate or personal tax return. How you take money from the business can also affect your tax bill. For instance, salaries may be treated differently than dividends on your corporate stock. Again, talk with your tax preparer to minimize tax liabilities.

Many entrepreneurs and most accountants don't know that you can also recover the costs incurred before you begin operating a new business, including start-up and organizational costs. The expenses you incur to investigate a new business are also deductible. For example, you could fly to Puerto Rico for a month and try to write it off if you have business contacts there to evaluate, say, the cigar shop industry.

If your business lost money, you may qualify for a tax loss "carryforward." This allows a company to apply a net operating loss in a given year to offset profits in a subsequent year, or as many subsequent years as it takes for the whole of the loss to be absorbed. Some states, however, may have a cap on the number of years the carryforward can be used.

Carryforwards are a useful means of cash flow preservation for businesses trying to stay afloat in the swamp. Not only do they lessen a business' overall tax obligation, they also shelter profits from other operations. The carryforward is an asset in its own right and you may benefit from buying a company and using its carryforward to shelter future earnings. In general, tax credits are as valuable as cash yet they are often overlooked in financial planning.

Tax savings are possible if one knows the law and all of the permissible tax "loopholes." This is legal tax avoidance, which is in sharp contrast to illegal tax evasion. Tax avoidance is not immoral and will become critical in your pathway to success. One study suggests that 65,000 accountants miss available tax credits each year. You must monitor everything and everyone.

A Powerful Agency

The IRS has powers that other creditors do not enjoy. And if you're naive, you'll actually believe what the IRS says and fall into their trap. When you can't pay your taxes, develop your reasons first. Generally, the government will cooperate and offer a payment plan but be mindful of stiff penalties and interest. In the 1976 Supreme Court Case US vs. Miller, 425 VS 435 (1976), the court ruled that bank customers had no legal right to privacy in financial information held by banks or other financial institutions.

However, you're not always responsible for your tax return. As your business expands, the demands on your time and attention can become overwhelming. You may need to depend on others to generate data, file returns and pay taxes. If and when they fail, it could become very expensive.

A penalty equal to the total amount of the tax can be imposed on a "responsible person" who willfully fails to collect, account for or pay over to the IRS any tax imposed under the Internal Revenue Code. The highest penalty is a felony tax evasion, which could result in five years imprisonment and either a $250,000 individual fine, a $500,000 corporate fine, or both. However, in one case the claims court held that the sole officer and shareholder of an incorporated medical clinic that failed to pay trust taxes wasn't liable for the penalty since he had delegated full control of the non-medical management of the clinic to an employee. The administrator made all decisions as to who would be paid, and the date and amount of payment. She did so without consulting the taxpayer. And, the administrator signed the checks with a stamp bearing the doctor's name. But don't fully rely on that one case.

Fresh out of college and new to the business world, I unwisely opened different accounts for different purposes and then transferred money between those accounts as needed. These transfers showed up as deposits in our local bank that triggered an IRS audit. The IRS wanted to know why my deposits were five times greater than reported sales. I explained the reason and satisfied the in-field review team but before our session started, they flashed their badges and announced they were from the criminal division. They had photographs of my residence and questioned how I owned such a beautiful home at such an early age. Those real-life experiences were petrifying at the time.

The Audit and Appeal

It's common to find you owe the IRS a large sum of money because of inept accountants, bookkeepers, auditors and inconsistencies in the law. The IRS defines an audit as "an impartial review of the taxpayer's return to determine its completeness and accuracy." Former U.S. Senator Edward V. Long compared the IRS to a "Gestapo preying upon defenseless citizens."

Examinations are handled either as an office or field audit. Office audits are usually conducted if you have a moderate income or you operate a service business that does not carry inventories. The field audit is usually conducted if the examination requires the review of records that are at the taxpayer's place of business. A revenue agent generally conducts field audits. A tax auditor usually conducts the audit on the IRS premises.

The tax auditor may conduct an exhaustive examination of every item on the return or audit one or two items in a review that may only require an hour. Agents are instructed to curtail the practice of auditing more than just the year under consideration. Only 0.9 percent of all returns filed in 2015 were audited and only 0.3 percent were audited face to face. The more you earn, the greater your chance of being audited. Aircraft, boats and seasonal homes draw attention to your return.

The IRS Discriminate Function Analysis is programmed to

identify returns with the highest probability of errors; its guidelines are kept secret by the IRS. Overpayment is refunded with interest at the federal short-term interest rate plus three percentage points, except when the refund is made within 45 days of the overpayment.

Typically, the "look-back period" for auditing is three years, however this time could double to six years if the IRS can prove that a taxpayer omitted at least 25 percent of his gross income from the tax return for years in that period. If fraud is shown, there is no time limit. When you appeal, penalties can be excessive, but many times they are forgiven, especially if it is a first infraction. After being improperly assessed significant penalties, I once raised the possibility of an appeal with the agent. He said, "Oh yes, I forgot. You may appeal my decision!" Remember, you must be vigilant.

Audit assessments always have an appeal date. If you miss the appeal date by one day, you could be "out of jurisdiction." This simply means that whether or not you have a strong case, the government won't hear it. Assuming that you file a timely appeal, there is a reasonable possibility that you can have the penalty abated.

Offer in Compromise

An Offer in Compromise is an agreement between the taxpayer and the government that settles a tax liability for a payment of less than the full amount owed. The IRS will generally accept an Offer in Compromise when it's unlikely the tax liability can be collected in full and the amount offered reasonably reflects the collection potential; it can be $1,000 on $100,000 or $50,000 on $60,000. And, know that if you can hide for ten years, your tax debt may be written-off. However, this timeframe is extended if an unsuccessful Offer in Compromise has been made.

One way to avoid higher penalties is to make certain that tax forms are filed, even if you do not have funds to make payment.

The Government

Remember that the tax collector is much like the school teacher who asks for your homework but may not bother to check it. Occasionally, the IRS needs to make an example of someone. You may find that audits or liens are publicized in local newspapers; the IRS issues news releases so all taxpayers understand criminal charges may be applicable. They specifically publicize this news prior to tax season so people are mindful of the threat. This, of course, is done without any regard to adverse publicity damage. If the matter is resolved in favor of the taxpayer, the positive outcome is rarely publicized.

One audit may trigger another. My company had not been audited for many years, but once we were audited, three different government agencies visited our offices shortly thereafter. So, to avoid disastrous audits, pay a tax advisor to make certain you're compliant. In theory, this sounds like a logical approach and it may help, but even a consultant is not always certain how tax laws will be interpreted. Remember that the tax laws are often left to the auditor and his supervisor and in many states, the policies and statutes are so unclear that no one can really understand them. The most you can hope for is the avoidance of large discrepancies.

Responsible businesspeople should want to pay their fair share of taxes. The disappointing situation is when an auditor's assessments were incorrect and you must retain a professional to present your position. After they have generated thousands in fees, they typically advise you to settle with a compromise — even though you may be correct in your position. It's simply not economical to fight Uncle Sam.

Our tax system is one of self-assessment described by Justice Robert A. Jackson as "taxation by confession." A claim of ignorance for a substantial underpayment of tax does not provide an adequate defense against the imposition of heavy penalties.

The Taxpayer Advocate Service May Help

The Taxpayer Advocate Service (TAS) is your independent voice in the IRS! Only the government would form its own agency to defend you against another of its own agencies. If you're audited or have an IRS problem, you may be eligible for TAS help if you've been unsuccessful in resolving the matter through normal IRS channels or if you believe an IRS procedure isn't working as it should. The TAS helps taxpayers whose problems are causing financial difficulty or significant costs, including the cost of professional representation. Obtain the TAS form and allow one branch of the IRS to attempt navigation through another branch.

To summarize, every one of your encounters with government will give credence to the Mises Institute motto: "Do not give in to evil but proceed ever more boldly against it."

Tips To Keep You Afloat

> Always keep your books in "apple-pie and audit-proof" order.
> Never assume your bookkeeper or accountant has everything in place; review their work before the IRS does.
> Research every legal allowance and deduction; they are all documented, but you have to dig for them and learn governmentese.
> Always remain current with trust taxes (such as sales or payroll withholding); they are not your operating slush fund. The money belongs to the government or your employees.
> If audited, do not panic. Understand the procedure and get professional help.
> Never assume the IRS has forgotten about you.
> Reduce your state taxes by relocating to any of the following "no-income tax" states: Florida, Nevada, South Dakota, Texas, Washington, Wyoming or Hawaii; or to zero/low tax corporate states: Nevada, Ohio, Texas, Washington, South Dakota or Wyoming. Do this even when your company may be located in your home state.

12. THE PROFESSIONALS

AT YOUR MERCY..SERVICE

"If you think it's expensive to hire a professional...just wait until you hire an amateur."

Unknown

There comes a time in the entrepreneur's career when the advice of a professional is indispensable. It might be when you start a business and need a lawyer to prepare the corporate papers, or an accountant to compile financial documents for your first business tax return. Depending on the nature of your business, you might require an architect to prepare plans for your facility or a space planner/ interior designer to best utilize your office, store or warehouse most efficiently. Engineers, contractors, plumbers, electricians, and carpenters are among the other types of professionals you may need in your business career. In each case, though, you should do three things before signing a contract for a professional's service:

1. Think about what you want to accomplish, and have a clear measurable outcome in mind. That could be preparing a document (lawyer), a tax return (accountant) or a clear picture of the issues facing your business (management consultant). But always start the process by establishing your goal. Otherwise, you could waste money.

2. Find the professional who seems best suited for your task. You can search online for an initial list of names, or you can ask family members, friends and business colleagues for their recommendations. Look for credentials and licenses of each professional, and see if any of them have faced disciplinary actions or sanctions for unethical or illegal behavior. Finally, interview at least two or three of the best qualified professionals to determine who would be the best fit for the engagement. If you're running an online store, for instance, you might want an accountant who has done similar work for other retailers and is familiar with the arcane web of state sales taxes.

3. Negotiate the fee. As a new entrepreneur, your funds are likely to be limited. See if the professional will give you a break on his or her rates in hopes of establishing a long-term relationship. Try to set a cap on the total fee with wording in your agreement, such as "not to exceed $5,000."

In some cases, you can include a timeline for completion, with penalties if the professional misses the deadline. Or, ask for a guarantee so if problems arise after the engagement, you can bring the professional back to resolve them.

Some professionals cause major problems and waste. Every profession has vultures that charge exorbitant hourly rates and submit unitemized bills. I've seen Certified Public Accountants (CPAs) charge $2,000 for absolutely nothing, either because their firm is forcing production or because the accountant is paid a stipend. If these professionals were truly working the total number of hours they're billing, they wouldn't have time to sleep! Some make an attempt at honesty by assessing an "appreciation fee," such as billing $5,000 because they saved the client $25,000. I'd rather pay this "value-added" fee than pay for bogus hours.

Professionals are no different from other humans. Some are good and some are not. Some will solve your dilemma and others might worsen it because of their incompetence or greed. Therefore, it's imperative that you select professionals carefully and be a good client by assisting them with your problem.

Remember that getting professional advice before problems arise is generally less expensive than waiting until you're served with a lawsuit or IRS audit notice. For instance, accountants can perform business audits to deter opportunities for theft while attorneys can perform legal audits that might identify and lessen risk.

In this chapter, we'll focus on three types of professionals you are most likely to need as an entrepreneur: accountants, attorneys and management consultants.

Accountants

For the most part, accountants are historians. History bores entrepreneurs. If you're working 14-hour days on the profit aspects of every business decision, then poring over financial statements is probably not going to be your top priority. But accountants can also be key contributors to your management team. They provide the numbers and projections that enable you to take the pulse of your business and predict success or failure.

New entrepreneurs rarely have the time to gather and analyze financial data without accounting support. Instead, they use Quicken, QuickBooks and similar software programs, because they can give you a quick financial picture of your business. They also serve as a reminder to keep thinking about the numbers, day after day! But these applications do not provide you with real bookkeeping support nor do they use the language of accounting. Capturing financial data is important and it will reduce your accounting costs, but if you want to maintain a real set of books then you should retain a real bookkeeper or accountant. They understand "double-entry" transactions and how to balance a set of books.

Assistance with Start-ups and Beyond

The start-up business owner should obtain the advice of a CPA when establishing a new company. This initial work forms a foundation for the future and the template design should not be left to public accountants or bookkeepers. After your company is established, you may want to save money by using a bookkeeper who will follow your template and generate reports necessary for an accountant to perform year-end tax work.

Your accountant's greatest ongoing involvement with you is in the preparation of financial statements and income tax returns. If you're borrowing substantial sums of money, your lender will most likely require that financial data be prepared by a CPA. The financial statement is an interesting work of art. If it paints a picture of high profits to the IRS, they're going to want a chunk. If it paints a picture of financial instability to the bank, they could call in your loan.

Make your accountant part of your management team and meet regularly for tax-planning purposes. Don't be intimidated by your accountant. Some accountants are strictly "play it by the book" while others understand the complexities of small business; you want the latter. Rigid accountants aren't going to do you any favors; they won't seek a lower tax bracket because they usually aren't creative enough to do it. When they're preparing tax returns, they're working for the IRS while on your payroll. When they go into an IRS audit, they seem to crawl from your side of the desk over to the auditor's. By nature, they are a squeamish bunch. You should select an accountant that is akin to an aggressive attorney. When you find one who is truly on your side, nurture that relationship by paying quickly; even a higher fee can be a good deal if the CPA can save you money.

Many businesspeople visit their accountant shortly before filing dates with a bundle of papers and canceled checks. You're begging to pay a premium rate, just like you would if you called a plumber at midnight.

There's a major difference between a tax preparer and a tax advisor. The preparer knows little more than which number goes in which space on the return. The advisor understands the IRS codes and regulations well enough to be able to lessen your tax obligations. A helpful accountant and tax specialist will prepare budgets and cash flow statements for your business plan and work to obtain all available tax breaks. Your accountant should also be a good teacher, able to help you understand the complex financial reports for your business.

Tax laws are subject to constant change and you should consult your accountant regularly to ensure that your business plan remains tax-efficient. In today's contentious political climate, who knows what Washington will do in terms of taxes in the next few years? Stay in close contact with your accountant and financial advisor, and don't hesitate to ask questions about the news articles you read.

Accounting Fees and Services

Treat your accountant as you do other business contacts and request an engagement letter to outline fees and services. Accountants tend to intimidate clients and many never question the bill. Determine the scope of work and ask whether your financial statements will be Compilation, Review or Audit quality; verify that a Cash Flow Statement is included in your reports. Assuming your data entry is processed in-house, request a quarterly Income Statement as part of the service. If you ask your accountant to prepare the payroll, compare that additional cost with that of companies specializing in this service.

Request reports that provide the prior year's data, current data, your budget, the variance and financial ratios for you and your industry. If you own a trucking company, obtain the trucking industry income and expense ratios and model your chart of accounts accordingly. Only after you receive this report* will you know where you've been, where you are, and where you are going.

Overall, accountants generally have your best interest at heart; you just can't always afford to pay their bills. While you may be struggling to earn $50,000 a year, they're spending 20 percent of your income on a two-week vacation. So, as with anyone else trying to reach into your pockets, you must negotiate. Don't retain them until you know the cost of the work. Just as you might try to sell customers accessories or get top dollar from the buyer who doesn't haggle, the accountant will quote top-shelf rates to the client who is too quick to open their checkbook.

I've only been able to find one foolproof way to avoid being overcharged for accounting services. If your accountant bills you $10,000 for $2,000 worth of real work, contest it and negotiate! However, if you go to court, you will most likely lose. Licensed professionals bill whatever they wish. Therefore, my next suggestion may save you from a very unpleasant experience. If your accountant quotes a fee of $100 per hour, tell him that's too low. Mention that their skills should generate more and you want to pay them $150. However, all of the work must be undertaken in your office, working alongside your staff. If the accountant really wants the job, they'll agree. If not, they were just planning to over-bill.

If, for some reason, you do not select an accountant who will work in your office, then offer 80 percent of the amount of the bill because they will most likely accept it. Before quoting a rate, the accountant always requests a copy of your last tax return. The first number their eyes fly to is what you paid for accounting services in the prior year, so you should black out that expense number, or merge it with other professional fees.

Accountants are not clairvoyant. I once amassed $1 million of net operating carryforward tax credits. My CPA advised me to accept fine art instead of money. In essence, I gave away tax credits to a client because my CPA predicted there would be an early cutoff time to apply those credits. But there wasn't, and I dealt away a million dollars of tax shelters in exchange for original artwork, which I eventually gave away. But I gave it to charitable organizations. In order to win the business chess game, you must understand all of the rules.

Silent Profit and Tax Obligations

A major shock for newer business owners is the realization that more inventory is taxable profit. Although your cash flow may dictate that you barely have enough money to buy groceries, the government assesses profit on the value of merchandise sitting on your shelves. Therefore, it's wise to have the advice of an accountant prior to finalizing your year-end reporting. Many businesses fail to properly and legitimately write down the value of inventory, which may lower the amount of tax you owe. Write-downs for obsolescence, technology changes and "shop wear" are perfectly acceptable to the IRS. While your decisions should be based on current operating data, inventory levels may cloud the picture.

Learn from Accountants

Build your library from the Institute of Certified Public Accountants. Call your state institute, order their catalog or go online, and purchase topics such as these:

- Small Business Structures
- Financial Management
- Understanding the Income Statement and Balance Sheet
- Analytic Financial Ratios
- Financial Forecasts & Projections
- Using Accounting Information for Effective Management Decisions
- Employee vs. Independent Contractor
- Business Insurance Decisions

Lawyers

There are two basic types of lawyers you'll encounter in the swamp. First, there are transactional lawyers who focus their practices on services like:

- Incorporating your business
- Drafting a Shareholders Agreement
- Filing copyright, trademark or patent applications in order to protect you intellectual property
- Preparing contracts for your customers, vendors, independent sales agents and employees

- Negotiating with landlords, real estate agents and suppliers
- Reviewing contracts and agreements

Remember that it's better to pay $500 for a lease review than to pay $5,000 trying to get out of the contract.

Other attorneys are litigators, including mediation and the arbitration of disputes. They represent your interests in matters like:

- Lawsuits filed against you by a competitor, customer, supplier, employee or anyone else hoping to take your money
- Lawsuits you file against someone who is trying to take advantage of you
- Legal actions to collect a bad debt

Hopefully, you will need the services of transaction attorneys far more than you will need litigators, but you never know! As Mark McCormick, an attorney himself and author of *The Terrible Truth about Lawyers*, wrote, "Lawyers are a clubby group, with the benefit of an arcane body of knowledge and under the smoke screen of an elaborate system of professional courtesies and rituals, they look out for their own — at the expense of the rest of us." So, proceed with caution.

Choosing a Lawyer

Lawyers are somewhat like weathermen; they get paid even when they're wrong. If they fail, you have no recourse. It's important to find the best one for your specific purposes. And remember, you can play games with your friends and your landlord, but be straightforward with your attorney.

Think carefully about what you want to accomplish, and then do your homework:

- Ask owners and managers of other businesses for recommendations
- Look for suggestions from other professionals who work with lawyers
- Seek out a lawyer who tries to solve problems — not a "deal killer"
- Find a lawyer who is interested in your business
- For routine matters, engage a young attorney, but select an established one if the stakes are big or complex

One of the best starting points is to search www.martindale.com – a site where attorneys and judges rate lawyers by specialty. Before selecting an attorney, learn how the rating codes and areas of practice are determined. You want someone who will creatively find a way to overcome difficulties. Yet, don't expect an attorney to make business decisions: they should serve as an objective sounding board. Remember that not all lawyers are all things to all people. You might find that one attorney has more experience and knowledge of zoning ordinances while another could be more effective at collecting a debt. And if you run into an obstinate attorney whom you immediately dislike, perhaps that attorney possesses qualities you may appreciate if you're dragged into future litigation.

Legal Fee Arrangements

It's your job to protect your money and there's a way to do it with respect. But if you sit by quietly, I guarantee you'll pay more than necessary for the service. Attorneys need business, so make a point of telling a good lawyer that you'll make a special effort to refer clients.

Legal fee arrangements can vary, based on the nature and complexity of the assignment. Transactional lawyers traditionally bill by the hour. In some cases, you may be able to agree on a fixed-fee for a certain service, such as drawing up the incorporation paperwork, reviewing an office lease, or preparing template contracts for your customers to sign.

Since there were approximately 1.3 million attorneys in the country in 2017, and the nation's law schools are graduating 400,000 new ones a year, you should have some power to negotiate the fees downward.

Beware of snakes in the business swamp. An attorney may advise you to retain them only because your opponent has hired a lawyer. It's actually one snake feeding another. Other attorneys are experts at feeding you a lot of crap that looks like complexity so you buy more of their time. They're masters of intimidation. A lawyer friend once told me, "I don't care if Rick and Barb want to accept the property settlement and divorce, it won't happen until my fees reach 5 percent of their net worth."

Come on, use one of your three Bs. Intimidate the enemy and negotiate hard with your lawyer. Otherwise, they'll think you don't even care what you pay. They'll be far less likely to 'pad' the time if they think you're sensitive to the cost. Why not rehearse with wait staff? Many people who serve your food have little training and concern. "Miss, excuse me . . . the food was okay, but your service was horrendous. Is there any reason you ignored us for the last 45 minutes while you were texting?" You shouldn't be hesitant to say the same thing to a lawyer: "Bob, while I appreciate your effort, you billed me $950 for virtually nothing and it took you two months to do it. If this is how the case is going to proceed, we have a problem."

Despite author and attorney John Grisham's quote, "There are few things in life worse than a long-winded lawyer," I can say that most lawyers are honest, committed and attempt to do their best for the client. Having thousands of encounters with law firms, I believe that the large majority want to perform in a responsible and ethical manner. Furthermore, complex cases place much demand and stress on a good lawyer so they deserve a bit of flexibility from their clients.

Lawsuits and Litigators

Depending on the nature of a lawsuit, a litigator may insist on an hourly rate or be willing to work with you on a contingency basis — if you win the suit and collect damages, the attorney will get a significant portion of the money.

When you ask lawyers to accept a contingent fee case without an hourly fee, they envision time, grunt work and risk. This is when your research and sales skills come into play. If you are a plaintiff, attempt to "sell your case" to an attorney on a contingent fee basis so the firm becomes a partner in your lawsuit. If you are the defendant, act quickly because the filing clock starts ticking the moment a lawsuit is commenced.

So, first prepare a Case Analysis for the intake meeting. Draft a written explanation of the entire dispute, with a sequence of events and details on the adversarial party. Provide a credit report on them, learn whether they have insurance and write a draft Complaint using the techniques in this chapter. Show the lawyer that you will be a good client and assist with the case. If you have a fertile mind, you'll enjoy the task, the lawyer will be impressed, more confident, and more likely to work with you on a contingency basis.

Here are some examples of the portion the lawyer may want to be paid:

25 percent — Contingent on your award

33 percent — Contingent on your award with you paying costs and expenses

40 percent — Contingent on your award with the law firm paying costs and expenses

50 percent — Contingent if an award is appealed

20 percent — Blended rate where you pay a lower hourly fee and the lawyer receives a percentage of the award, if any.

Use Lawyers Wisely

Good lawyers can be invaluable in your business. An investment in their time can pay off substantially, as shown by this personal example:

One of my clients owed $12 million to a bank. His loan was in its "special assets division," which is charged with bringing the money home. He was special all right – his account was specially singled out to recover the loan balance any way possible. If you're expecting these workout bankers to resemble the guy who gave you the money in the first place, grab your life vest because you're in rough waters.

My client's workout officer summoned me to his office and we knew the "writing was on the wall." I did my research to identify one of the premier bankruptcy lawyers in the East. We met in his ostentatious office and at the end of the meeting, he quoted his hourly rate; it was $1,000 and like all skilled lawyers, he acted as though he could care less if we utilized his services.

I retained him despite the high rate because I had a strategy that had been effective in the past. When you attend a meeting with a bank workout department, take a bankruptcy lawyer with you. The bankruptcy legal industry is small and the players know each other. And if they don't, the first thing they do is research the name in the Martindale Directory.

Applying my negotiation skills, I was able to convince this attorney to simply ride with me to the bank meeting, even though it cost my client an extra $500 when we stopped for a sandwich. When we entered the meeting, the bank was present in full force with about six executives and their lawyers. Our lawyer walked into the room, they glanced at him, we exchanged cards and the bank counsel said, "Excuse us." Having a top bankruptcy lawyer on our side changed the entire tenor of the meeting from aggressive browbeating to "how can we help" mode. The one-day cost was $11,000; the benefit was invaluable.

Settle

Most lawsuits are settled before judgment is rendered in the courtroom because even the bitterest of adversaries will sit down at the same table when they can be shown there is a greater advantage in negotiating rather than fighting.

Whatever it is you want, or want to avoid, can be the subject of a settlement if you can convince the other side to determine how the terms work to their advantage. It is possible to settle your own case. If someone sues you, pick up the phone and talk to them. These calls should be formally designated as "settlement negotiations," so they may not be admissible into evidence and there is no harm in making them.

No, you're not supposed to contact the adversary directly. But, do it anyway. Attorneys don't want clients contacting adversaries because they may jeopardize the case, but worse, they might, God forbid, settle it! Many people place everything in the lawyer's hands, including their checkbook.

If you didn't settle before the commencement of litigation, you will still have many opportunities before actually facing a trial. Your primary goal is to mount a defense, or threaten litigation, with postage stamps as opposed to money. And use the Department of Justice, Consumer Protection Agency, Better Business Bureau and other state or federal agencies to place pressure on your adversary by filing complaints if they are warranted.

How to Represent Yourself

More consumers are turning to self-representation to handle basic legal matters. There are two technical Latin terms for this: appearing in propria persona (as yourself) and appearing pro se (as an advocate for yourself so you are held to the same standards as if you were an attorney).

By acting pro se, you will save thousands of dollars and will often perform as well as if you retained counsel. Acting pro se is derived from General Sun Tzu: "You get inside the opponent's head and upset the form and rhythm that the opponent typically follows to achieve their goal." Another reason for pro se defense is that any lawyer you are likely to retain will think within the constructs of their legal training, but probably will not strategize outside those limits.

However, practicing law yourself can be as dangerous as treating yourself for cancer. It's necessary to distinguish important legal issues that require professional assistance from the day-to-day routine legal needs that you may be able to manage. If someone owes you money or has done something improper, you can threaten to file your own lawsuit. Like the scared tadpole, they'll swim away, hire an attorney and start to spend money. When you go into small claims court, let your adversary bring an attorney. Represent yourself and if you lose, simply file an appeal.

If you've failed to bluff your way out of the mess by yourself, there may be another tactic you can try. Each state publishes its Rules of Civil Procedure, which explain how you must do business within the court system; go to the law library or search online for the latest edition. While difficult to decipher, this publication can provide a rule you should cite or rely upon. Some pro se-friendly states, such as Florida, provide staff to assist you in preparation while other states, such as Pennsylvania, slam the door and tell you to paddle to your nearest lawyer. This is lawyer lawmakers feeding their own profession.

There are also local rules of civil procedure that even many lawyers fail to follow and kind judges may help you through this process. But it's always best to prepare thoroughly. And, don't be shocked when your own pleadings are more exact and professional than some prepared by a busy or sloppy lawyer who barely passed the bar.

Filing your own lawsuit against a corporate giant is no big deal for your adversary, which may face hundreds of suits every day. The big company will soon recognize it has a "nuisance claim" and will be willing to pay thousands of dollars just to have you go away. It's called a "settlement value." Many attorneys understand the process, overlook the rules that are supposed to guide them and file frivolous claims just to make an easy buck.

Representing Your Corporation

Wouldn't you think that if you were the only officer and shareholder in your own corporation, you could represent it in court? Not necessarily. You must first understand your state law. For example, in Pennsylvania, a corporation may not appear in court and be represented by a corporate officer and shareholder who is not an attorney, or is not an officer of the court. See Walacavage v. Excell 2000, Inc. 480 A.2d 281 (331 Pa Super 137.1984). This is because lawmakers are lawyers and judges, and it's just another scam to protect their turf.

The rule may have merit if you are representing other shareholders, but it remains the law because legislators don't want to fix it. So, place a provision in your agreements that your corporation can assign the contract to you, individually, without the other party's consent. Formally assign it, and then protect yourself. You just "beat the system." Always weigh the outcome of self-help versus self-destruction.

The Court Clerk

While there are many online and law library reference books for legal pleadings and forms, the easiest way to get pleadings is to copy them. Go to the court clerk's office and ask to review case files. This is your courthouse and oftentimes the files are available online. If you must prepare a complaint or response, read the Rule Book and then use the same format you copied in a similar lawsuit.

Photocopy a half dozen different legal actions. Then lay out your lawsuit patterned after those examples. I recently sued Apple myself. Large companies will often settle, and if you make a mistake in your filing, you might not have gotten your money anyway.

Understanding the Law

Once you acquire more knowledge of the law, it will help you to retain a competent attorney – possibly under a contingent fee arrangement – which will turn up the lawyer's greed knob.

There are several ways for you to sharpen your legal skills. First, you may find that local colleges offer paralegal classes. The barriers that long insulated lawyers from outside competition have begun to crumble and now those competitors are clamoring more insistently for a place in the legal services arena.

Self-help materials abound, and in some regions, tasks once handled almost exclusively by lawyers are being performed by accountants, real estate agents, title companies, bankers and others. However, the Federal Administrative Procedure Act prevents laypeople from representing themselves against federal agencies.

The most significant development, however, may be the growing presence of paralegals (also identified by such terms as legal assistants, legal technicians, non-lawyer practitioners or free-lance paralegals) who provide basic legal services directly to consumers without the supervision of lawyers.

"Legal technicians" allow for greater public access to legal services. The bar now refers unauthorized practice of law complaints to county district attorneys, who may, but seldom do, prosecute them as third class misdemeanors.

You may stop short of wanting to represent yourself in court, but you should still use lawyers' resources to educate yourself on legal matters. For example, if you ask some lawyers a legal question, they say they will research it. Next you get an opinion letter and a bill for $500. In fact, they pulled a $35 "crib book" off the shelf that contains most of the relevant information on the topic. Or, you can attend bar association seminars and get the same book, or just buy it. These books will address most of your questions on the topic of interest.

In a 1986 report, the ABA Commission on Professionalism concluded, "It can no longer be claimed that lawyers have the exclusive possession of the esoteric knowledge required and are therefore the only ones able to advise clients on any matters concerning the law."

Legal Topics Published by Your State Bar Association

They may be white in Wisconsin and yellow in Pennsylvania, but inexpensive "crib books" cover specific topics of law and are available in every state. So, if you're operating an accounts receivable system, you might want to understand credit and collection law, or if you're renting real estate, you might want to understand landlord and tenant law. Simply go online to your state's bar association and start to shop for topics such as:

- Civil Procedures and Rules
- Litigating the Business Dispute
- Real Estate Transactions
- Commercial Leases
- Troubled Real Estate Projects, Bankruptcy & Tax Implications
- Drafting/Negotiating Commercial Loan Documents
- Buying and Selling a Business
- Corporations & Partnerships
- Credit Sales & Other Consumer Transactions

Be sure to add these books to your office library: "Black's Law Dictionary" and "West's Business Law." These publications contain Latin and legal jargon — tools used by lawyers to confuse the hell out of everyone.

Bad Legal Advice

Expect to get some poor legal advice during your business career. I once drove an 80-year-old client to Philadelphia to meet his wife's divorce lawyer. He was in poor health and I held his power of attorney to make business decisions. Once extremely wealthy, he still owned many assets and his ex-wife wanted them all.

This successful man paid me to represent his interest because he respected my business acumen and over six decades, came to despise lawyers. The litigation had gone on for a decade and he wanted closure. He told me to offer what I felt was appropriate given all of the numbers. So, I did: an immediate cash settlement of $2 million.

The wife's lawyer advertised herself as "counsel to the stars." She was flamboyant, pushy and arrogant, and liked to point out the photographs of celebrity clients throughout her office. She said we would go to trial and she would not consider any settlement less than $6 million. When my frail client heard that number, he actually passed out. His head dropped to the conference table. She gave him a glass of water, said she felt sorry for him, but rejected our offer.

Six months later my client lost his business. He died and the wife got nothing. The wife called me saying she wanted me to assist her in suing her lawyer! I hung up on her.

Sue Your Lawyer

If you feel you've been financially damaged by bad legal advice, there are a number of ways to bring overreaching lawyers to their knees. You can hire an attorney who handles professional malpractice cases and sue your lawyer. Do your homework, negotiate the fee and hopefully you can recover at least some of your losses.

You could also seek legal sanctions against your attorney. Review the Code of Professional Responsibility in the Rules of Civil Procedure Book if the matter involves a state court. The Federal Rules of Civil Procedure 26(g)(1)(b)(ii) provides for sanctions against an attorney who seeks to increase your costs of discovery in a piece of litigation "for any improper purpose, such as to harass or to cause unnecessary delay or needless increase in the cost of litigation."

Disciplinary Action Board of the Supreme Court

You may raise alleged inappropriate conduct against a lawyer with the Disciplinary Board of the Supreme Court in the state in which the action took place.

Some lawyers occasionally cross the line between bold advocacy and a breach of ethics. The Supreme Court of each state has jurisdiction over its licensed legal practitioners and regulates the Rules of Disciplinary Enforcement. These rules contain various levels of punishment based on what the Disciplinary Board considers to be the severity of the offense. The board itself can usually issue private or public reprimands. The Supreme Court, based on the recommendation of the Disciplinary Board, imposes more severe penalties like suspension and in cases of severe misconduct, disbarment. Disbarment prevents an attorney from ever practicing again.

A very sweet and very elderly real estate investor placed a sizable amount of cash in a Florida condo project, which is higher in risk than vacant land. She lost it all to a Florida speculator and her physician son engaged me to help her through the mess. She and I flew to Florida and confronted the two enemies: the developer and her lawyer. The developer didn't develop and the lawyer took $75,000 of her money and accomplished absolutely nothing.

Her lawyer was a retired judge and we met in his former bank office surrounded by a balcony of law books. I told this portly, gruff, overbearing ex-judge that I wanted a refund of half of her money and he laughed at me. "Do you know who I am? Why son, I eat people like you." I was hoping he would do the right thing, but was sadly disappointed.

I left, contacted The Florida Bar and learned there was a required important notice missing from his engagement letter. I filed a disciplinary complaint. The attorney was reprimanded and I recovered all of my client's legal fees. On another occasion, I reported a Florida woman for holding herself out as an attorney when, in fact, her license had been revoked. The state brought criminal charges against her. It's the balls "B." If there is any intimidating to be done, you do it.

While it's rare to encounter these scoundrels, they're out there and there are remedies for clients who become victims of their greed. Without client complaints, their entire industry would go unregulated.

While a seemingly small number, some lawyers are simply licensed thieves and will steal your money or violate the law. When I was only 33, a lawyer did something in my case that appeared to be unethical. I prepared my own 60-page complaint with exhibits, submitted it to the Disciplinary Board of the State Supreme Court and he was disbarred.

Successful businesspeople are tough. They simply don't allow others to bully them, not even lawyers. Attorneys will want to avoid a private or public reprimand, suspension or disbarment and they will typically be a little more cautious if they know you're aggressive and crazy enough to keep them in line. The law protects everyone. By filing your complaint, you're doing something positive to protect those who follow you.

Like most regulatory agencies, the referees of legal disputes follow Milton Friedman's law, which states that regulatory agencies, to justify their existence, will support the industry they are empowered to regulate. Therefore, your complaint must be air tight.

It would be ludicrous to suggest this book, or any publication, could competently replace good legal advice. Rather it's only a guide for the layman to even the playing field with lawyers. Armed with an awareness of your rights, you can seek the advice of counsel trained to advocate the law as it applies to the particular situation.

The Management Consultant

Management consultants can be teachers, coaches, analysts and trusted advisors, helping entrepreneurs solve perplexing problems and stay on the path to success. A consultant will give advice on concepts like business strategy and operational techniques, and also offer skills such as time management.

It's said that an expert is someone with a briefcase that drove more than 100 miles to your meeting. Most consultants are unlicensed, but not necessarily uncertified. Someone who measures your living room drapes or is a website designer can call themselves a consultant, so the designation carries little prestige. Few people understand what services a business consultant can provide.

Yet, management consulting is now becoming a well-utilized service and somewhat glamorous field. Major corporations and small businesses alike are reaching out to independent consultants for advice. They can obtain expert, specialized guidance without having to employ people full-time. Some have extensive or particular expertise in very complex issues.

Once again, be sure you understand why you are bringing in a management consultant, what problem you want to solve or opportunity you want to exploit in the market. Ask them to put their terms in writing in an engagement letter. Always demand the right to terminate them without cause.

Saving Dollars and Jobs

As a certified management consultant in the field of "turnarounds and workouts," I accepted an assignment as President and Chairman of the Board of Charles Chips, a snack food company losing a significant amount of money.

When the company was founded in 1950, the owner decided to deliver his homemade potato chips in a yellow tin can, door to door, using a step van much like the milkman of yesteryear. The concept took off and customers anxiously awaited their chip and pretzel cans every week. Eventually, the products were also sold through markets in bags, competing with the other 300 chip companies that exist today. The cans were trucked to the West Coast and available in 37 states.

With high revenues and high consumer demands, why were there losses? My staff and I first eliminated costly expenses, like corporate airplanes. We reduced the number of upper-level managers, trimmed back the massive expense accounts and fine-tuned the operation. Yet, the business still generated annual losses in the millions.

Realizing my consulting expertise was not sufficient, I retained another consulting firm to review wage programs, initiate time studies and produce cost reports. The losses were eventually found in the tin cans. This analysis revealed that by the time my client purchased the cans, replaced damaged ones, retrieved only some of them, trucked them back to the plant, washed them and then shipped them as far as California, every can sold cost the business half the value of the product!

I immediately shut down the can lines and only sold Charles Chips in bags in markets off the shelf. The retired owner was devastated, customers were distraught, and I had not one ounce of support from anyone in the plants. However, my decision was a big success. We left the company in the black, 1,000 people retained their jobs and customers are still munching on one of the best chips in the marketplace. There are times that management consultants are irreplaceable.

Tips To Keep You Afloat

> Learn the basics of professional advisors businesses.

> Recognize when you need professional advice.

> Get the advice of colleagues, including other professionals, before hiring one.

> Find the professional whose skills and experience are best suited to the assignment.

> Demand and negotiate an Engagement Letter specifying fees and services.

> Demand fees be in proportion to services rendered.

> Don't allow professional people to "baffle you with science."

> Educate yourself to expand the areas where you can represent yourself.

> Review your professional's work for errors.

> If your professional has been negligent and you have suffered financial damage, you may consider filing a malpractice lawsuit.

> If you're not sure about an important business issue, consider engaging a management consultant for advice.

13. THE INSURANCE GAME

"There are worse things in life than death. Have you ever spent an evening with an insurance salesman?"

Woody Allen

As an entrepreneur, you need to protect your assets by playing the insurance game. Here's how it works. Your goal is to embark from the starting point of your venture and cross the swamp successfully without tipping over. Along the way, you might encounter high winds, rainstorms, dangerous swamp creatures, and perhaps a thief who wants to steal your oars. Part of the journey will require insurance protection.

Today, insurance companies play a different game. Oftentimes, the insurer will try to squeeze as much money as possible out of your business through premiums and optional coverage that you may or may not need. Then, if you suffer a loss and file a claim, the insurer may attempt to negotiate the lowest possible settlement and procrastinate before paying the claim.

Even if you work with a supportive agent or broker, when you file a claim, the company may send in a stranger to review your documents and damage to determine if you complied with every specific requirement. Many claims adjusters pay you as little as possible and delay payment as long as possible. When their telephone recording says, "This call may be recorded for quality assurance purposes," you should say, "I don't consent to a recording." These people aren't there to help you out so let's shed the rose-colored glasses.

A close friend worked for a major insurance company. Over dinner I asked, "What do you do?" He responded that his job was to step in once it was determined a claim had to be paid and delay payment through any means possible so the company reserve would continue to earn interest and dividends. At times their financial investments would exceed the amount of the claim. My friend was rewarded for "dragging it out."

Types of Coverage

Insurance is an arrangement by which one party, through a contract called a policy, and for a compensation called a premium, assumes for another party certain types of risks of loss. While business owners must protect their assets, they tend to sign almost anything thrown down in front of them. Mark Twain said, "Why not go out on the limb? That's where all the fruit is." That may be true in some cases, but not for asset protection because going out on a limb with fine print will only bear spoiled fruit.

Today, insurance costs needed to protect your assets can be an overwhelming burden for business owners, and a savvy entrepreneur cannot afford to make mistakes. That means understanding what coverage you need, such as:

- Property and casualty insurance to protect your physical assets such as inventory and equipment.
- Liability insurance to protect against personal injury or other

types of lawsuits filed against your business by customers, employees, and others.

- Umbrella insurance to protect against claims in excess of your policy limits.

- Business interruption insurance, which can cover lost revenue if your company can't operate for an extended period due to damage to the building, extended loss of power, or other causes.

- Business Expense (Overhead) Insurance to pay a portion of your monthly operating expenses if you are unable to work.

- Malpractice and errors and omissions (E&O) insurance to protect against a lawsuit filed by someone who feels damaged by your professional advice or actions.

- Life and disability insurance to keep the business going in the event of your death, serious injury or other medical problem.

There are other types of insurance coverage that come into play on a personal and business level. As an employer, you may want to purchase group health, life and disability policies for your employees. You will also need to pay into the federal Social Security insurance fund, as well as your state worker's compensation insurance fund, which provides benefits to employees who are injured on the job. The government sets those requirements, so you'll just have to live with them.

Our focus in this chapter is on insurance that will protect your business and personal assets. That includes talking with your attorney to find the best ways to shield your home, car, bank accounts and other personal assets from a business creditor, such as a plaintiff who prevails in a lawsuit against your company.

The same holds true on the business side. It's one reason why large real estate companies, for example, set up separate corporate structures

for each property, along with an overall holding company. They know if you can properly isolate your biggest business assets from potential liability, your need for insurance decreases. If your corporate restaurant owns nothing but food in the cooler, someone who chokes on a chicken bone can only attach the food. Plaintiff attorneys become discouraged when they discover the corporate defendant has minimal assets. If you are a corporation that doesn't carry insurance, lawyers may go away. In fact, the more insurance you have, the more vultures swarm the claim.

Get the Best Deal

Before purchasing a policy, be sure that you actually need the coverage. Then, be a savvy shopper. Talk to several insurance agents, or better yet, find a seasoned independent broker — a broker who contracts with a variety of companies and has experience with business policies in your industry. Unlike captive insurance agents, who produce policies on behalf of one specific company, independent agents who write for a number of different companies focus more on the customer, rather than the wants of the insurer, making them the most valuable resource in "shopping" for insurance.

The Insurance Game

One good, basic question to ask an insurance broker or agent is the structure of the insurance company. For the most part, they are either "stock" companies, owned by shareholders and expected to earn profits for them, or "mutual" companies, owned by the policyholders, who are the principal beneficiaries from the earnings of the company. Premiums are generally lower in mutual companies, but these insurers are financially limited in comparison with stock companies because they cannot use debt to fund their operations. A few companies sell insurance directly to the customer, but this usually occurs on the consumer level, not in the business world.

As you investigate the types of coverage available, you can begin to compare their features, deductibles, premiums and the "exclusions" inserted into policies so the insurer doesn't have to pay certain types of claims. For example, a property and casualty policy in California might not cover damage due to earthquakes, and one in Florida might not cover hurricanes. You may need to purchase an additional policy — and pay a substantial premium — in order to guard against those risks.

Here are some other questions to consider:

- Does the policy cover the most-likely risks?
- What are the exclusions?
- How large is the deductible?
- Does it pay for legal defense fees and expenses if you are sued?
- Is there a limit on damage claims or does it cover "replacement cost" for damages?
- Can the premiums go up after the first year?

Small companies can often purchase a "business owners policy," referred to as a "BOP," which pays the agent a lower commission but provides more protection for less money. Apartments and offices are typically covered by this type of policy. Coverage is provided for real and personal property on a replacement cost basis and there is no coinsurance clause in the policy. Property of a real and personal nature may be insured on an all-risk or named peril basis. In a BOP, loss of income is generally included on an actual loss sustained basis. It also includes employees, medical payments, employee dishonesty, plate glass, boiler and machinery, outdoor signs, floods, burglary, and robbery losses.

Finally, it's important to have your policy reviewed at least every two years. By changing your deductible and reviewing policy limits, you may often reduce your cost of coverage. Your insurance company now operates like your friendly airlines; it will exclude risks and hike rates depending on factors that have nothing to do with fairness. Because of this trend, the carrier you've been with for many years may no longer want to insure your tavern because it has a dance floor – just like airlines and hotels hike or lower rates based on changing circumstances.

Property and Casualty Insurance

It's important to understand that there are three different types of property and casualty coverage available: basic, broad, or special.

Sadly, I learned this when a roof collapsed on one of my buildings and I was denied a six-figure claim. We settled the three-year lawsuit for $33,000 on a $100,000 loss after we paid $7,000 to AccuWeather to determine if the wind speed was more than 5 mph at the exact minute the roof collapsed. Special coverage, which I ordered but the agent didn't write, would have paid the claim. You can sue the agent and the carrier.

The lesson here: Read the fine print and understand the covered perils. Your policy will be written as one of the three types and there are significant differences in the protection afforded by each. In most cases, you'll find that your property insurance policy is written with special coverage, but there are instances where it may not be.

Basic Coverage	Broad Coverage	Special Coverage
Form 1	Form 2	Form 3

When a property insurance policy is written under a basic form, coverage is limited to those items damaged by a cause of loss specifically listed in the policy. There are 11 causes of loss: fire, lightning, explosion, windstorm or hail, smoke, aircraft or vehicles, riot or civil commotion, vandalism, sprinkler leakage, sinkhole collapse, or volcanic action. If damage is caused by anything else, there may be no insurance protection.

Within the 11 causes of loss, the insurance company can limit or exclude how the insurance applies. For example, if your business is damaged because you didn't maintain your sprinkler system properly, there may be no coverage; however, if a fire causes the sprinkler system to go off, the policy should pay to repair the resulting water damage.

When property insurance is written on a broad form, four additional causes of loss are added to the original 11: falling objects, weight of ice, sleet or snow, and freezing of plumbing systems and burst pipes. The only exclusions on this form are those designed to further define how the 15 causes of loss are applied. Note that with both the basic and broad forms, the insurance company has the duty to specifically include coverage. If it's not included on the list, it's not covered. The most common form of insurance, therefore, is special form, which is not limited to those causes of loss named on the policy. Always consider special form coverage, which the agent may not quote in order to present the lowest premium and procure your business.

Fire Insurance

With fire insurance, as a general rule, the insured agrees to carry coverage of no less than 80 percent of the actual cash value of the property at the time of the loss. If you carry less than the agreed percentage of insurance, you will not be entitled to collect in full for a loss, but will have to bear part of any loss yourself.

Here's how the insurance company calculates your claim:

- "Should" – the stipulated percentage of the actual cash value of the property at the time of the loss
- "Did" – the amount of insurance actually purchased
- "Loss" – the amount of the loss
- "Amount" – the amount for which the company is liable

$$\frac{\text{Did}}{\text{Should}} \quad \text{x} \quad \text{L} = \text{A}$$

Since most fire losses are partial in extent, many property owners are inclined to carry only coinsurance, or partial insurance, on their property, counting on the chance that a fire at their premises would be brought under control before it exceeded the amount of their insurance. That makes purchasing real estate near a fire station wise.

Deductibles

The deductible is the amount you must pay out of pocket before the insurance pays anything. Agents earning a commission often recommend a low deductible, because low deductibles mean higher commissions. Many people accept this advice but it's not necessarily good business advice. Gauge your risk and make the deductible $1,000 or $5,000 and watch your premium drop. This form of "self-insurance" allows you to assume more risk and lower your costs.

In a few real estate investment situations, when cash was tight and where there was no mortgage requirement, I dropped property insurance entirely for six months. I gambled that there would be no catastrophe or damage that would be more than the savings, as I put the insurance company's premiums in my pocket. Listen to your agent and then do what you think is in your best financial interest.

Malpractice and E&O Insurance

People who earn their living by providing professional services, such as attorneys, accountants, insurance agents, real estate brokers and medical practitioners, should carry professional liability insurance to protect against claims for damages that occur as a result of their professional actions. This type of insurance is often called professional liability, malpractice or errors and omissions insurance. The E&O policy protects the practitioner or business advisor from things that they did wrong (errors) and also things that they should have done but didn't (omissions).

Claims-Made Liability Policy

Think twice before signing up for something called a "claims-made liability policy." These policies provide coverage only for claims made during the time the policy is in effect. In contrast, an "occurrence" policy protects you even if the claim is made years after the policy has been terminated.

Directors & Officers Insurance

Companies will occasionally carry directors and officers insurance, referred to as "D&O," on their board of directors — some of whom are appointed from outside the company. Non-profit organizations also insure their boards of directors in this manner.

This type of insurance is generally written on a "claims made" basis, which means that actions taken during the lifetime of the policy are covered against claims initiated during the same period. Additional insurance, covering actions taken before the policy became current, can be purchased for an additional premium. This is called "nose" insurance, and likewise, coverage can be purchased for claims arising after the policy has ceased to be effective; this is called "tail" insurance. These premiums are high so many smaller organizations assume the risk. The IRS once collected money from one of my non-profit clients, causing all of the good-hearted volunteers to pay employee withholding taxes. Insurance isn't important until you need it.

Life Insurance

Insure your business and yourself. Personal lines of insurance are complex and it's difficult to make a wise choice of an agent and company. But if you're an independent business owner, purchase an amount of life insurance that will pay all your obligations, and if you have family, provide for them in the future. Whether you decide on a universal policy, whole life or term coverage, life insurance is typically inexpensive while you're young and in good health. Check "Best Ratings" to determine if a company is reputable. Life insurance policies have, at times, paid a higher interest rate than a bank on your cash value. Moreover, while life insurance is not protected by the FDIC, it is generally exempt from creditor attachments and it carries tax advantages. Shop this hard. The confusing illustrations are designed to present a high return.

First to Die Insurance

This is a specific type of life insurance taken out on the lives of a married couple or a pair of business partners. One policy covers both lives and whenever one party dies the proceeds of the policy go entirely to the other partner. This type of policy is less expensive than having both parties insure their life in favor of the other, but not all insurance companies offer these policies since they receive lower premiums than they would if both parties were carrying individual life insurance.

Disability Insurance

Disability policies are designed to pay cash benefits for stipulated periods to individuals who are unable to work by reason of illness or accident. They are generally based on the earning power of the insured.

Most business owners should carry disability insurance. These policies typically include a waiting period and are determined by a percentage of your income. The less known Business Expense (Overhead) Insurance is extremely important in the event the principal cannot participate in the business. For example, if your monthly expenses are $30,000, you could insure that a portion of those expenses are paid in the event you are unable to work. Like the casualty lines, the insurance company will fight with you on the payment of these claims and hire investigators to actually trail you to be certain you are not working. Once, when disabled, I noticed a van following me. I lured him to a parking lot and called the police; they frisked him on the hood and sent him back to New Jersey. Did you ever imagine these things could happen in a business career?

Key Man Insurance

If your business is heavily dependent on one, or a few people, for its future success, consider buying key-man life insurance to cover against the loss of their life.

Buy-Sell Agreements

Insurance is not the only way to protect your business assets. For instance, a Buy-Sell Agreement can be utilized by sole proprietorships, partnerships and closed corporations to divide the business share or interest of a proprietor, partner, or shareholder who is disabled, deceased, retired or who wants to sell his interest. A typical agreement requires that the business share be sold according to a predetermined formula to the company or to the remaining members of the business. Before the interest of a deceased partner can be sold in this way, the deceased's estate must agree to sell.

I convinced one of my best client/friends to buy life insurance while we were still in high school. He later founded a company that grew dramatically. He indicated that he wanted his company to eventually transfer to his son, who had a keen interest in sales. I suggested a Buy-Sell Agreement. My friend was tragically killed in an accident. His son immediately stepped into the business with all arrangements made in advance. The entrepreneur must possess a general knowledge of all of these asset protection vehicles.

Tips To Keep You Afloat

> Ensure that your property has appropriate coverage for likely risks.

> Reduce insurance costs by isolating your assets from your business operations wherever possible.

> Become familiar with the insurance industry jargon and monitor your policies.

> Keep your insurances under constant review. Automatic renewals can be wastefully expensive.

> Ensure that you carry enough personal insurance to cover the obligations of your business and provide for the needs of your dependents.

> Carry errors and omissions insurance if you provide professional services for a living.

14. THE CHALLENGES

> *"In the middle of difficulty lies opportunity."*
> *Albert Einstein*

Just as every canoe runs into rough water at some point, business ventures face a series of challenges. The successful companies find a way to overcome their problems, while the others go into bankruptcy or simply close their doors. As noted business coach and author Tony Robbins said, "The only people without problems are those in cemeteries." So get accustomed to dealing with the issues and the stress that will surely surface as you cross the business swamp.

What kinds of challenges will you face? Many are related to sales and marketing, such as a change in customer preferences, an aggressive move by a competitor, or an innovation that decreases demand for your products or services. Your bank might "put the squeeze" on your loan, or you could be hit by an increase in the cost of supplies, raw materials or insurance. Other challenges are internal, such as a slacker on your management team, a disagreement in goals with your partners, or a loss of productivity in your workforce.

Even with precautions in place, it's normal to face ruthless people, delays, uncertainty and risks as you paddle across unfamiliar, dark waters. Business isn't failure free. It's more like war and you'll hear it in the lingo: we "capture" a market and "make a killing." To beat those odds, the best approach is to be prepared for the challenge and address them effectively.

As an entrepreneur who cares about your business, you may have an emotional reaction to bad news about your market, customers or people:

- Regret – How did I get into this mess?
- Doubt – Maybe I'm not cut out for this business.
- Blame – If that damn customer had paid his bills, I could pay my staff.
- More Blame – If that jerk banker had granted our loan, we'd be fine.
- Fear – What if we can't recover?
- Shame – I'm a failure.

- Escape – I want out. I want someone to buy this company and let me walk away from it.

It's important to understand and acknowledge those emotions without acting on them. Rather than dwelling in depression, shame or fear, you should take action. If there's no clear solution, then call for help.

My profession as a management consultant focuses on diagnosing and treating daily business problems that my clients face. Many entrepreneurs don't recognize the signs of trouble, thus delaying seeking professional assistance. In this book, my goal is to help you overcome those challenges using your own ingenuity and hard work. As you try to stay afloat on a sea of troubles, remember that you may be able to turn those daunting challenges into new opportunities for your business.

Reasons for Business Trouble

Let's take a closer look at some of the reasons your canoe may take on water as you try to cross the swamp:

- Lack of adequate planning and financing. Often enthusiastic start-up entrepreneurs fail to prepare an accurate business plan with financial projections. A fluid business plan should be the blueprint for success, not a fiction to impress lenders or investors.

- Lack of capital. This is the number one reason that new ventures fail. It's easy to overestimate incoming revenue and underestimate your costs. As a result, you run out of money. You need adequate operating capital in order to have enough time to penetrate your market and become profitable.

- Ego and emotion. Nobody should open a business without a clear conviction there is a sustainable market for the product or service. The majority of people who start a business choose to do what they enjoy, not what they know will survive. That's why your typical art gallery is owned by an art lover. And remember, your business can't live on love.

• Lack of training. Most people do not believe they need formal training to operate a business. Owning a successful business takes no less skill, nor is it any less of a profession, than any other enterprise. Successful businesspeople study the science of business.

• Lack of professional support. Don't cut corners by hiring inexperienced accountants or lawyers. Having good professionals on your team will help you manage the risks and overcome the challenges.

• Lack of advice from others. Supplement the experience of professional advisors by contacting people who have been in a similar business for years and allow them to scrutinize your plans.

• Disregard for your customers. Never forget that it is your customers who keep your business alive and pay your salary. Being rude or ignoring your customers will quickly destroy your venture.

• Overconfidence in "good old boys." The essence of good business is looking at the numbers. So avoid the temptation to buy overpriced insurance from your golfing buddy or to get a loan at a higher rate from your brother-in-law at the bank. By all means, give friends an opportunity

to compete, but there's no line item on your P&L statement called "Friendship Allowance."

• Ignorance of the law. Never ignore laws and regulations that govern your business. Seek all available advice to ensure you are compliant.

• Other causes for failure. These include inadequate sales, heavy operating expenses, receivable problems, inventory difficulties, excessive fixed assets, a poor location and competitive weaknesses.

Recognizing these types of challenges, in time, is crucial to finding the right solution for your business. Again, if you're not sure of the issue, get professional advice – pronto!

Early Warning Signs

One of the first early warning signs is a decline in your sales. In some cases, a drop may be due to economic conditions beyond one's control. In that case, the solution may be simply to cut back on  your spending and ride out the recession. But at other times the problem lies within your organization and will persist even in times of economic recovery. A mix of practical and psychological "rules of thumb" can guide business owners through the swamp.

The "Business Diagnostic Review," developed by Philip Scherer, is an excellent tool for understanding how far a business has regressed:

Early Decline

• Shortage of cash to meet current obligations
• Current assets decreasing while current liabilities increase thereby reducing working capital

The Challenges

- Increase in aging accounts payable
- Increase in aging accounts receivable
- Return on investment decreasing by 20 percent to 30 percent
- Lack of sales growth
- Several quarters of losses
- Three quarters showing losses in any given year
- Increases in employee absenteeism and accidents
- Increase in customer complaints about product quality, delivery, back orders or service
- Late financial and management information

Mid-term Decline

- Inventory increasing and sales decreasing
- Financial margin erosion, with revenue declining as expenses increase
- Advances from banks increasing in dollar amount and frequency
- Financial and management information unreliable or late
- Customer confidence declining and the customer base noticeably eroding
- Vendors demanding payment on delinquent accounts and placing the business on a cash basis
- Bank overdrafts becoming a form of interim financing
- Accounts receivable delayed by opportunistic customers
- Loan covenants violated and compliance with loan covenants demanded by banks
- Bank borrowing more frequently used to cover payroll
- Interest rates on indebtedness increased by banks

Late Decline

- Profit decreases ignored by management in attempts to raise cash
- Attempts made to reduce operating costs without analyzing the causes of business problems
- Overdrawn bank accounts becoming permanent loans
- Cash crisis
- Accounts payable 60 to 90 days late
- Accounts receivable 90 or more days late
- Further decline in sales owing to loss of customer confidence
- Employee morale extremely low
- Company credibility eroded
- Inventory turnover excessively up with inventory supply down
- Suppliers requiring payment at the time of order
- Fewer reports issued to the bank
- Accountants qualifying their opinion of reports
- Checks returned because of insufficient funds
- Further decrease in financial margins, indicating imminent bankruptcy
- Cash flow turning negative
- Increase in uncollectable receivables as customers find new sources
- Management team trying to convince lenders that company is viable and that liquidation or bankruptcy will not become necessary.

A business in mid or late decline must evaluate its financial ratios such as liquidity, solvency, profitability and turnover to compare financial profiles with industry standards. This will provide the basis to complete a "Z-Score" analysis. This study predicts the long-term viability of the business and the likelihood of it going into bankruptcy.

A business in late decline may lack management skills necessary to recover. Fewer than 20 percent of business failures are caused by external elements while the other 80 percent are caused by management's failure to control internal elements. The causes of the financial problem were most likely overlooked by management, and management's ability to define and solve those problems may not exist.

Addressing Your Financial Problems

If your business can't pay a bill, it's always best to call the lender's credit manager. This will make you a hit in their parade because few debtors call credit managers and collection agencies, so most will do anything to cooperate by offering a payment plan. The largest reason people fail to resolve credit matters that could disrupt their business is because they hesitate to be proactive and communicate. If you owe $10,000 and send $4,000 they will usually accept it with a smile. If you say nothing, companies will eventually turn the matter over to a collection agency that will charge up to 50 percent of the amount you owe, making it more difficult for you to settle for just a portion of your debt.

Your lender's collection agency may "sell their client out" and give you a discount on the debt so they can earn something rather than nothing. However, your delinquency or "charge-off" could appear on your credit report and the debt reduction may be treated as taxable income. When debt is forgiven you may open your mail to find a 1099 for the amount written off! Recently, I was able to obtain a $500,000 reduction in a client's debt only to find the creditor filed a 1099-C, thereby creating a $200,000 tax obligation.

If your account is in collection, remember that attack is the best form of defense. Collection agencies are like rabid dogs. If you run away they will chase you, but if you stand firm and bark at them they will cower and hang back. So tell them that you refuse to pay the full amount. Tell them that they can sue your corporation, but it has no assets. Tell them that you intend to defend the matter on principle regardless of the cost. Tell them that you have fought disputed claims before and if they are unwilling to reach an amicable settlement they are free to go ahead and sue. Yell at them. Become irrational. Become a crocodile. Make like a crazy person. Remember this exercise is not free for them either. They face incurring collection expenses and some lawyers are lazy. Tell them you will settle for a portion of the original debt paid over time as full settlement. Make certain to demand a signed release* and, finally, mark the back of your check with a settlement endorsement.

The collection agency may be five states away and have no intention of suing, because too many noses get in the trough. They may have their own attorney, and he will need local legal counsel – eating away at the commission. They may even give up and go away if you have a valid and stout defense. But if you are sued you must answer the complaint promptly and robustly. You can answer the suit pro se as we discussed earlier in the book.

It's possible to settle most of your disputed bills without the assistance of an attorney. Many trade creditors aren't savvy enough to grasp the process so they will be anxious to "bail out" with part of the obligation. Slick negotiators will learn the creditor's industry's profit margin so your offer will at least reimburse their cost. If you owe a jewelry store where the mark-up could be 70 percent, offer 30 percent. If you owe a car dealer where the mark-up could be 25 percent, offer 75 percent.

Once you agree to settle, explain the debt was disputed and that you would view any negative credit report to third party clearing houses as a "slander of credit" and that you will take appropriate legal action; the disputed obligation should be reported as "satisfactorily resolved." Require that they do not file a 1099-C because the obligation never existed in the first place.

The Stretch-Out

Another financial strategy is the stretch-out. This buzzword simply means that if you owe your lender $100,000 and there are 32 months left on your loan to repay the debt, ask the institution to "re-do" the loan and stretch it out to a longer term, thereby reducing your payments. If you intend to approach the lender with this request, you might simultaneously ask for some additional money as well. This is the time to prepare a Source and Use of Funds* so the lender knows what you will do with the additional cash flow that you will experience. Don't hesitate to ask for a lower interest rate, "interest-only" payments for a term, or a complete moratorium on some payments.

Because restaurants, golf courses and other seasonal or weather-impacted businesses may experience lower revenues during certain times of the year, provide for that situation. It's an "easy-sell" because lenders do not want you to become delinquent. Suppose your golf course is closed during the months of December through February. You could request no payments during that time frame and spread them over the remaining nine months. Few borrowers consider this type of request and loan officers never suggest it to avoid accounting challenges.

Composition Agreement

A composition with creditors is an agreement between the debtor and the creditors but also between the creditors themselves, to accept less than what each is owed. Once you settle for less than what is due, you're viewed as a "financially pressed debtor" who owes money to more than one creditor and your future payment is to be divided among them in full satisfaction of their claims. Settling with creditors is simply a negotiation process and you may have no choice. Your other option may only be to lay off people or close the doors entirely.

Remember that if you don't pay your bills, many creditors will swim away. Eighty percent of your creditors to whom you owe under $1,000 will settle for pennies on the dollar. If you're "judgment proof," most creditors will settle for as little as 10 percent of your debt.

Lender Liability Claims

Visiting the banker always is akin to a visit to your proctologist. Stripping down to have your financials examined is submitting to an emotional examination. This opens them up to lender liability claims.

Because banks can look at your innards and have access to confidential aspects of your business, federal laws require they treat borrowers fairly. If they don't, they can be subject to borrower litigation under a variety of legal claims that can be brought for breach of contract and/or fraud claims. The bank has an "edge" dealing with your company because of this open relationship.

We've discovered since the savings and loan crisis of the late 1980s, with the intervention of the FDIC and the RTC, that many bankers are crooks, with those in Colorado and Texas leading the pack. Often small banks are owned by lawyers or thieves who would rather have your property than your money, and big banks are virtually impossible to deal with.

The lender liability claim is a weapon you may not realize is in your arsenal and it is seldom wielded by the business owner who may be under extreme pressure with a line of credit demand notice or foreclosure. Your solo practitioner lawyer, most often familiar with state laws and divorce cases, isn't going to suggest that you sue a bank. Moreover, they are reluctant to sue because much of their work surrounds local banking transactions. You'll need to contact a litigation firm familiar with banking laws.

If the bank sues you, sue them. First, they want no part of a lender liability lawsuit or you filing a free and easy complaint with the State Banking Commission. Next, they're sensitive to bad publicity, which is why they give money away to community fundraisers. So, calling on one of your three Bs (balls), you're going to threaten or file a Federal lawsuit. Lawyers will often take your case on a contingency fee basis because they know the bank's defense firm is going to bill them to death. The bank will often back off, re-do or stretch-out your loan and offer other goodies to keep your mouth shut.

Watch Your Cash

When a business is in financial trouble, it's doubly or triply important to pay attention to cash flow. You need to use every dollar wisely, spending as little as possible until you can make it through the rough waters and come out of the other side. Hopefully, everyone around you will recognize the need for cash and be willing to accommodate your needs, at least on a short-term basis. Consider these tips when you feel cash flow pressures:

• Don't be embarrassed. Cash shortages, decreasing sales and other business problems may be the result of external forces beyond management control.

• Face the predicament. The problem will not fix itself – things will get worse if neglected.

• Don't borrow. Often owners find that borrowing more operating capital is the first easy answer to the problem; this pattern can snowball. Moreover, it consumes valuable time that should be spent working on the root of the problem.

• Obtain accurate numbers. If financial statements are not factual or timely, devote time to correct the deficiency.

• Seek assistance. Depending on the problem, consider meeting with an accountant, attorney or business consultant. Don't overlook free help such as that offered through universities, the Service Corps of Retired Executives (SCORE) and government-subsidized programs.

• Avoid playing games, such as paying part of an invoice, marking checks paid in full, attempting to avoid debt with endorsement releases, intentionally not signing checks to buy time, stopping payment by mistake, purposely making the amounts differ, and other gimmicks found in pocketbooks should only be used in a dire emergency. These practices erode company credibility.

Keep Your Airboat Moving

Dealing with financial challenges can be incredibly draining. You need to put your time and attention to these types of survival strategies, while continuing to serve your customers and motivate your workforce.

As the owner of a business in trouble, you may want to form your own Crisis Management Team where each member is focused on a particular aspect of the business such as financial, operational, management, sales, marketing and human resource issues. Time is always a factor so if you or your board members do not possess the right expertise, you may need to go outside of the organization and engage a professional turnaround crisis manager.

In my profession, crisis managers are most often bold, aggressive, experienced, driven critters with immense fortitude and determination. We thrive on change and instability. We possess a basic command of business, finance, accounting, law and marketing. As excellent communicators, we're often able to convince people to do things that they never would have done otherwise.

The best management consultants will want to roll up their sleeves, push you into the broom closet, take control and bring about massive change. We often form a new management team and quickly draft a Business Diagnostic Review and Management Report. Conversely, some consultants write talk about it and charge a fee, but never jump into the water with you. Terminate their services.

So, when selecting this important advisor who could save your company, make certain the consultant isn't "all talk and no action." You might want to offer a good consultant a piece of the company, so you can avoid a situation where you could end up with 100 percent of nothing.

One should never intentionally avoid their obligations, but if you have customers with warranty claims, employees with families and your mother's retirement on the line, then you need to survive. You took a big risk with potential big rewards. Now, it's time to live up to the old saying, which goes, "When the going gets tough, the tough get going!"

Succeed While Sinking

You may now have a revenue stream but can't pay your bills. It might be helpful to read a few books on ethics, but now might be the time to borrow more money, form a new entity, buy another business and slowly walk away from the old one that you threw into the swamp as lawyers bob around looking for any fish food you left behind.

One should never intentionally avoid their obligations – but if you have customers with warranty claims, employees with families and your mother's retirement on the line, then you need a way to survive. You took a big risk with potential big rewards. You did your best. You fought like hell. It didn't work. Do it all over again because the next one might be a winner.

Future Trouble Pitfalls

For those who have been fortunate to develop a successful business, pay attention to possible pitfalls:

- If you're bored, get out

Most people tire of their profession at times. This is dangerous when you're the entrepreneur. Many companies fail because the CEO lost interest.

- Take an outsider's look

Being too close to the forest to see the trees can result in missed opportunities. Take time away from daily operations to discuss your medium and long-term objectives with others. Ask your accountant for management reports or ask business acquaintances to review your business trends and ratios.

- Get help when it's required

Tips To Keep You Afloat

> Maintain a current and realistic Business Plan
> Don't allow emotions and loyalties to cloud your judgment
> Watch for the signs of business decline
> Stay abreast of the latest business thinking
> Attack problems early
> Recognize the need for professional advice and assistance

15. THE BANKRUPTCY

> "At that darkest moment, while drowning in the abyss of Emotional Bankruptcy, reflect on this universal truth: the difference between success and failure is one more time."
>
> Ken Poirot

If your canoe is sinking, you could jump out and swim to the shore, leaving your business behind. You may wind up dodging calls from your creditors and unhappy employees as you look for ways to find a new job and repair your credit. You could also give away your business to one of the "alligators" lurking nearby that might find your canoe to be a tasty snack. Those exit strategies are likely to leave you with nothing to show for all the time, energy and money you poured into your business venture.

But those aren't the only ways to deal with a struggling business that's about to go underwater. You could also file for bankruptcy and try to find a solution with your creditors that might allow your venture

to survive. If you have a healthy cash flow and a solid customer base, but find it almost impossible to meet your loan payments, then bankruptcy might be the right solution. Your creditors might write off some of the debt in exchange for a share of the equity in the company, or they might extend your loan to reduce those onerous payments.

Even if things don't work out and your business must be liquidated, you should be able to retain your personal assets and walk away "clean" without worries about debt collectors knocking at your door. Hopefully, you will learn some valuable lessons on the "dos and don'ts" of running a business that will serve you well in your next venture as an entrepreneur.

Because bankruptcy can be an expensive, time-consuming process, you should consult with an experienced attorney in your region to see if there might be alternative ways to clear up your debts and make a clean start. For instance, Florida has an "assignment for the benefit of creditors (ABC)" statute that allows companies to reach financial solutions in a state court, rather than U.S. Bankruptcy Court. In any case, the legal process may provide you with a better exit from your business than simply closing the doors and walking away.

Reasons for Bankruptcy

If you're considering filing for bankruptcy, you are far from alone. According to the American Bankruptcy Institute, there were approximately 24,115 corporate bankruptcy filings in America in 2016. The SBA says that 30 percent of new businesses fail within the first two years.

Why did they file? Dun & Bradstreet has compiled the following statistics on the causes of business failures:

Insufficient profits
22.2 percent

Poor growth
19.8 percent

Too much debt or too little capital
14.7 percent

Inexperience
12.0 percent

Heavy operating expenses
11.7 percent

Industry weakness
10.5 percent

High interest rates, poor location, and competition
5.3 percent

Neglect
2.0 percent

Fraud
0.9 percent

Poor planning
0.9 percent

What is Bankruptcy?

Most cash-starved debtors believe bankruptcy is their last resort, but if you heed the early warning signs, obtain professional support, and launch a successful turnaround plan, you may never have to file for bankruptcy. You may also run out of cash or not have enough assets to cover your debt. This condition is called insolvency and may be remedied by obtaining additional equity capital from an investor or credit from a lender.

Technically speaking, you are bankrupt when you cannot meet your ongoing financial obligations as they become due. Bankruptcy is simply a legal process that relieves debtors of all or part of their debts and allows for a fresh start. It's possible for creditors to force an individual or business into bankruptcy, but only under special circumstances and with more than 11 creditors.

There is a U.S. bankruptcy trustee appointed in every Federal judicial district. They, in turn, appoint local trustees – frequently attorneys – and oftentimes a debtor's assets are turned over to such a trustee. These assets are then converted into cash by the trustee and distributed to those creditors who asserted claims against the individual or business that filed bankruptcy.

If you're a creditor, you must file a Proof of Claim to participate in the distribution of assets in a bankruptcy. Otherwise, a creditor is limited to collecting only what is on the debtor's schedule, which is frequently less than the amount owed. Pay attention to Proof of Claim filing deadlines. Missing the deadline could be the end of your claim.

Occasionally, creditors favor a bankruptcy filing over a business' continued operations because it generally ensures them equitable treatment by the court. Without bankruptcy, a debtor might give preferential treatment to certain creditors.

How Does Bankruptcy Work?

There are three major types of cases specified by chapter in the U.S. Bankruptcy Code:

- Chapter 7. Liquidation: All the business assets are sold, and you could be left with a Bible and $300.
- Chapter 11. Business Reorganization: "Debtor-in-Possession," with you retaining control of your own company, according to your Plan of Reorganization.
- Chapter 13. Personal Reorganization: The individual debtor is given three to five years to recover under a plan approved by a court-appointed trustee.

Let's take a close look at these three options, always keeping in mind that you may have alternate ways to pull yourself out of financial trouble than filing for bankruptcy.

Liquidation

A Chapter 7 plan liquidation of assets may be filed by a business or an individual. A Chapter 7 filing is designed to lead to a complete liquidation of all your corporate assets. Often a personal bankruptcy filing will be necessary if you and/or your spouse guaranteed loans. You may be forced to retain a second, independent lawyer because your corporation's best interest and your personal best interest may not be aligned. If your business is not incorporated, you may be personally liable for all debt.

In a liquidation, all assets (except for exempt property) are sold and the proceeds are apportioned to all creditors based on priority as established by law. In this form of bankruptcy, all nonexempt assets are delegated to a trustee for distribution.

Reorganization

With a Chapter 11 filing, your business continues to operate while you devise a plan to service debt over an extended period of time at reduced sums. You or your lawyer negotiate with creditors and shareholders to formulate a workable plan that is then presented to the judge.

Reorganization differs from liquidation in that all debts, along with your plan for their payment, are turned over to the court, which immediately issues an order preventing creditors from all attempts to collect debts. A reorganization enables you to make regular payments to the trustee, who then distributes the funds to creditors under a court-approved plan.

Typically, secured creditors get paid in full if there are available funds. If they object to the Plan of Reorganization, but the court believes it's in the best interest of all parties, the Plan should move forward. The judge can also impose a "cram-down" which will force a lender to "take a haircut." This is an action that is talked about more than approved and yet remains a threat to your primary lenders, especially if they are over-secured. Understanding these basic legal principles will aid you with successful negotiations.

A Chapter 11 plan may be filed by a business or individual debtor, but is rarely adopted by individuals due to the expense and complex nature of the proceedings. The typical business plan requires nine to 12 months to make its way through the system and obtain approval. A business can remain in reorganization for years.

The Plan of Reorganization

This formal document, the content of which you may be able to partially write yourself, explains what steps you intend to take to stay afloat and how you are going to pay the obligations. Creditors will vote on this Plan of Reorganization. However, most unsecured creditors are confused by the process and conditioned to think that they'll never recover money. Therefore, they often fail to file a Proof of Claim and ignore the proceedings. As a result, those obligations may evaporate. But if a debtor fails to identify a creditor, the creditor may have grounds to sue after the case has ended. The court will schedule a creditor's meeting where creditors interrogate the debtor in the presence of a trustee. Few creditors attend these meetings. Those that do attend are often ill-prepared and ask irrelevant questions of debtors.

Barriers to Bankruptcy

Remember when we discussed the reasons to avoid granting a personal guarantee on any debt? Nothing complicates a company's troubles more than the personal guarantees of the stakeholders. Without a loophole in the language of the personal guarantee, or a condition in the state's law pertaining to when a guarantee is applicable, this condition places all corporate and personal assets into one bucket. It is then necessary to persuade the secured creditors to think twice before forcing the company and the stakeholders into bankruptcy because it may signal the end of the fight to stay afloat and the creditors may end up with assets instead of cash.

Pre-Bankruptcy Steps

"Cash is king" in bankruptcy, so you should create a "safety valve" account prior to filing that may be used for leverage in debt compromises or costs of litigation. You can also use this time to restructure your operations.

After filing, don't fall into a false sense of security because your

creditors are no longer "banging at your door." Your business could even be reporting a paper profit because some of the old debt is not being serviced. You might fall into the trap of thinking that being a "Debtor-in-Possession" of the business is a safe corner of the swamp. But sooner or later, the alligators may find you and devour your business.

A Bootstrap Recovery

By age 32, I had created quite a business empire, but the economy crashed and I lost more than $1 million in one year. Our bank "called the loan" so we had a meeting in its boardroom. I was represented by my accountant and two lawyers, while the bank invited its loan officer and two lawyers. Every one of them agreed with the messenger: "Steve, I know this is difficult, but you need to face it. You will never, ever be able to pull yourself out of this dilemma." They laid financial projections on the table, the bank said it wouldn't wait, and they all concurred that it was time to call it a day.

One of the "Bs" kicked in. I was emphatic that I would not file bankruptcy and that I could fix it. Sick to my stomach, I walked out and went to work, negotiated with creditors, slashed expenses, closed some stores, sold-off underutilized assets, and two years later I was back on top, paying my creditors.

However, only about 10 percent of debtors who file for reorganization under Chapter 11 emerge successfully because:

- They wait too long to file.
- An emergency demands they file immediately.
- Their lawyer doesn't want them to succeed.
- The lawyer takes so much of the estate that there's nothing left for the debtor.
- The debtor failed to build a "war chest" before filing.
- The debtor pledged all of his/their personal assets.
- The debtor fell into a false sense of security.

Bankruptcy FAQ

In weighing your options for restructuring, consider the following questions:

- Will suppliers continue to provide critical services and products needed for continued operations, while accepting extended terms of payment?
- Are there other sources of supply that are easily available?
- Have I been direct, honest, kept my word and paid bills on time for the most part?
- Are there any large creditors who might begin legal action when I attempt to reorganize my affairs?
- Is the local competition making it impossible to sell our products or services at a reasonable profit given the stigma of bankruptcy?
- Do our financial problems have their origin from within my business or from outside market forces?

- Do others view us as responsible businesspeople with sound common sense?

- Do we have loyal, competent employees and specifically, do they possess skills necessary to contribute to a reorganization? Are they emotionally and mentally up to the task? Do we have their trust so they will swim in murky waters?

- Am I up to the job of rehabilitation? Do I have the necessary emotional stamina?

If the answers are yes, then you have a good shot at emerging from the swamp. If not, you should consider liquidation or other alternatives.

Prepackaged Bankruptcy

Many companies are now opting for "prepackaged bankruptcies" rather than traditional proceedings. It was Donald Trump's strategy to exit Atlantic City while preserving his other holdings. In a prepackaged plan, you strike a deal with your creditors before filing a petition, greatly increasing the probability of survival. Yet it is still protected under the code.

Lawyers rarely suggest this enhanced bankruptcy strategy because it might actually succeed with minimal risk and fewer legal fees. In essence, you develop a plan, take it to the creditors, obtain their blessing and then go to court to approve and formalize it. Legal fees for this strategy are as dry as the mud around the swamp.

Borrowing in Bankruptcy

Most banks will want out and would rather accept a large hit at the auction than keep the loan — or worse — receive an "adverse" classification by the FDIC. This "C loan" irritates the bank because they can no longer offer your loan as collateral to underwrite other loans. So, if you present a good proposal to "take out the lender," they may cooperate. And those who loan to a debtor in bankruptcy may be entitled to a "super-priority" lien, which is superior to old liens and the likelihood of being paid could be much greater.

Bankruptcy Nuances

Payments made to insiders and creditors in the three months prior to filing may be reversed by the court. Payments made to managers or significant stockholders, such as management fees, within 12 months prior to filing may also be reversed. This power prevents self-dealing in a manner that protects creditors, but can harm a company in bankruptcy.

If the company pays a pre-petition debt to one or two creditors but not to all, that may be a criminal act. Therefore, all of the small, but important bills should be paid in full before filing; some (not all) credit cards should be paid down to zero because, after filing, the pre-filing bills cannot be paid and charge privileges could be revoked.

Bankruptcy Pitfalls

Most lawyers won't raise the following factors because your interest may not be aligned with their own. The Bankruptcy Code is complex and the Rules of Bankruptcy Procedure even more so. Therefore, the bankruptcy lawyer is one of the most specialized, greedy critters in the swamp. These attorneys typically ask for a big retainer claiming that the court won't allow them to collect from you for months after the case is filed and the judge could, at his sole discretion, write down legal fees. This becomes their justification for demanding a fat retainer at the outset.

The moment a bankruptcy is filed, the debtor is quickly pulled into quicksand with a myriad of filings, motions and hearings. The code seems to have been written from Newton's Third Law: "For every action there is an equal and opposite reaction."

The bankruptcy filing imposes an "automatic stay" that prevents creditors from initiating or continuing debt recovery actions; there are potentially heavy penalties if they do. Nevertheless creditors may move to have the automatic stay lifted. Debtors will want to continue to use their liquid assets. Some creditors may file a Motion for Cash Collateral in order to seize the debtor's cash.

This all provides opportunities for lawyers to draft motions and responses, attend hearings and generate fees as their client watches them paddle through these infested waters.

Debtor options are limited because:

- They waited until the major, secured creditors foreclosed or called loans.

- They failed to communicate with creditors and internally work through problems.

- They didn't stop paying non-essential unsecured creditors six months before filing in order to reserve needed cash.

- They opened their pocketbook to the lawyers who know they had no alternative but to immediately give them money under onerous terms.

Big Bankruptcy Paradigm

The debtor's idea of a successful outcome may conflict inherently with the lawyer's best interest. The debtor wants to save the baby, while his lawyer may want to throw it out with the bathwater.

Like anyone experiencing grief, a debtor won't sleep. They

may feel shame from family, friends, employees and creditors and get up every morning and work twice as hard to save the assets, emerge and stay in business. Conversely, the lawyer is on the top of the Money Totem Pole with an "administrative claim," which means that he gets paid first from the spoils, regardless of the outcome.

The debtor will be mystified by the process and take comfort in the thought of his lawyer doing battle for him for months or years while he rarely, if ever, receives a bill. He begins to think he's on welfare. He doesn't question the purpose of a hearing; the process grinds on slowly as the lawyer bills the newly created estate hundreds of dollars an hour.

If the debtor does complain the lawyer may say, "Our fees come out of what you owe creditors so don't worry about it." There are court costs and trustees to pay. But because the primary obligations are to pay the bank and insurance carriers after the date of filing, the Debtor-in-Possession Financial Statement (prepared by an accountant) appears as though the debtor is now making a lot of money! It's a delusional good feeling. No lawyers are sending nasty letters, creditors have gone away, and the idea of "being in the black" is an illusion.

As the end of the case nears, the debtor finds himself at the bottom of this Money Totem Pole and left with only table scraps. The lawyers took a chunk, the IRS took a chunk, the state took its slice, the bank got most of its money, the bank recovered its legal fees, the unsecured creditors picked up a few pennies, his accountant got a fat fee, real estate brokers got their commissions, trustees were paid, expert witnesses profited, and he is in the 90 percent group that fails or moves to file a Chapter 7 liquidation. He may, or may not, keep his home.

The Bankruptcy

DebTor FRIENDLY Judge

Worse than all of this is the damn lawyer who periodically evaluates the case and says to himself, "Do I want this guy to emerge? Let's see, if he's forced to sell off the plant, the inventory, cut his employees, screw some of his necessary suppliers so they won't resell to him, he'll close the doors, we'll hold an auction, there will be a pile of cash and I'll be the first vulture to dip into that big pot and snatch a hundred grand." Being qualified to testify as an expert witness since the mid 1980s, I've spent many days in the courtroom. Even with a "debtor-friendly" judge who may give my client time to recover, there are other alligators eating the whole pie.

Much like a protracted divorce case without a pre-nuptial or post-nuptial agreement, you and your bankruptcy lawyer may swim together for years. The average attorney can't muddle through a bankruptcy case and the ones who can are expensive and difficult to identify.

In one market where I'm experienced, there are only a few bankruptcy specialists and some operate like a wheelhouse, cranking out the same documents in huge numbers with no change in strategy from one client to another. In another market, there are seven bankruptcy lawyers. Some only work for banks, some are open for private business but only one accounts for his time, charges a reasonable fee, does only what is necessary and works for his client's best interest. He's about to retire. Therefore, select the right lawyer very carefully because if you select the vulture, you'll drown.

Shady Bankruptcy Tricks

It may be considered an "abuse of process" if your lawyer should file a petition in order to effectuate a debt settlement. A denture technician once owed back rent and while I pleaded with him for a payment or settlement, he simply ignored the obligation. I sued, obtained a default judgment, filed a Writ of Execution and began to seize his property. Having no use for false teeth, I spotted his golf clubs hanging out of the trunk of his red T-Bird parked in front of a bar. I called the towing company and they hauled his car down the street. The deadbeat ran out of the bar chasing his car on foot, trying to pull his golf clubs out of the trunk as the vehicle was moving.

He found an attorney who called to say the "golfer-on-the-run" filed bankruptcy so I must take no further collection action. However, his client would pay twenty cents on the dollar as a full settlement. Not being a golfer and knowing a bankruptcy could last a good year, I accepted the payment on a Wednesday and on Thursday, the sleezeball lawyer withdrew his petition.

I offer this example in the event you encounter mean creditors. You're not constrained by the Canon of Ethics of a lawyer. If someone threatens your company or your personal assets, reverse this strategy and file the Petition yourself. Or, if you look under enough rocks, you'll find a lawyer who will, for a thousand bucks, direct his paralegal to file a Petition. Even if the sleezeball lawyer also saves you a percentage of what he collected with the sham Petition, you may avoid the debt. At times, you might need to stretch "situational ethics" a bit to protect your family and company. The water is deep here, so be careful.

Bankruptcy Alternatives

As the CEO, you will be the lightning rod who takes most of the strikes from creditors and the press for company problems. The smaller the community, the greater the personal attacks because the filing can cause disruption and unemployment. As we've mentioned before, you do have alternatives to filing for bankruptcy.

- Self-liquidation. You simply sell all business assets, pay your bills, and close shop. You avoid the expense, stigma, lengthy legal proceedings and costs that accompany bankruptcy. This is much easier if you've protected your personal assets.

- Self-reorganization. This is the best choice if you want to save your business and you're willing to make the effort. You must negotiate on an individual basis with each creditor, stop all legal or collection threats, create new cash flow for your business, pay some debt and give yourself valuable time and space to reorganize and rethink your affairs.

- Hire a turnaround specialist. This is your last desperate attempt to stay afloat. Hire a professional or become your own turnaround specialist. Take over as the authority in all matters concerning money flowing in or out of the company. This often means immediately terminating some employees, restructuring jobs, halting all debt payments except absolute necessities (such as trust taxes and utilities) and initiating very harsh collection methods with customers.

A comprehensive "turnaround plan" will typically address these factors:

- Purpose
- Background
- Preliminary study
- Past problems
- Procedure
- Financial ratios and comparisons
- New accounting system

- Development of company
- Image of company
- Company ownership
- Company management
- Human resources
- Turnaround strategy
- Financial information
- Operating budgets
- Debt reductions
- Funding issues
- Business development
- Sales and marketing
- Waste reduction

As your business' new "crisis manager," you must do everything in your power to buy time and use your negotiating skills. You'll have to go out and find cash, defend the organization from enemies, manage operations and develop and implement a redirect and growth plan. It's time for the biggest business battle of your career.

But don't rely on a white knight to come to your rescue. Often debtors simply cannot accept the fact they're losing their business or home. Perhaps they caused the problem

with drugs, gambling, airplanes, expensive cars and oceanfront condos. They'll not let go of hope. The White Knight is someone with a lot of cash or someone who relies on his mouth and a sales pitch. If you believe his flattery, you may shun reality or professional advice. The gullible do need a lawyer. Otherwise, you'll do anything the knight asks, which often results in a theft of your company or application processing fees that represent this scavenger's sole income, knowing full well they're never going to loan you a dime.

Bankruptcy is a Buyer's Opportunity

Now, let's take a different perspective. Let's say your business is running successfully and you're ready to expand and take on a new challenge. In this case, another company's bankruptcy could create a buyer's opportunity for you.

Suppose you're in the heavy construction business and one of your competitors files bankruptcy. Invite your competitor out for a drink and explain that you feel badly about his demise. Whether at this initial meeting, or a subsequent meeting when their creditors are knocking on the door, you can offer to be part of their Plan of Reorganization and purchase their stock, tender a loan convertible to stock or buy all or part of their assets.

You'll get their customers free and pay nothing for goodwill. Offer the debtor a job; cut any deal you want. By this time, the option for the court and creditors is probably an auction which will routinely bring as little as ten cents on the dollar. Your offer of thirty cents may be "music to their ears." Align yourself with the debtor and go in as a team.

If you have standing with the court, file a motion to purchase the assets or offer to buy the bank loan. You'll quickly become a main player in the case. The lenders do not want keys to the business – they want money. They'll begin to place pressure on the debtor to accept your lowball offer.

If you attempt to buy a bankrupt company, don't worry about being branded as a "bottom feeder." Call the debtor, because they're now desperate for an "angel" to fly into the swamp with cash. After they come to realize the cost of the case, requirement for monthly operating reports, court fees, continuous hearings and stress, they'll listen to anyone. They and/or their spouse could have signed personally for company loans so their home and other assets may be in jeopardy. They may have filed a personal bankruptcy to protect those assets. By this time, the debtor could have half a dozen lawyers pulling them under. Make the call. The court and creditors will want to hear any viable plan. Being the bottom feeder that you've come to be, you won't need a lawyer early in the game. And, you could become a hero.

If your efforts fail, attend the auction and perhaps pay even less. The disadvantage to that strategy is that you're now buying non-performing assets rather than an intact operation with customers, employees and other intangible assets. Worse, there may be competing bidders. Obviously, each "angel" will have individual own goals and objectives. But remember that when a federal bankruptcy judge hands down an order that you purchased the assets free and clear of any liens or encumbrances, it is less risk than if you buy an operating business with hidden skeletons in the closet.

The Bankruptcy

Undertake due diligence in order to value a business, and apply those same tactics to acquire the bankrupt firm. You may want to maintain some obligations of the debtor. If not, a "Debtor-in-Possession" may reject leases and contracts and can "clean house" before you assume control. You may have the benefit of some net operating losses carried forward that potentially could be used to offset future profits. You may find the debtor holds claims against others that you could pursue in their stead.

There are few bankruptcy suitors because most people are intimidated by the court system and the word "bankruptcy." Bankruptcy can actually be good for a buyer, so go to the courthouse and review open cases; these are all "diamonds in the rough." Wouldn't you prefer to buy your Mercedes at a dealer's auto auction than in the showroom? Why not buy a company for half of what it's worth through a bankruptcy court?

I didn't have the required cash when I purchased 175 pianos out of bankruptcy. I handed a Federal judge a bad check because they were priced at ten cents on the dollar. After the courtroom auction, I raced to call my banker and said I must have a loan today and I'll pledge every asset I have as collateral. I didn't get sanctioned by the court and I made a fortune selling those instruments. High risk equals high rewards for those with the 3 Bs.

Tips To Keep You Afloat

> Be proactive with creditors; generally they prefer to work out a delinquency rather than deal with you in bankruptcy.

> Explore all your alternatives before filing for bankruptcy.

> Become familiar with the basics of the Bankruptcy Code.

> Don't allow your attorney or other advisors to "lead you by the nose."

> If it seems like there is no way out, look for a way through.

> Watch for profit opportunities from businesses in bankruptcy.

> Never be afraid to grab assets at bargain prices that may also benefit the sellers.

LEAVING THE SWAMP

Exiting Your Business

Now is the time to realize the rewards of your hard work, business skills and financial acumen. You can sell your business or use it as a springboard to building wealth in real estate, launching another entrepreneurial venture, or becoming a philanthropist — or all three. Congratulations on reaching the other side of the swamp!

16. THE SUCCESSFUL EXIT

Now, you've almost paddled your canoe across the swamp. You're probably happy that the goal is in sight and you'll be able to capitalize on your entrepreneurial venture. But now is not the time

to relax and start drifting. You could still be swept away by the currents of business life. And there are some dangerous swamp critters standing on the shore, ready to haul in your canoe – after tipping you overboard. Rather than take a risk themselves, they let you do all the work and then try to buy your business at a steep discount.

In order to make it safely to shore, you'll need to take a realistic look at the current state of your business, as well as your short- and long-term goals. For instance, are you ready to cash in on your hard work and live a life of leisure? Or do you plan to use the proceeds from the sale of your company to invest in real estate or to start a new venture?

You'll also need a good business lawyer or management consultant who can help you maximize the value of your business investment, as well as an accountant and a personal financial advisor. They can help you create a financial plan that aligns with your long-term goals and shows you how much income you'll need to be comfortable when you retire.

There are many ways to exit a business. You could sell it outright for a lump sum of cash. You could sell your share of the business to your partners. You could find a new partner and work out a gradual exit. You could sell to your employees. Or, if you're really fortunate, you could attract the interest of private equity investor or even go for an initial public offering (IPO).

I sold and financed a company in 2009 with an agreement to provide pro-bono support for one year and I'm still providing it today. Like me, you may want your buyer to succeed — not only because you have provided owner financing, but because it's the right thing to do. This was your ship.

There are many sale variations that could be attractive to you and the buyer. Perhaps a merger of your two companies might be more favorable than the sale of one. Or, there could be a benefit in spinning off a segment of your company while retaining part of the operation. You could become a consultant or an employee of the new company. Explore the benefits and create a transaction that satisfies the needs of both parties.

Hopefully, you've already been thinking about your exit strategy for some time. That will accelerate the planning process and help you avoid the sad scenario of the entrepreneur who gets fed up and just unloads the business for less than its true value. Selling a business can be emotional, even traumatic, if you don't prepare for it in advance.

Even if you don't think you're quite ready to sell, there are steps you can take to make the transition easier (and gain a higher price). For instance, you could place your assets in a different entity, and sell it as a smaller part of your business for more money, create a desirable image, and boost incoming revenue. It's a good idea to manage your organization as though you have buyers "in the wings" today, since buyers may surface at any time. Just as you would wash and wax your car before trading, you'll need time to prepare your business for sale. Also, consider what might happen if you're disabled or deceased. You should have bound insurance and perhaps drafted a Buy-Sell Agreement in the event of a forced or unexpected sale.

When to Sell

The purchase and sale of companies is not necessarily tied to the market, because different buyers want different businesses for different reasons, at different times. For example, I once had a buyer approach me to purchase a company at a price that was well over market. After the transaction was completed, I learned that his intent was to acquire its revenue stream in order to enhance his public company's P/E ratio. He wasn't necessarily concerned about losses, employees, or assets; he only wanted to "drive revenue."

Recently, a client of mine was operating profitably with no plans for an immediate sale. However, when I read of an active, public company acquiring similar operations, I reached out and made contact. That cold call resulted in a sale for significantly more than the owner expected, and made the difference between "just doing well" and "getting rich."

Value Your Business

Before you start counting the cash you hope to receive from a sale, take a realistic look at the current state of your business. One of the first questions to ask is: "What is its value?" That's an easy question to ask, but a difficult one to answer.

There are several different ways to value a business. One is to consider the "book value," which is basically the value of your assets if they were to be sold tomorrow. Those assets might be physical (your property, inventory, office furnishings, etc.), or they might be intangible (your brand, customer list, etc.). The difference between your accounts payable (what you owe vendors) and your accounts receivable (what your customers owe you) may also be considered in the book value.

Another approach is the income method: how much revenue does your business generate in a year? If it produces $1 million in income, for instance, a business expert might apply a multiplier factor such as "3x current income," placing a value of $3 million on your company.

There are other ways to develop a value for your business, and plenty of other factors to consider. If you have a small business and generate most of the revenue yourself, for example, the value to an outside buyer might be minimal. On the other hand, if you have been grooming a successor to take over your business, you might be able to command a higher sales price – particularly if you are willing to accept a stream of payments from the new owner, rather than a big lump sum at the time of sale. Or you might decide to sell to a family member for less than the market value in order to give that person an opportunity to keep paddling the canoe through the swamp.

Take the time to prepare a Business Valuation to demystify all of the numbers and factors. But remember that ultimately, the value of your business will be determined by whatever a buyer is willing to pay.

Types of Buyers

Buyers come in all shapes and sizes with unpredictable behaviors. You may find trust fund babies, wealthy professionals, government workers, and educators, all of whom are interested in your business. Let potential buyers know that you will be with them during the transition, and then follow through. Never pre-judge your suitor, but, instead, treat every prospect with respect and earn their trust. Once a small businessman contacted me to nationally launch three new products. Skeptical, I drove four hours to learn that Ted Nugent, rock star and TV personality, would finance the deal.

Sellers typically encounter ten potential buyers to purchase their business before finding the right one. Eight will be "tire-kickers" (someone who shows a lot of interest but ultimately will waste your time); two may be serious, one of the two may not have the finances to consummate the deal, and the tenth one might just be your prize.

When it comes to finding buyers, consider some of these alternatives:

• An Employee Stock Ownership Plan. Perhaps you employ loyal people who could collectively, afford to buy your company, with or without outside financing. This qualified defined-contribution benefit (ERISA) may commensurately offer significant tax benefits.

• The competition. Regional competitors not only have the advantage of adding your profit to their bottom line, they have the ancillary benefits of eliminating a competitor, enjoying economies of scale or adding breath to their product lines or resources.

• Regional advertising. Craigslist, Facebook, regional publications, trade journals and online sources should carry a well-written advertisement that might read something like this:

> Established wholesale business in northern Virginia offered by highly motivated seller with financing to qualified buyers. Must sell now! Clean financial data. Priced right with stable income and opportunity for growth with tax advantages. Brokers protected. Call in confidence: 800#

Business Brokers

After you've allowed one year to sell privately, it may be time to contact a business broker. Just remember that the broker's fee will come right out of your profits from the sale, and they typically charge 6 percent to 12 percent of the selling price for the service.

Unless you operate a commercial real estate business, don't bother engaging a real estate agent to sell your business. Many real estate agencies designate someone in the office as a "commercial expert." That person typically has no knowledge of the valuation, solicitation process, or mechanics of a business transaction. While a real estate sales agent's commission may be half that of a business broker, here is where "you get what you pay for." A sales agent's strategy is usually to list the company for sale and then hope that someone "falls out of the sky" with their commission. Save your time, as most self-proclaimed commercial agents will only delay your transaction.

Basics of the Sale

Now, let's look at some of the issues involved in structuring a sale. Lawyers make money on this aspect of the transaction because one of the first issues to address is whether the deal will be a stock or asset transaction. In other words, are you selling shares of stock in your corporation or selling assets to the buyer? Routinely, the buyer's counsel will insist on an Asset Purchase Agreement to be assured there are no "ghosts in the closet," as old debts or problems may not be extinguished under a stock transaction. While many owners blindly follow that advice, this is an outline of my more successful transactions:

If you're a corporate entity, sell your stock, which requires only a few transaction documents, transferring a stock certificate, and meeting filing requirements. Finance all or part of the transaction with the buyer, so that you're now the bank. Add a paragraph to the document that says you are attesting to the fact there are no undisclosed obligations or pending litigation, but if there should be, offer a mechanism to deduct that amount from the loan balance. You just cut the lawyer's legs out from under them and dropped the cost to complete the deal by 70 percent.

The age-old demand for asset transactions only serves to extend the closing date from several months to a year, during which time "buyer's remorse" could set in. Another benefit of the stock transaction is that it's less of a disruption to customers and clients; contracts do not need to be assigned, credit worthiness is no longer an issue as the name of a company is not changing, there is no need for any announcement, and it's "business as usual." Your accountant should also be involved because there are depreciation or capital gains issues that could be a benefit or disadvantage to you.

Consider owner financing, because it could defer capital gains taxes and buyers are usually more focused on obtaining a lower selling price than the financing terms. So, the smart owner will lower the selling price, raise the interest rate, allow a payment moratorium, and impose stiff prepayment penalties. At the time this book was published, money laying in a bank account paid less than 1 percent and a buyer may pay you 12 percent. More importantly, if there's adequate collateral, your transaction will not fall apart because the buyer's loan officer wasted six months to ultimately reject an application. I've seen deals fall apart when half a dozen lenders and professionals were unable to work out the financing. Most companies can be sold within a few months, yet most take six months to a year. Step in and take control before the opportunity dissipates.

My last restaurant transaction involved a buyer's lawyer who insisted on an asset purchase even though the seller financed the deal. A stock sale would have cost $2,000 in fees and closed in 60 days, but this transaction required more than a year and tens of thousands of dollars were paid to the professionals. You're the businessperson; you hold the checkbook. You tell your professionals how you want to proceed, and don't allow them to turn your deal into a frustrating, expensive tragedy. Buyers are also damaged with this archaic process and could lose a year's worth of profit or witness a seller getting "cold feet."

Why Deals Fail

These are the paramount reasons that business transactions crater:

- Bank loans. The moment you hear the words "loan application with a local bank," you're in for a six-month delay, often culminating in a denial.

- No owner financing. Don't expect a quick and successful sale without offering creative owner financing, including securing the obligation with assets being purchased, a reasonable down payment and additional collateral or loan guarantees. If you fail to do this, you've wasted an opportunity for additional profit, placed the spotlight on the selling price, and delayed the closing.

- Not knowing the value. Don't "place the cart before the horse" by searching the market to find a prospect while possessing no understanding of your business' value. Often a seller will try to omit this step to avoid paying a valuation fee. Instead, they may sign a Letter of Intent to sell without a formal Business Valuation, potentially leaving lots of cash on the table. Without obtaining a valuation, everyone involved in the transaction is completely in the dark.

A seller who fails to address the financing and valuation issues is headed for failure. The catastrophe often begins to unfold when the empty-handed buyer meets with his loan officer, who has no intention of recommending a credit approval without an independent valuation opinion in the file. Or the buyer will approach his own accountant who will dump some numbers into a software program, push a button and create a value without assigning any weight to other factors that should be considered. Instead, the buyer's professionals will simply tell their client to pass on the deal.

Absent a business valuation, both parties are exposed to risk, because the buyer could be paying 30 percent more than the company is worth or the seller could be selling for 30 percent under market. Everyone must be comfortable with the numbers.

Tips To Keep You Afloat

> Understand your current financial position and your goals in life.
> Know the value of your operation by obtaining or preparing a formal Business Valuation.
> Identify prospective buyers and market directly to them.
> Offer owner financing to avoid the loss of a sale.

17. INVESTING IN REAL ESTATE

> *"The biggest mistake you'll make in real estate is not buying enough fast enough."*
>
> Stephen Poorman

A wise man once explained to me that most business operations are only a conduit to create cash flow to invest in real estate. Lease or buy your business location and start investing in other properties when it's practical.

Whether you provide tenant management or contract it out, losing money in the real estate game is difficult. And each night, when you crawl into bed, tenants are paying you an hourly fee to sleep as they reduce your debt. One day you wake up and the buildings are paid for! You've met your wealth-builder.

So, once your canoe gets moving across the swamp, it's time to seriously consider real estate as the foundation of your long-term financial strategy. For entrepreneurs, this chapter is as important as the day man rolled a rock to the entrance of a cave to create a shelter for his family.

About Real Estate

Real estate is any "space created by man to contain activity for a specific period of time." Including buildings, real estate is often referred to as real property. Personal property is all property subject to ownership that is not real property. Personal property may be classified into two groups: tangible property and intangible property. Tangible property has a physical existence, such as an automobile. Intangible property does not have a physical existence, such as a patent.

Real estate investments offer a tax shelter through depreciation, leverage to generate profits, increase in asset value through appreciation, cash flow, opportunities to acquire other real property, and the pride of ownership.

Real estate is one of the safest investments because it is a commodity in demand, difficult to replace, an effective hedge against inflation and it throws off tax benefits. The asset appreciates, you build equity, and it generates cash. What more could an investor want? It's your vehicle into a strong future and solid retirement.

But your timing is important. There is an expression: "If you take care of your business, it will take care of you." When your company does well, the next step might well be to buy your own home. This can be your first real estate investment! If now is the right time, make your home a four-unit townhouse complex and live in one of them – free. Try to secure four or more units in one building; they usually produce a better return because you can spread expenses. If your choice is between a boat, which stands for, "Bring Out Another Thousand," or a building, go with the building. Boats, or personal property, depreciate and sink, while buildings, or real property, appreciate and rise to the top.

Commercial Real Estate Versus the Financial Market

Some people contribute to retirement plans like a 401(k), and believe Social Security will offer a reasonable retirement income. While FDR introduced Social Security back in the 1930s, he promised that it would be voluntary and that participants would only pay one percent of the first $1,400 of income, and that payments would be tax deductible, only be used to fund retirement and not be taxed as income. Presidents Johnson, Carter and Clinton reneged on those assurances to the point where Social Security is now insignificant for the small businessman's retirement portfolio. Consider that fact when accountants tell you to draw more income from your company so you contribute to FICA for retirement. These assurances are simply more broken promises of government – and politicians wonder why we don't believe a word they say.

A 401(k) account, IRA, Social Security or the stock market will rarely outperform real estate returns. If you've invested in the stock market, you've found it declines more than 20 percent about every

3.5 years for one decade. Commercial real estate investments seldom experience that same volatility. Without a high employer-contribution 401(k) match — which has become a rare perk — playing the market would have yielded little wealth in recent years. Instead of feeding yourself, you're the banquet for an army of bottom feeders who slice up your investment dollars.

To depict the power of real estate returns, I compared one of my typical real estate investments with an index fund tied to the S&P 500 for one decade. I heard of some aging physicians who owned an office building in Florida. I then organized my own doctor investment group to buy them out. This was a return versus the S&P:

COMMERCIAL OFFICE BUILDING		S&P 500	
Cash Down Payment	$ 40,000	Cash Investment	$ 40,000
RETURN ON INVESTMENT		RETURN ON INVESTMENT	AMOUNT
Management Fees Generated	113,076	Market Return	48,162
Accounting Fees Generated	22,153	Stock Dividends	58,517
Less Expenses	(27,315)		
Less Opportunity Cost of Down Payment	(26,680)		
Capital Distributions	113,000		
"Equity Kicker" - Syndication Fee	89,000		
10-Year Total Net Return	337,229		
TOTAL RETURN		TOTAL RETURN	
Real Estate Appreciation	1,325,000	Stock Returns and Dividends	106,679
Total Real Estate Gain after Sale	1,662,229	Total Stock Market Gain after Sale	146,679

The management and accounting fees, "equity kicker" syndication fee, and nontraditional gain will be explained later in this chapter. Business is not run on formulas, but instead on real visions. Cash-on-cash returns, internal rates of return and other salient factors should not be tossed aside in any purchase decision, but private real estate returns tend to dwarf the market investments, and they are safer. Certainly money has time value; it's simply compound interest in reverse. So before you even think about trying to calculate these performance formulas, purchase real estate investment software, dump the numbers in, push a button and voila; you'll have a comprehensive analysis of the potential deal.

You don't have time to study all of the internal returns. It is far more important to employ leverage, and remember my quote at the beginning of this chapter. Instead, buy more buildings, fast. If the monthly rental income will pay expenses and service debt, it's probably a good deal. Pull the trigger.

Investment Considerations

I was once attempting to buy a $200,000 building and was negotiating hard to drop the price. The impatient seller refused my $180,000 offer, and the deal died. Instead, someone else bought it and enjoyed a handsome long-term rental income with an established tenant. While visiting with a friend and his elderly merchant father, I told him of my foiled attempt. He said, "Son, you made two mistakes. Your first was not moving quickly enough. Your second was not realizing the additional $20,000 in the selling price throughout 15 years at 8 percent interest would have only increased your payment a few hundred dollars each month." So, each month I saved $190 and lost $8,000 in rent; long-term I lost $1 million!

The swamp water is always colder as the investment amount goes up. Early in my career, I avoided large deals because I didn't want large losses. Instead, I preferred many smaller deals. Buying larger, high-ticket properties can yield higher returns in a good market, and they can sink your canoe in bad markets.

Today, many of my financially distressed clients are bigger players. Ironically, it can be easier to buy big because banks prefer larger loans that are easier to service. The only difference between finding, buying, financing and leasing a $1 million building compared to a $5 million one is the number of zeros on the loan. But, when the economy slows, it can be a crater.

When purchasing my first property, a seasoned lawyer, who

ultimately became a long-term friend, told me not to make the typical mistake of purchasing everything in my own back yard. He said, "If your local economy dips, so will the occupancy and value of your real estate." So I made investments from Pennsylvania to Texas.

Manage Your Expenses

In order to profit from real estate investing, you need to monitor and manage your expenses carefully. There is a long list of costs you will need to address, including:

- Building maintenance, such as repairing a roof or replacing an air-conditioning system
- Damage and "wear and tear" to the interior
- Landscaping, such as taking care of the grounds and parking area
- Insurance coverage, as discussed in the prior chapter
- Marketing your property
- Leasing to new tenants
- Verifying property taxes are based on the property's real value

Depending on your skills, as well as the type and size of your property, you may be able to handle some of these tasks yourself. That will reduce your out-of-pocket costs, but take up a significant portion of your time. Therefore, it may make sense to engage a "Mr. Fix-It" to take care of maintenance issues and perhaps a property manager or leasing agent. As an entrepreneur, you want to pay attention to your business, while carefully monitoring and managing the expenses on an investment property.

Tenants Will Steal Your Profit

By the time you subtract the expenses from your rents, your effective profit in real estate will likely be about 10 percent. But if your tenants don't pay 10 percent, you made nothing. One of the first realizations of real estate investing is that not all tenants pay their rent — particularly in residential properties. As they attempt to make their personal woes your financial responsibility, 5 to 10 percent of them won't pay. By the time you go through the eviction process, they are in your building for another 45 days, rent-free. Some are skilled at working the system, which could actually tie you up for six months.

Laws are being passed to limit residential landlords' rent increases, require that they provide notices in advance if the lease will not be renewed, and even require that the landlords pay the tenant's rent. These types of onerous anti-business laws will influence young entrepreneurs. Always research how political candidates could impact your business and vote accordingly.

If you're not prepared to understand the basics of the legal system and if you're not the type of person to take immediate action when the rent checks don't show up, don't get into the business. If you are, however, here are some ways you may be able to lessen the risk:

- Obtain a tenant's written consent on the application and then run a credit check
- Always call the former landlord references on the application
- In addition to the security deposit, add the first and last months' rents, if permitted in your state, for questionable applicants

- Get corporate signatories and officer's personal guarantees
- Demand both husband and wife as parties to the lease
- Ask for a guarantor if there are any credit concerns
- Establish an ACH account so monthly payments are automatically deducted from the tenant's account and sent to yours
- Make credit card services available and hold signed blank slips that can be processed in the future
- Accept post-dated checks for the first three months
- Require 10 percent late payment assessments after five days
- Require a Confession of Judgment if permitted in your state.

Most importantly, don't let time pass. Hang a reminder on their door for all the neighbors to read the day the rent was not paid and begin an immediate dunning process. They must understand that you are their first obligation each month and that you do care if the rent comes in late.

Understand the Legal Terms

The very basic rights associated with an ownership interest or estate in real property include the right to use, abuse, enjoy, possess and dispose of specific real property. And there are some very basic concepts you should understand in order to play in the sandbox. Professionals throw Latin around to create a mystique so you feel the need to pay them money, but you're going to ignore those games.

The Contract

In order to be valid and enforceable, a contract must at least

(1) identify the parties, (2) state the terms and conditions of the transaction including the consideration or price to be paid and, (3) sufficiently describe the work or property so that it can be easily identified. Unfortunately, contracts are broken as much as they are honored.

The Statute of Frauds and Parole Evidence Rule

Real estate transactions must be in writing as required by the Statute of Frauds adopted in most states. The Parole Evidence Rule states that when parties put their agreement in writing, all previous oral agreements merge into the writing, and the written contract cannot be modified or changed in the absence of a plea of mistake or fraud. These concepts are important in the world of real estate, and when dealing with contractors.

Specific Performance

Specific performance is an equitable remedy that compels the breaching party to carry out the specific terms of the contract. So, when a buyer or seller of a building develops remorse, you can sue them and force the transaction. Because 90 percent of lawsuits seem to settle after lawyers have generated ample legal fees, you will most likely achieve your goal without a trial.

The Freehold

All estates in real property are either "freehold" or 'non-freehold." The term freehold dates back to feudal England, where it meant that land was possessed by a "freeman" for an uncertain duration. If you are the landlord, you'll want to preserve your freehold rights; if you are a tenant, you will want to modify the lease to enable you to remove personal property upon its expiration or termination. While repairing the holes in the wall should be your obligation, giving your equipment away is not. When you see the phrase "attached to the freehold," think of something that is attached to the wall or building, and something you either own or don't own.

Liens & Judgments

Liens and judgments are important for you to obtain from debtors, and important to keep off your own real estate. A lien on real property is normally filed as a result of litigation or because you failed to pay the government. A judgment lien may terminate by lapse of time. Each state has its own time limits on the life of judgment liens, and they may need to be renewed and revived every five years, for example.

Mechanic and materialman's liens are non-possessory security interests in real property to secure payment to workers and suppliers for services and supplies provided for the improvement of real property. The labor and material incorporated into the real property enhances the value of that property, and a property owner who failed to pay for the improvements would be "unjustly enriched" in an amount equal to the value of the improvements. Lawyers use the term "quantim meruit" for unjust enrichment. You can use these terms in demand letters and litigation that you should learn to file pro se, or in propria persona. Unless you insist on having your contractor or supplier execute a no-lien contract– often referred to as a Waiver of Mechanic's Lien* – he could place this cloud on your real estate until the dispute is resolved; this act can make your lenders anxious. You simply must document everything with a contractor in order to avoid the abuse discussed later in this chapter. Because I didn't understand this early on, I once watched my brand new sports car being towed away from a parking lot to pay for what I supposedly owed.

Tenant Assignment

In the absence of an express or implied lease provision to the contrary, a tenant has the right to assign or sublet possessory interest in the leasehold premises without the landlord's permission. If a tenant-assignor assigns his or her interest in the leasehold premises to an assignee, the assignee figuratively stands in the shoes of the tenant-assignor. The assignee becomes a third party to the landlord-tenant contract. You'll demand the right to assign, but you won't extend it to a tenant.

Subleases

On the other hand, if a tenant subleases the leasehold premises, a new contract comes into existence to which the landlord is not privy. Thus, even though the subtenant may take possession subject to the terms of the original lease, the landlord cannot proceed against the sublessee for unpaid rent because the landlord is not a party to the sublease contract. Therefore, from the landlord's point of view, the assignment situation is the more favorable method of obtaining an alternate tenant, because then he can collect from either the assignor or the assignee, whereas in the sublease situation the landlord can look only to the tenant for satisfaction, unless a new three-party contract is written.

The commercial tenant can typically assign and sublease for any legal use by a business similar to their own. But if your landlord rejects that provision — and says he will help find a replacement tenant if your business should fail or if it needs to expand — pretend you believe them. They will be chuckling after you leave the office. The only way that will ever occur is if they are completely filled in all of their properties and someone else begs them for your square footage. The tenant will be responsible to pay the rent until a replacement tenant comes along at which time the landlord may mark-up the rent even more to capitalize on the former tenant's improvements to the space.

Shelter Your Income

If you invite others to make real estate investments with you, become familiar with the passive versus active tax regulations and percentage of ownership required to enjoy depreciation. The beauty of real estate is that you can generate a profit but report losses that shelter income from other sources. After paying expenses and a mortgage, you should have cash left. But on your tax return, you will deduct interest and depreciation, which may generate a paper loss. Suppose you are a school teacher with taxable earnings of $60,000. You may be able to use the real estate loss to shelter your income, thereby reducing your taxes. As time goes on and your equity increases, your interest expense drops and your tax credits decline. This is one of the reasons some investors ultimately utilize a 1031 exchange where you can "swap" properties to restart the depreciation cycle.

The real estate investor should understand basic tax consequence regulations, and depreciation is crucial. The Economic Recovery Tax Act of 1981 established the Accelerated Cost Recovery System (ACRS), which permitted real property to be depreciated throughout a 15-year-period. The 1981 tax law provided liberal tax credits for those who rehabilitated qualified older properties.

The 1984 Tax Reform Act disincentivized passive investors from enjoying some tax credits. A rental activity is considered passive unless it is a real estate activity in which you materially participated and you were a real estate professional. You should review the IRS website to obtain current qualifications.

The Deficit Reduction Act of 1984 also modified ACRS rules, increasing the depreciation life of real property from 15 to 18 years.

More importantly, perhaps, the holding period necessary to realize long-term capital gains was reduced to six months from one year. Further changes in tax laws affecting real estate were passed in both 1985 and 1986, creating an 18 to a 19-year depreciable life.

Prior to the 1986 Act, investment property held for six months or more was entitled to preferential tax rates if the property was sold for a gain. This sort of tax preference had been incorporated in the tax code since 1924. As far as the Tax Reform Act of 1986 is concerned, it doesn't matter if property is held for one day, six months, or 10 years. If it is sold for a profit, it is to be taxed at the rate of 28 percent. The 1986 Act had dictated the useful life of the improvements in (a) residential rental property, and (b) nonresidential rental property. In the first instance, property must be written off in 27.5 years, and in the second instance it must be written off in 31.5 years.

Lower Your Real Estate Taxes

Land, houses and slaves were first taxed 2,400 years ago in ancient Greece. In 1646, the colony of Massachusetts began collecting property taxes. And we obviously must tax to support a need for community services, like roads, utilities, schools, fire and police protection. Whether you support a tax on income or property, you need to become aware of how the government is digging into your pockets.

If you now own or plan to buy real estate, it's critical that you monitor the assessed value. Ad valorum taxes (an old Latin phrase that means "according to value") are taxes levied when the city, county, school district and other taxing bodies tell you how much something is worth when they truly have no clue. On top of all that, they are going to tax you based on the opinion of assessors (who may or may not even conduct a drive-by).

Most assessors, whether appointed or elected, do not need experience or education. And the tax millage is established by politicians; a mill is 1,000th of a dollar. A tax rate of 10 mills is 1 cent per dollar of assessed value. It can be stated in dollars per 100, or 1,000.

If your property is a home, assessors in some localities generally will try to assess it based on current market value using recent sales of similar properties. If you own income producing properties like stores, industrial or apartment buildings, they may use the Income Approach by capitalizing, at a "fair return," the net income of the property. Some use the Cost Replacement Approach, either in conjunction with the Market Approach or Income Approach, or alone.

But generally, values are thrown around as guesstimates because assessors are over-worked, underpaid and under-qualified. Moreover, their task is virtually impossible because of the sheer number of properties within the taxing district. Next, there is often interference from politicians more interested in re-election than tax fairness, so some friends or industries may get a break. Some government taxing bodies offer free taxes for five to 20 years, even to retailers! This is all good news for you, because you are going to appeal values.

It will become your job to understand common level ratios and formulas to convert assessed values into market values, because it directly affects your bottom line. Assistance is normally found in the county assessor's office. If you believe the assessed value is greater than the market value, request an appeal form and make your case. If your property is losing money on paper (after adding management fees and other appropriate costs), it is one of the reasons you will offer to lower your taxes. You may need a new roof and other improvements you cannot afford to make — and these needs may bolster your case. If your local taxing body reassessed the property value for what it calls "tax fairness," it is a tax hike in disguise and most likely it will automatically be greater than market value.

A word of caution: If you appeal the tax and it is determined the current market value is actually greater, it can (but rarely will) hike the tax. So don't make an appeal until you are confident that you have a valid case. Confused? There are many firms who will file the appeal on your behalf for all, or a percentage of, the first-year reduction. But, it is often best to learn to make the appeal process yourself. And, if the assessor refuses to lower it, sue the taxing body; this will require that three or four government taxing bodies to retain a lawyer. Normally, they will settle the lawsuit with a compromised reduction before you step into a courtroom. The squeaky wheel gets the oil.

Restoration Tax Credits

Become familiar with the U.S. Department of the Interior, National Park Service and the Historical Preservation Certification Application in order to receive handsome restoration tax credits, not only for yourself but also for investors you may secure. Here are some factors of this playing field:

• Some properties may be within the "historical district" of your town. If they are, having them certified is a relatively simple process. If they are not within a district, having them certified is still an important step in ownership and worth the time and trouble of facing bureaucratic red tape by completing the applications.

• Architecture isn't the only criteria to be considered for certification. I once had a ho-hum building approved because it was the site of a scandalous murder. Make your application interesting.

• Work up the history yourself. Most communities have an "Inventory Sheet" that will provide relevant data surrounding the property; they can usually be obtained from your local historical society. While this provincial group may flex its muscles, grit your teeth and cooperate with them. They usually have no real authority and most members don't ever personally complete a historical project; they just talk about them and tell you how to spend your money. However, they're a well-intended lot.

• If you've not yet come to appreciate the importance of preserving our heritage or haven't enjoyed the proud satisfaction of owning a beautiful old building, then do it for the money. There's a 20 percent dollar-for-dollar tax credit available for construction and long-term preservation costs if the property is certified. Recently I observed an acquaintance spend $1 million on an uncertified historical property; he threw away $200,000.

• It is a myth that if you have a building certified the government will dictate specifications and make it almost impossible to rehabilitate. While there will be guidelines, they are normally practical and in good taste. If too costly or restrictive, you will seek a variance.

• The key historical word is "preservation." The goal is to maintain, in an appropriate manner, the style and existing design, not necessarily to return it to its original condition. Therefore, a new roof could qualify for tax credits if it will protect the property.

• You may be referred to individuals who prepare applications; they often charge $5,000. But you can do this yourself. As Earl Nightingale said, "We all walk in the dark and each of us must learn to turn on his own light." Part One of the application is called an Evaluation of Significance and Part Two is called a Description of Rehabilitation. They come with instructions and the state provides staff that will guide you through the process. Call on government employees to help do your job; they're not overworked.

• Often there are design review committees or members of a local historical society who may be willing to assist with the design process. There are often 50 percent matching grants that will pay for façade improvements, awnings and sign costs.

• Your property will be more attractive and more valuable to both buyers and investors after it has been properly and tastefully rehabilitated.

• You should begin with the state application before you commence rehabilitation work. Once approved, you will file with the federal government in order to qualify for the tax credits.

• While the property is to be inspected after completion in order to qualify, that step rarely occurs.

Finding a Deal

In 1998 my wife and I flew to Florida to sell a golf driving range to a Mr. McDonald. We met for lunch in a Tampa hotel. We ventured into the dining room and sat with a Ronald McDonald and his aide. Soon guests came by seeking his autograph, so of course, we asked, "Why?" He responded, "I'm Ronald McDonald." I said, "I know that. But why do they want your autograph?" He said, "Because I am THE Ronald McDonald." How would we have known without red hair and big shoes? Sure enough, he was a family member of Richard and Maurice, who founded the chain. Extremely congenial and certainly no clown, Ronald was preparing to start a new foodservice venture because the family restrictive covenants had expired; it was to be called "Mad Mac's International." He would retrofit four ships to visit seaports and offer a floor with fine dining, a casino, a playland and of course, a hamburger shop. The vessel would float from city to city, keeping the concept fresh at each port-o-call. That idea transcended into a freestanding burger chain and went public.

We spent the afternoon looking at real estate and burger shops while he talked about recipes, origins of the Golden Arches, franchises that offer the healthiest items and other topics contained in his book, *The Complete Hamburger — The History of America's Favorite Sandwich*. It was a delightful afternoon and certainly had nothing to do with a driving range; he wanted the land. The plan others have for real estate may have nothing to do with your ideas. So erase all of your thoughts on motives, realtor's opinions and all of the other unconfirmed seemingly rational reasons you think there is, or isn't, a deal to be had. Buy some junk on a high-traffic corner, collect enough rent to meet your mortgage payment and then wait for Starbucks to buy it for twenty times your purchase price. Ronald McDonald never really had an interest in the driving range . . . he wanted 50 building lots.

Location, Location, Location

While many are tired of this over-used phrase, location is certainly a major decision factor for your investment decisions. Consider factors such as bus routes, airports, geography, nearness to your market, labor supplies, availability of raw materials and anticipated future growth of the area. Talk with other business people because there are often idiosyncrasies associated with buildings, neighborhoods and cities. For example, you might find that a river will create two separate commerce markets in the same city, or tenants in the building you're considering roast on hot days because the mechanical system was not properly engineered. These are the factors you need to understand before you make a purchase.

The Wonderful World of Realtors

Everything is negotiable. By now, I trust you've come to appreciate the need to study both the art and science of negotiations. Whether you're buying or selling, you must be sharp because this is the sales agent's profession. These are some real estate dynamics that you may not find in "how-to" books:

If Buying:

• Brokers typically work for the seller. If they claim to have the best interest of both the seller and buyer at heart, remember that no professional can truly serve two masters. Yet, the "dual-agent" concept was born. In reality, brokers represent the deal to get paid, and they will beat the seller or buyer up or down in order to chin up to the closing table. There are times they may act for an undisclosed principal who desires to remain anonymous. That would be me.

• Retain a buyer's agent. This will cost the seller's agent half of the commission. It may annoy the seller's agent but gain you a smidgen of representation. Since the seller pays the commission, you get a free agent.

• Make lots of offers with $500 refundable good faith or earnest money deposits and a host of contingencies, especially contingencies that are within your direct control. While some states require earnest money checks actually be deposited, some agents will simply hold your check to first get the seller's response.

• Consider 10 buildings that may suit your business needs or be a viable investment property. Don't waste your valuable time chit-chatting with agents. Instead, ask a ringer-friend (someone who makes an offer at, say 60 percent, of the listed price) to make an offer — sometimes referred to as a "straw offer" — even if it will likely be rejected. Then you make an offer on the same property at 70 percent of the listed price. All of a sudden, your offer is more palatable. Keep in mind that sellers will often list for 30 percent more than the property is worth. You need to be as ruthless and unreasonable as them. If your offer is accepted or countered, it's time for you to bring contractors through the building to determine level of your seriousness. You, not a pushy Realtor, should control the process.

• Your ringer-friend will request the right to assign. I wanted a very important property and knew the seller would never deal with me because of a prior confrontation. And, I knew he would attempt to capitalize on deep pockets. So I had an associate make the offer, and it was accepted. The seller "smelled a rat," but because it was an all cash deal with no contingencies, he had to sell or face specific performance litigation. He was infuriated upon learning I was the real buyer, yet the deal went down. We've since become civil to each other (since we both made money).

• In any transaction, "he who holds the checkbook calls the shots." As we saw in the 2008 market debacle, values can go down as quickly as they go up so it's imperative that you buy properties at the lowest possible price, including foreclosures and bankruptcies. As Midas Muffler's slogan says, "Don't pay too much for that muffler."

• Attend county tax sales. Some are sheriff's sales that may carry with them liens and encumbrances whereas others are judicial sales that may provide a clear title. If you want to buy at a tax sale, make certain you undertake a lien search to determine how many people are above you on the totem pole.

• Run a cheap classified ad:

"Willing to pay full price for your investment property with flexible terms and minimal down payment. Other collateral available. Save Realtor's commission. Call Jack."

This type of ad may attract "don't wanners," anxious to sell and get out from under the property. And, you may need to give them the title to your truck to sweeten the deal. Just make sure the "don't wanner" doesn't want it because of hidden problems that will become your own.

Watch for investor-sellers who are approaching retirement, absentee owners or those with trauma in their life — and be the first person to talk to them or send a cold-call letter. Monitor death notices, auctions and divorce filings. Encourage lawyers to apprise you of these occurrences and explain that you would want he or she to handle future acquisitions so there is a hope for a long-term relationship.

• There may be mortgage financing available without resorting to a third-party mortgage lender, with the seller acting as lender-mortgagee for the transaction. This arrangement is called a "purchase money mortgage." Under this arrangement, the seller conveys ownership interest to the buyer and as part payment of the purchase price, takes back from the buyer a promissory note or bond secured by a mortgage on the property.

• Always ask for owner financing, and don't depend on an agent to sell the concept; they are market-oriented, not investment-savvy. Smart agents attempt to keep the parties away from each other — but you must insist on being in this loop to relay all the financial benefits to sellers. (See Chapter 6) Make friends with the seller; he will be more flexible with a friend than an unknown entity who wears the face of an agent.

• Lower your offer but agree to share in the Realtor's commission, pay all of the transfer taxes/stamps and assume other expenses that are normally prorated to make your offer "sound good."

• Research the time your target property has been on the market. It can easily require one year to move a commercial building. Unless you recognize the deal is sizzling, don't exhibit signs of being anxious. Leaving a month or two between offers can be worth tens of thousands of dollars.

• Ignore the traditional 5 percent vacancy factor reported on the seller's Income Statement and replace it with the actual or a more reliable percentage. Is the current rental income achievable long-term? Sellers' hide repair costs; compare them with maintenance needs and industry standards. Sneak in a conversation with the maintenance man; he will gladly spew out every defect in the building.

• If the building has not been reassessed recently, or if there have been recent improvements, project higher taxes.

• Talk to neighbors and the local code officer. You need to dig for gems and uncover the adversary's weaknesses.

If Selling:

- Shop the agency. Tell them you want to review the regional Board of Realtors Sales Report depicting which agents and agencies are selling the most commercial properties. They usually tell you they can't share that information with the public, but they'll eventually cave in (especially the star producers). If your agent objects, he's a loser.

- The more agents in the agency, the better. In order to receive 100 percent of a commission, agents tend to keep their own listings "in house," so you want to list with the most successful agency; it will be more incentivized to expose you to more potential buyers.

- Select the star commercial agents; they have different talents than residential agents.

- Franchised agencies may attract buyers out of the area; local agencies may lack national prospecting networks. Research the franchise success as well as the agent and agency's success. For example, RE/MAX agents pay a monthly expense contribution fee to the broker, as opposed to sharing the commission, so those agents are oftentimes more aggressive because they retain a bigger piece of the pie.

- Ask the agent to cut their commission when they ask you to lower the asking price, or after an offer is received. Even your own agent should never believe that you are anxious to sell.

- Beware of listing maniacs. They are easy to detect because they have signs posted on every commercial property in town. That is because they send postcards and telemarket, offering to list anything at any price. Next, they sit back and pray to God that other agents will do all of the legwork, sell something, and then, out of the sky, a commission check will float down upon their desk. They have no interest in showing or closing a deal – only collecting. Oddly enough, they are perceived as being more aggressive.

Navigating the Business Swamp

• Agents aren't just required to advise you that their commissions are negotiable, they really are. Representing that you may sell yourself or list elsewhere tends to drop the standard commission. The danger is that if you negotiate too low, only your listing Realtor will become aggressive because the split commission will be a deterrent to outside agents.

• The listing agent may hiss when you offer to pay only a four percent commission – while offering thousands of dollars as a bonus to the selling agent. This very non-traditional little plot keeps your total commission down while at the same time, adequately rewards those hundreds of outside agents who might find and close a deal.

• Don't blindly sign the "standard" listing contract Realtors obtain from their real estate Association; read it carefully. More often than not, it will grant the agency and agent indemnification for almost anything that occurs with the transaction. Why should they be indemnified if they are at fault? Strike it and anything else that you don't like. Insert a sentence that reads you can cancel the listing with a 30-day notice.

• When Realtors tell you they "have a buyer," it's usually a lie. Just say, "no problem, I'll give you a buyer-specific non-exclusive Listing Agreement," so you're protected with your one buyer. I once owned a large agency. Trust me, they don't have a buyer.

• Demand a detailed explanation of how the agent intends to market your property and an identification of the specific media with frequency. Make it a condition of the Listing Agreement.

• The Realtor's bag of tricks is full, including the market analysis. They are not appraisers and they can only give you a "ballpark" value. They may estimate low because they would rather sell it quickly at your loss. So add their commission and an extra cushion percentage on the top of their estimate of value. You can always drop. Ignore their comment, "If it's too high, it won't move." Test the market. Go in high. When prices eventually drop it actually attracts more attention to the property.

• Conversely, some agents list substantially over market to make the seller feel better, and then, after the ink is dry, start banging them down to a lower number or worse, let it set for three months until their client becomes discouraged with no showings. Some unscrupulous agents traipse non-qualified buyers into the property so the  seller believes they are actually trying. This cheap maneuver normally occurs right before the Listing Agreement is about to expire.

• Ask the agent to add a provision that says you will finance to qualified buyers with a small down payment. That will neutralize a higher listed price and bring you more prospects. This could violate a "due on sale" clause in your first mortgage; be aware of that dilemma. Generally, owner-financing will increase the selling price, relieve you of management duties, provide a higher interest rate than other investments, expose your offer to more potential buyers and delay transfer, capital gains or other taxes. Determine if the buyer has any other personal or real property that you can encumber in order to increase your collateral.

• Structure your first private sale with an accountant and an attorney. You may be able to defer capital gains' taxes and obtain favorable terms on others. Recent Stimulus Act laws provide for stepped-up depreciation on assets, so there are times the sales' price allocation to various assets can be critical. Sell your property with a Deed in Lieu of Foreclosure so you would own it upon default. Or, in the alternative, require the deed be held by your lawyer in escrow. More importantly, remember this. I didn't know any of these tricks or precautions when I made my first purchase at age 20. I just scraped up the deposit and bought the damn thing.

Navigating the Business Swamp

In my early twenties, I attempted to buy a vacant food market and two apartments for $80,000. A local Realtor, who I believed was a trusted mentor, initially pushed to close the deal but then suddenly gave me some 'fatherly advice." He said that after thinking about it, the risk was too high because the food market space was vacant. I took his advice and backed away from the deal. Three weeks later I drove by to find backhoes demolishing the building. One of the heavy equipment operators informed me that McDonald's bought the land. Sales agents, summed up. As stakes rise, greed follows.

If these comments seem edgy or pessimistic, and if you think you can trust Realtors or believe they won't deal under your terms, you're mistaken. However, they must win too. Agents can be very helpful by providing financing sources, documents and data. They can also act as a neutral "go between" if your deal begins to crumble. If you're active, you'll be a volume client — you'll treat them with respect and you'll go out of your way to send them business. Be tough, but fair. I worked with one agent who I truly put through the paces. She was smart and always tried to accommodate me. I knew of a large transaction and hand-delivered the buyer to her office. Her commission was $138,000. Tell them straight out, "You may not make a lot of money on my deals but I will bring you other business." Then, do it.

Is The Flip Game Profitable?

Economists say the pure buy low/ sell high situation is when you buy at wholesale and sell at retail without having to wait for appreciation. While reality TV shows have dubbed it "the flip," savvy investors have been applying that practice forever. It isn't easy, but it can be done. It requires a keen sense of value on the part of the investor, coupled with the ability to move the property quickly.

Recently I purchased a speculative a property for $127,000. There were no tenant prospects. Six months later a bank called and purchased it for $375,000. Then, to meet the IRS one-year capital gains holding requirement, I leased it with the option to purchase. But just as with land that is producing no cash flow, this game is for the buyer who is able to absorb holding costs. You are not going to experience many deals with this rapid rate of return, so buy properties with existing cash flow and only play the flip game after you're established, or if you're a hands-on contractor with extra time on your hands.

Some creative real estate investors implore a modification of the flip. Under this little known strategy, you execute an assignable purchase contract directly with the property owner. Under the contract you have 90 days to close with the understanding you'll market it to others and if you are able to resell it, you'll keep any sum over the price you contracted to pay. Next you plaster yard signs all over town and hold open houses, or "auctions." If your seller wants $60,000 and you sell it for $90,000 because of your marketing expertise, you keep the $30,000 gain – five times more than a Realtor would earn on the same transaction. Like the Realtor, you only have marketing costs at risk. Unlike the Realtor, you do not need a license because you're selling something that you are buying. While the reward is greater with this flip, the risk increases as many sellers are not ecstatic when you earn $30,000 in only 90 days, and they may try to renege or do an "end-run" to the ultimate buyer. Also, don't expect Realtors to embrace your little maneuver, either. These non-traditional approaches can work only if you are creative, energetic and a nonconformist. This is the real estate version of the pyramid game. You try to make money on others with no investment.

Isn't Land a Good Investment?

"They're not making any more of it" or "land always increases in value," are two proverbs that have recently gained some credence as the burgeoning gas industry creates "shale-ionaires" throughout Northeast states. But they will, more often than not, initially steer you in the wrong direction. Speculation on land is more risky than playing the slots. It's referred to as the Alligator Investment because debt service can eat you up. Pre-developed land projections often depict a 50 percent return. In my experience, the unknown infrastructure and holding costs will more often drive it into a negative. While there may be a high potential for gain, most novice developers are disappointed. When you buy land, you simply buy the opportunity to incur risk.

Wait — How Do I Buy Real Estate If I Don't Have Any Money?

Leverage, or the use of borrowed funds, is the key to building wealth in the real estate game. By borrowing as much as you can, a small amount of cash can give you access to a lot of real estate. While some believe borrowing should be avoided, in a situation where the property produces a positive income, you can enjoy appreciation and tax benefits as the loan is repaid. Your goal should be to break into the game as soon as possible — then worry about whether or not you can make a reasonable down payment.

Remember that putting little or nothing down doesn't always mean the seller receives nothing down; it only means the payment doesn't come from you. It means that you need to find the right seller, be creative and practice your negotiation skills.

One way to leverage is to use the "paper-out" strategy. This is when the seller reduces the sales price in an amount equal to his equity and you then pay him that equity back over time. This will greatly increase your ability to obtain conventional financing because the loan-to-value ratio will improve, and there could be some tax benefits for both parties. However, if the bank asks the question whether there is any side-financing, admit it. Realtors must reveal the side obligation. Two of my sales agents had their licenses suspended and paid large fines because they withheld knowledge of a second loan.

Some buyers offer to pay more for the real estate in exchange for a lower down payment. Others finance all or part of their down payment with the seller. But whatever trick you invent, the real winner simply thinks out-of-the-box, and tailors his terms to fit the needs of the parties and the transaction.

After a friend retired from a bank lending board, he disclosed the slang term bestowed upon me by our local banking industry: "The Leverage King." He thought I might be offended but I took the designation as a compliment! Starting with little money, I managed to acquire, develop and then sell-off the largest private real estate package in the history of my hometown county. A high-leverage model was my key to make small down payments so I could buy more properties–faster.

Borrowing from friends and family can be a win-win, especially when prime rate interest rates are low. You could substantially increase the return on their money by offering over-market interest rates.

Effective negotiation may convince sellers to accept personal property as down payments, the assignment of cash values of life insurance or equity in land or other real estate. Ask the seller to grant a lease-option or time to make the down payment, which may well come from tenant income. If you close at the end of the month as opposed to after the date rents have been paid, you can utilize tenant income for that first month. Or, assume the seller's existing mortgage and then offer him a mortgage for some of his equity, thereby lowering your down payment. It is more important to sell yourself to potential sellers than struggling over perceived transaction roadblocks. Many people will be enamored with your ingenuity.

Finding Money for Investment

Pay attention. I'm about to explain how to get rich with my own proven model. Let's begin with these all too familiar circumstances. You just graduated, or not. You're broke. You foolishly swiped credit cards, and drove your credit score down to 480. But, you want to be rich. You believe you have what it takes to be an entrepreneur and you've got the brains and the balls, but no backing. You don't have a Realtor's license and you don't want one anyway, just to compete with a few hundred other people. But you may not realize that doctors and other professionals often need a safe place to put their money.

Some of these circumstances led me to investigate distressed properties and then, at the courthouse or from nearby tenants, I discovered who owned them. One of the properties had 20 apartments and seven retail stores — all vacant! A former "developer" remodeled one apartment to show it to the surgeon-owner in order to fraudulently access his cash. The thief never installed any electrical or plumbing to the apartment, but charged the good doctor $110,000 to present one attractive and "completed" unit.

I made a cold call to the doctor and explained that I develop "troubled and historical projects." He called other physician friends and we held our first meeting. I made a glossy presentation and convinced them I could rehab the building and fill it with tenants. I would pay my share of the upfront cost over time and dilute their investment by 20 percent for a "value-added" benefit, which we will refer to as an "equity kicker," in exchange for (i) my development expertise (ii) elimination of the typical 15 percent overhead and profit a contractor would charge and (iii) avoidance of a six percent commission the owner would pay a Realtor to dispose of the property. In addition, I would receive 8 percent of the rental income as an owner-manager. We prepared a Partnership Agreement and funded the project. This relationship gave me access to other physician-investors. Here's why this strategy was a success:

- Doctors only believe other doctors. They will accept physician advice on taxes and law over their own accountant or lawyer because they think they are smarter than most. They probably are. So, if you prove yourself to a few doctors and do the right thing, physician referrals will keep you funded forever.

- I worked tirelessly and treated their project with more care and concern than if it were my own.

- I documented everything so they fully understood all aspects of the development, construction and leasing phases of the project — and to protect myself.

- I placed properties on the National Register of Historical Places and structured the deal so they were "active" investors who could enjoy lucrative tax credits.

- Their friendship and trust was as important to me as the money.

As shown in the Return on Investment chart at the beginning of the chapter, "equity kicker" is an upfront gain transferred to you, as the developer, for finding and syndicating the project. Imagine, you own 20 percent of the real estate out of the gate! The investors enjoy a reasonable, safe return in a local project they can see and touch and you lock into an ongoing cash stream with long-term ownership.

"You have to spend money to make money." Even though non-discretionary cash was tight at that time in my career, my foot was in the doctor door, so I gathered all my new physician-clients and their friends for a very unusual experience to cement our relationship. We began with a champagne party and string quartet at my home. Next, 136 guests boarded a leased railroad train fully equipped with a bar and bluegrass band. We traveled to a gourmet restaurant for a fabulous dinner and entertainment. Everyone had a memorable evening. By the end of the event, a half-dozen more physicians set an appointment to invest. Wham! I was a fully funded real estate developer with one cold call and a rented train.

Never allow intimidation to stop you from exploration. We are all mesmerized by the healthcare world. Yet, I mixed neurosurgeons with bricklayers at the party. Think of it this way. You can make a lot more money than a doctor, and many doctors want to be businesspeople. Today, a family practitioner out of training annually earns $80,000 to $120,000; when they are established, the total income might creep up to $200,000. To do this, they may work long ER hours and often have 2,800 annual patient encounters, or one every eight minutes. Healthcare criminals (people in suits disguised as health insurance providers), through capitation and other controls, deliver nothing to patients but instead, reduce physician income. Now physician assistants perform many of the same services for $60,000 per year, lessening demand for the family doctor. Without creative accounting or investments, the government takes a good third of the doctor's income.

The U.S. Department of Agriculture says it takes $250,000 to raise a child to 18, and doctors' children routinely attend private schooling, which can be $140,000, per child, for the first four years. Most family practitioners must service their own student loan debt. The family shuns anything less than an S-Class Benz, and its mortgage payments probably equal the median income in your county. They're oftentimes broke with little left over for retirement, let alone investments. So, include them, but focus on specialist physicians and then partner-up. You, as a real estate investor, can make more money than a doctor by owning an office building that you visit four times per year to make certain it's still standing upright.

Doctors are your real bankers. Partner with just one, and prove that you have their best interest at heart. The investment will allow them to brag to all their country club friends about the things they own. They love investments like golf courses, hotels, restaurants, land deals and vacation-market properties.

If one doctor says yes, your first decision and early choice of ownership should be based on your long-term plans to own and operate real estate. You may want to consider a joint venture, or a special type of general partnership formed by investors for the purpose of owning a specific property or set of properties. While a joint venture is similar in most respects to a general partnership and is usually treated as such in many states, there is no intention on the part of the investors to enter into a continuing partnership relationship or to assume general partnership obligations and liabilities. You will find that your physician-investors and types of investments will change throughout time.

Syndicator, Developer & Entrepreneur

Whatever legal entity you select to do business, you've now become a syndicator! You, or an organization you will form, will purchase real estate investments that you identify, acquire and manage for the group. Syndication can be defined as a device by which a real estate professional – the syndicator or sponsor – obtains investors who provide the funds required to engage in a real estate enterprise. Some people consider it to be a legal form of ownership; others view it as a type of financing – one that offers smaller investors the opportunity to invest in real estate ventures that would otherwise be beyond their financial and management capabilities. It will be easier to pick up a physician's check if you are Crystal Real Estate Associates than if you're Bob Smith.

You'll produce, or borrow the basics from one of the big players, a brochure touting all of the benefits such as local ownership, appreciation in value, tax credits, diversification and other investment factors. But your real first step is finding the property, finding a willing seller, leveraging, preparing a financial forecast for that property, and then taking it to wealthier private investors.

"All of life is a stage." I love young guys and gals who have big ideas and talk about being in the real estate business even before they've closed the first deal. It's that mental attitude and conquering FUD that is the true ingredient for success — not the science of it all!

Drive around your community and search for distressed properties with potential. And if you've subscribed to the entrepreneur work ethic, this is something you can do while you operate another business or hold down a full-time job. Research the ownership and prepare a proposal for those absentee owners, busy professionals, widows or others who simply cannot manage their properties.

Or, nudge your way into the sandbox with another nontraditional strategy. In most states, you can't legally manage a property unless you are a licensed broker, so convince the owner to transfer one percent of their holdings to you and now you're legal! Tell them you will absorb all of their management headaches but you want an option to purchase 25 percent of the building over time. Or, accept in-kind ownership for your energy and expertise. Make it up as you go. There are no rules. You're an actor. People deal with people. People will adapt your plan.

One of the most interesting characters I've ever met is a Rockefeller descendant. He carried a stuffed monkey into one of my restaurants, bought it dinner and carried on a conversation as though it were human. As a pastime, he flies a Russian MIG fighter jet around our town. Obviously, cash flow is not his problem. While one of the most likable men I've ever met, he wasn't the most astute businessman. He bought a building to house his new car dealership, which ultimately failed. The building sat vacant for years.

One day I drove by and cold called him. I offered to work on the project at no charge but if I found a tenant, he would be required to transfer ownership in the real estate. Within 90 days, I signed a car dealership lease and received equity in a million-dollar property. You need to be convincing and show a desire to benefit the other party. These paradigms will only come to fruition if you do a heckuva job and your modus operandi is "win-win."

Whether you want to invest in a few properties, find a way to syndicate or whether you want to actually become a real estate developer, you're on your way to becoming an Intrapreneur! This personality type is one level above those characteristics described in Chapter 1. Here you need guts. This is not a game for the weak. You must not only look beyond immediate challenges; you must be completely focused and driven to succeed.

The true real estate developer is often a successful real estate broker or contractor who understands the necessity to be familiar with financial data. Now your narcissistic characteristics will blossom, you'll recognize the fact that trampling on everyone from city planners to property owners to the government is simply a way of life for you. During part of my master's thesis research, it became clear the temperament of a real estate developer is unlike most all other personalities. So think about whether or not this is a compatible field for you considering your work and behavioral tendencies.

Offer a Mortgage

If cash is tight, offer a Purchase Money Mortgage to sellers as part of the purchase transaction. Alternatively, offer the seller a Balloon Mortgage, which is a short-term mortgage with a final payment to retire the balance coming as one large installment at the end of the term. But if your doctors are on board, you can have more fun by purchasing bad loans. Here's how it works.

Few entrepreneurs consider purchasing paper instead of properties. Suppose you've located a distressed property and you know or suspect the owner is experiencing financial difficulties. Go to the courthouse and learn who holds the mortgage. If a lending institution, it will typically have a workout department, or what they like to call a "special assets" division. This department is staffed by a bunch of meanies whose performance depends on bringing home troubled loan obligations under any means.

Institutions regulated by the FDIC need to report delinquent debts.

Contact one of these bankers and tell them you're interested in purchasing the mortgage. If they respond positively, start talking, and ultimately make an offer. You'll need cash to play this game, but isn't it better to buy a mortgage at half-off, own it at its full face value and collect interest than to pay retail? You can now afford to "re-do" the loan to the borrower. If the mortgagee is not able to pay, you too may need to foreclose in the future.

If you decide to buy a mortgage, you must have counsel "scrub the deal." If the lender is in first lien position, it may be a great opportunity. If the borrower performs, you just doubled your money, plus interest. If they file bankruptcy, you'll spend some of that gain on legal fees.

I once represented a divorcée who owned a business with her husband; it was purchased with her family's money. The husband, unbeknownst to his wife, placed the stock in his name and didn't think it should be part of their eventual property settlement. No, you don't need to be a lawyer to represent a client to negotiate a financial settlement for a fee.

Next, to throw some gas on the dispute, the husband dated his brother-in-law's wife! Because of that we'll call the brother-in-law Frank Furious. Frank was mad as hell and I was batting zero with my attempts to reach an amicable property settlement. The company's mortgage was in arrears so I suggested to Frank that he buy the mortgage! The bank wanted out. I drove to the bank's special assets department and handed over a check for 70 percent of the debt. They took the cash, my client profited 30 percent overnight, and then held the leverage to force the property settlement. It was a financial chess game. So, if you want to own or control a business or real estate, don't buy it; buy its mortgage!

Conversely, if you're experiencing financial trouble, be careful. You can lose your company or real estate to a shark like Furious Frank overnight and never feel it coming.

How to Protect Yourself from Contractor Abuse

Unless you're a contractor, you're at a disadvantage in owning properties because you are always at the mercy of others. You will often find that contractors own real estate because they steal materials from other jobs, perform the labor for half the market rate and utilize their crew during slow times. If you're a contractor, you should clearly be in the real estate business. For the rest of us, we are your dinner.

Recall, I've already apologized for generalizations. Unless you're a hands-on person or working smaller projects, most real estate investors can't do business without contractors. Except for trying to keep employees happy, it is often the most distasteful relationship you will encounter. So, here are some ideas that might prevent you from getting the "short end of the stick":

1. Unless they come with an office, employees, references, insurance and equipment, most contractors are bandits. They hold more debt than you and are looking for someone to dig them out of it. They rarely generate a profit because their skillset isn't running a business. So, they buy a pad of one-page proposal sheets and try to do business with Post-it-Notes and a shoebox. This can be good for you because when they try to screw you, which they will inevitably do, you'll be wearing protection with a contract*.

Just as landlords may tell you, you'll tell them, "it's your standard contract" because you retain a lot of contractors; this will start the salivation process, especially if it is their off-season. Those contractors who can barely read will just sign it, while others may want revisions. But no matter what most people believe, most sign it "as is" and as individuals — even if they are a corporation. They already mentally spent your deposit. Of course, if they have no assets, you'll never recover your loss so it's important to monitor the drawdown of funds.

2. Decide how you want to pay them:

• A lump-sum bid. This allows you to maintain a budget and limit cost overruns. It can be the preferred approach if you obtain three bids and then apply my "92-percent rule" to the lowest bid. However, contractors usually build-in a cushion because most projects contain hidden costs. So, the guaranteed limit may ultimately come as an expense to you with incomplete work.

• Time and material. Don't do it. They are going to be working on other projects while billing two people for the same hours and they'll pad the hours. This arrangement keeps them in your nice, comfortable building and delays completion times.

• Time, with a "not to exceed," plus material. This is my favorite for various reasons. First, they're quick to accept it because they don't know how to estimate costs in the first place. This approach will give you an idea of what the job is really worth — as you "nail them" on the estimate. Here's how the conversation between an owner ("O") and contractor "(C") will often unfold:

O: How long do you think it will take to do the job?

C: We can knock it out in 10 days! (This means six weeks.)

O: Now tell me, what is the hourly rate for you and your crew?

C: I get $30 an hour, my electricians get $25 and the illegal immigrants get $16.

O: How many will be working during the 10 days?

C: Me, two electricians and four laborers. (This means half of them.)

O: Okay, that sounds fair. Now you said the total job will be $38,000, right? How much of that is material anyway?

C: $19,000.

O: Sounds about right. (They don't know. Someone once told them materials are about half). Well I understand it's difficult to know how much time it will take to do the job, so why don't we do this? I'll buy all of the material. You just give me a copy of the invoice (there goes his 15 percent overhead and profit on materials) and I'll pay the suppliers directly (this may dissuade them from charging materials on your job they plan to use on other jobs) and I'll pay the labor each week.

C: Okay. Can I get the deposit today?

Do the math: 10 days is 80 man hours. The contractor should receive $2,400 (even though he won't be there half the time), two electricians are $4,000 and laborers are $5,120, or $11,520 plus 17 percent for payroll taxes and insurance for a total labor cost of $13,478. The materials are what they are. In your follow-up meeting, tell the contractor you'll pay his wage rate with a "not to exceed" of $13,478 plus materials at cost. He will now realize he quoted you $5,522 more than the math conclusion. Watch him try to squirm out of that one! Don't feel bad though, because he already doubled the hourly rates and should be making a profit of $5,760. Just say that your math indicates he will be paid the rate he requested and if that isn't acceptable, you'll need time to obtain three bids. He won't want that.

3. Never verbally change the scope of work. This is the contractor's "get out of bid free" card. They often lowball the quote knowing full well you will want or need to change specifications, thereby creating the golden opportunity for them to quadruple their cost of labor*.

4. If you must have the work completed on a strict timeline, include a liquidated damages provision so you can fine them each

day they are late. Contractors' rarely adhere to start and finish dates. Excluding large firms with oversight and ramrods, they'll drink beer over lunch and only work about 75 percent of the time. That is why that when you visit the jobsite, they are always "out for materials."

5. Before you sign, demand the names and numbers of their last two customers and then actually call for a reference. Make sure it's not their brother-in-law; inspect the workmanship.

6. Before anyone picks up a hammer, require that a Certificate of Insurance and Waiver of Mechanics Lien be received and signed; have it signed by sub-contractors. Under the "New York System," a subcontractor is limited in the amount that can be collected by the amount due the contractor from the owner. Under the "Pennsylvania System," the subcontractor has the right to file a mechanic's lien for labor performed even though the entire contract price has been paid by the owner to the contractor.

7. Scores of contractor notices, Mechanics Lien conditions and dozens of other state laws could supersede the terms of the sample contract*, so have your agreement reviewed by an attorney. Even if you know a reliable contractor, you should develop your own set of documents to do business. Document everything!

There can be situations where you should bend. Create "tight" deals and be in a position to make concessions when circumstances warrant. Contractors often admit they made bidding mistakes or experienced problems they simply couldn't predict. That is the time to be fair and pay more than your contract requires. Everyone needs to make a profit.

Beware of Scammers

If I convinced the naiveté to trust no one in Chapter 1, you should survive con artists who can truly destroy you long-term.

A North Carolina surgeon requested I assist in recovering several hundred thousand dollars she paid to a contractor to build a new Hikau home. I made a surprise pilgrimage to California to meet the old devil. I found that he owned nothing but a desk and a 10-year-old Jaguar. He lived with his mother. He hadn't undertaken any construction in a decade. These tales of woe are meant to reinforce the fact that you cannot trust anyone, and there are very slick scammers all around you. Other scammers brought me wild deals to consider because my doctor clients pay so much income tax and all tax avoidance investments sound enticing. Many scam deals are hydrocarbon investments which combine three tax credits that make it sound good even if they discover no gas or oil. Likewise, questionable real estate investments may sound enticing to the highly taxed.

Some of my partners purchased Texas real estate, financed 100 percent by using their credit rating and collateral. The scammer said he needed nothing down — only their signature. He would first purchase, then flip the properties in one year, for a gain, while during the interim, the doctors would receive all of the tax credits and rental income. That year came and went, leaving the investors with no principal recovery and only debt. In one case, the obligation was $1,900,000 due a Savings and Loan Association.

I began to make actual site visits to investigate the transactions and inspect the properties, only to find some condominiums sold to my clients for $160,000 were run-down cement block boxes in depressed neighborhoods. Ultimately I learned that one of the brokers was a disbarred lawyer working with another group of lawyers who owned savings and loan associations. They paid-off appraisers to overstate values and based on those documents, sold the properties to my clients, pocketed the money and left behind a pile of junk.

During this time, Texas was in a recession due to the peso exchange rate and S&L and oil crisis. Real estate wasn't worth a fourth of its former appraised value, as pawnshop cases were overrun with Rolex watches.

I retained a litigator and began to file government complaints and civil lawsuits against those who sold the over-valued and depressed properties. Soon, the FBI requested I meet with them at a post office in Beaumont, Texas, and I complied. With little knowledge of the purpose of the meeting, I recall that day well. The storms in Texas are as big as the state. By the time I reached the post office, water was gushing from my shoes. Drenched, I was escorted to the basement in a room with about 10 agents, who began to ask questions about my knowledge of the oil and real estate deals. By this time I had accumulated a good amount of information. Soon thereafter I found myself in Dallas, wearing a wire and meeting with dishonest brokers, bankers and lawyers in restaurants. The scammer's offer: I was to bring them physician investors and for each one delivered, I would be paid $200,000. I recall them handing me one prospectus for a nightclub. The slick brochure made this place look like Hollywood's Highland Club. Curious, I did a drive-by to find an old frame barroom.

Next, I was commissioned to write a report for the FBI. I completed the six-inch-thick documents, shipped them off and heard little about the outcome. I did get one phone call; the agent said he could not release specific information, but thought I might want to know they were indicting some of the players, and the key crook died from AIDS.

This did not solve my client's dilemma. So I began the process of selling off the properties to recover as much cash as possible. And, there was one nice complex in the bundle. By this time, the FDIC had assumed the notes from the crooked savings and loan associations. So, off to the FDIC I went and struck a deal: we would pay them $1.8 million for 48 deluxe condominiums known as Inwood Place. I invested in the project, under the same model explained earlier in this chapter, and raised the capital. We paid $200,000 down and signed a Sales Agreement — with the government. We were preparing to close when a newly created bureaucratic ape known as the Resolution Trust Corp. usurped the FDIC and took control of all the assets. They sent our deposit back and said the price wasn't high enough and they did not need to honor the FDIC contract because they had sovereign immunity!

Of course, my clients were distraught because this one deal would have lessened losses on the other transactions. So, I retained an attorney, ultimately paid him $200,000 and we sued the government. It settled. I purchased the units and leased them for seven years. The then-Charlie's Angel Jacqueline Smith purchased an adjacent country club and poured millions of dollars into the facility at the request of her father. This drove the value of our condominiums up, and I sold them off for a substantial gain.

In another debacle, seven physicians retained me to travel to Nags Head, N.C., because they purchased 21 piles of sand drudged from Roanoke Sound, which someone labeled as "cays." The cays were "free" because the government simply needed a place to dump sand. After a two-year effort, I unraveled the entire real estate mess to learn a broker sold the cays as developable, knowing that utilities could not be provided. The engineer falsified reports on the ability to build, the appraiser over-stated values, the bank only made the loan because of seven doctor signatures and a lawyer, with few scruples, orchestrated the deal. An audit revealed the son of one of the doctor investors was stealing money to support himself. And you wonder why I'm a bit untrusting? There are scammers everywhere!

What are the lessons? First, just as in other arenas, there are slick real estate scam artists who can destroy your future. Any deal "too good to be true" isn't true. Never bite on tax credit deals without ample cash flow. Next, there are crooked brokers, bankers, lawyers and appraisers. Finally, the government can help you with one arm and tell you to go pound sand with the other.

So, how do you trust anyone? Don't make big decisions without significant due diligence and investigate the professionals you retain. If you retain a young architect, hire a seasoned general contractor and vice versa. Ask for references on everyone. Negotiate your contracts well and include "what-if" provisions and contingencies. And remember that most of the good real estate investments will be the ones you find, not the ones people from afar try to sell you.

Tips To Keep You Afloat

> Turn your business profits into real estate holdings.
> Partner with other investors to purchase income-producing properties.
> Make sure your tenants pay rent on time.
> Understand the roles Realtors play with buyers, sellers and investors.
> Play the mortgage game and create more financial opportunities.
> Take precautions to avoid contractor abuse.
> Beware of scam artists – undertake due-diligence.

18. ENJOYING YOUR SUCCESS!

"We make a living by what we get, we make a life by what we give."

Winston Churchill

Y ou've paddled across the swamp and you're marked with battle scars. You've squeezed much out of the business and invested in other endeavors. You now understand how to finance your business, protect your assets, acquire real estate, manage people, market your brand, train salespeople, and manage professionals and government. You've built a tool chest that allows you to unleash your creativity and achieve your Business Plan. If you're uncomfortable with your ability to grasp financial basics, then explore studies at the Stephen Poorman College of Business, Computer Science and Human Services on the campus of Lock Haven University, located in the heart of Pennsylvania.

You're fully empowered and ready to turn your canoe into a "cigarette boat." You've totally conquered FUD, you possess the 3 B's and you're a true entrepreneur. Now it's time to have some fun with success in the wonderful world of business.

What is Success?

Success is being in good health, and having enough money to live comfortably while providing for your loved ones. With the knowledge you've gained from this book, you have the tools you need to become successful.

You work hard. Risk turns you on. You're not intimidated, especially by those people trying to steal your paddles. The confidence you've gained with this book has empowered you to set the rules of the game. If your corporation (that never owned any assets) fails, you'll change the rules, stay focused and move on to your next exciting venture.

What is Wealth?

We all know people from modest circumstances who "made it big" and flaunt it. The nouveau riche tend to demonstrate success by adopting an ostentatious lifestyle. It's their way of proving to themselves, and to the world, that they've become very important people. While it's okay to purchase a Ferrari once you've made it, real wealth is when you drive a modest vehicle knowing that you could buy the Ferrari dealership.

There are plenty of professional athletes, actors, and musicians who get paid massive incomes, only to wind up penniless. They aren't the only wealthy people to lose track of the meaning of financial responsibility.

I believe that you should share your good fortune with your God, those who helped you become successful, and those less fortunate. It's a bumpy road to success so cherish it once you're there.

Remember that as you inch your way to the top of the steep money mountain on your hands and knees through rocks and snakes, lots of people will be rolling big boulders down the side to crush you and your dreams. If you make it to the top, you'll finally achieve the opportunity to become a philanthropist.

Philanthropy

Begin this process early in life. Being driven by capitalism should only be a part of your road map to success. As motivational speaker Tony Robbins said, "Life is a gift, and it offers us the privilege, opportunity and responsibility to give something back." You don't want to place your education, your company and your employees in jeopardy, but there are always ways you can improve the lives of other people.

Even the IRS will encourage you to "give rather than receive." They allow tax breaks for giving to qualified charities.

Always help others. Walk up to someone you know and ask about their personal goals. Then say: "I really want to help you achieve those goals. What can I do to help?" Once you hear the reply, follow through on your commitment. Some people will never possess your business acumen so use your talents to help and encourage them. These gestures are always returned tenfold.

I was inspired by Luke 6:38, and by my Mother, who taught me to help those in need. Her handwritten notes are still framed in my office: "Don't look for flaws as you go through life. And even though you find them, be wise and kind and somewhat blind, and look for the virtues behind them."

At an early age of 26, I funded and became the "Founding Father" of our local Women's Center, an organization that protects people from abuse. Later in life our wealth multiplied and we were able to give back to our community. Everyone leaves a legacy — so start to think about leaving a positive one early on.

The real joy of living is found in giving. And when others witness your generosity, it will awaken their need to give, and they will follow your lead. Life's most urgent question came from the Rev. Martin Luther King, Jr.: "What are you doing for others?"

Life not only drove me to success, but to also share that success with others. It is why I wrote this book — in hopes that it might touch you, fuel your entrepreneurial spirit, protect you in murky waters, and encourage you to give back. Because only then will you truly be wealthy.

ABOUT THE AUTHOR

At the tender age of eight years old, Steve Poorman traveled door-to-door in a small Pennsylvania town selling trinkets. By age 10, he employed four salespeople and at age 12, clerked in a retail music store. Poorman taught music, played piano, and sold musical instruments throughout his high school and college years.

During his senior year in college, Steve opened his first music store. His company grew to a 17-store operation in New York and Pennsylvania. In 1977, he was recognized as the highest U..S. volume Kimball keyboard producer in Copenhagen, Denmark. This chain gained national recognition for its non-traditional marketing programs.

With retail profits, Steve purchased more commercial and apartment buildings. He formed multi-million dollar real estate syndicates with projects in three states. However, Poorman's primary profession is management consulting.

Steve's firm provides support to troubled companies, sometimes referred to as "turnaround consulting." Past projects include work with gas and oil investments, retail, wholesale, snack food, manufacturing, medical, restaurant, airline, communication and insurance firms. Services include management audits, diagnostic reviews, business plans and valuations for banks, attorneys, insurance companies, investors, and even the FBI.

Poorman has also owned or operated golf courses, restaurants, collision centers, surgery centers, real estate agencies and various other business investments.

In recent years, Steve has lectured on topics such as entrepreneurship and corporate strategy. His many articles have appeared in publications throughout the country including *Companies in Trouble* and "Turnaround Strategies" for the *Florida Business Review*.

Steve obtained his bachelor's degree in Business Management from Elizabethtown College in 1972, paralegal certification from Penn State University in 1987 and master's degree from Vermont College of Norwich University in 1990. He also studied at Lock Haven University. Steve is certified by the Institute of Management Consultants and the Institute of Real Estate Counselors.

Honorary positions held by Steve include a seat on the Pennsylvania Retailer's Association Board of Directors and with Transcriptions International, Bangalore, India. Governor Richard Thornburgh appointed him to The Pennsylvania Crime Commission. For ten years, Steve acted as assistant to the chairman of the board of directors of a publicly-traded cancer treatment and ophthalmology group. He served as CEO and Chairman of the Board of Directors of Charles Chips, and President and CEO of Nibble With Gibbles, two large snack food manufacturers.

Achievements include Businessman of the Year and the Heritage Award for the restoration of historical properties. Steve was recognized as Elizabethtown College's "Most Enterprising Graduate" and received the O'Reilly Memorial Award for outstanding leadership and vision. In 2017 he received the "Service through Professional Achievement" Award from Elizabethtown College.

Steve and his wife selected fourteen hometown organizations to receive philanthropic gifts. In recognition of a $7 million bequeath to Lock Haven University, the largest gift in the history of the Pennsylvania State System of Higher Education, the University honored him by naming its business college the Stephen Poorman College of Business and its central campus and theatre The Poorman

Amphitheatre and The Poorman Commons. The Poormans created a Student Investment Fund that allows students to buy and sell stock with real cash. The gift will also be used for facility upgrades, entrepreneurial studies and Scholar-In-Residence programs.

Steve enjoys a "second career" in music. He became an accomplished musician by his teen years. He was engaged by the Hammond Organ Company to play concerts throughout the east and produced his first vinyl at the age of 17. His most recent CD is titled, *Pipes, Pops & Patriotism.* As a hobby, he performs several annual benefit concerts.

CLIENT COMMENTS

"You came to my office just when I needed you most. Most people would have walked away from a very difficult situation but you took it as a real challenge. I must tell you that I have never seen anyone who could keep more balls in the air and still be so organized. Many people said it couldn't be done, but you made it happen, with the help of both God and our employees."

D. Gibble, President
Nibble With Gibble Snack Food Manufacturing
Chambersburg, Pa.

"We would sincerely like to thank you for all your masterful efforts to untangle the North Carolina mess. You accomplished more in weeks than the other professionals accomplished in five years."

W. R. Somers, M.D.
Cogan Station, Pa.

"In my long very business experience, you were the toughest and most successful opponent I have dealt with. You work like a New York professional – get everything you want."

F. D. Winner, M.D.
Dunedon, Fla.

"You're a tireless worker with a keen understanding of many complex issues."

A. Bergman, Esq.
Dallas, Texas

"Without the outstanding efforts and extremely hard work by Stephen Poorman, we never would have successfully completed this deal."

J. Lash, M.D.

A. Roque, M.D.

J. Ibarra, M.D.

Brooklyn, N.Y.

"In all my years as a trial lawyer, I have never received such well organized, professional assistance."

H. Pomerantz, Esq.

Palm Beach, Fla.

"Congratulations to you for being able to resolve the divorce issues. Your leadership and negotiations were obviously effective and has been a great benefit to my client."

G. Morrison, Esq.

Harrisburg, Pa.

"I will forever appreciate my son for introducing me to you. You got me out of the 'mess that took on a life of its own.' I want to thank you whole heartedly for your participation in this matter and the solving of same."

L. Powers

Hartford, Conn.

"Your efforts to get refinancing and work with our family in producing viable plans to generate future profits enabled us to obtain the necessary funds we needed to go forward. When we first met in my office, we had all but given up on the prospects of saving the Company."

G. McBeth
The McBeth Corporation
Chambersburg, Pa.

"You've made many changes in our Company which will protect us in the future, and your work resulted in immediate savings and increases in revenue."

C. Bloom
Grampian, Pa.

"I would like to commend you on the excellent job you did in negotiating a sale. The arrangement far exceeds what I thought was possible given the financial condition of the Company. I thought you were aggressive, yet tactful and professional in the negotiations. You certainly exceeded my expectations."

J. Rose, CEO, CPA
Charles Chips Snack Foods
Mountville, Pa.

"Thank you again for your consultation and expert testimony on this case. My partner and I felt that you were extremely well prepared to testify. Your conference and demeanor went over well with the jury."

R. S. Costantini, Esq.
Jacksonville, Fla.

"You've been extremely supportive and guided us through the recovery process. You've been effective, efficient and always helpful in our business dealings."

Dr. J. E. DeFinnis

Dr. S. G. Bishop

Berwick, Pa.

"We especially appreciate the tireless hours you spent trying to resolve hundreds of issues surrounding the transaction. You not only handled the business issues, but also worked to get the legal documents revised and amended to meet the requirements of our client's counsel. Had it not been for your efforts, this sale would have never closed. No matter what obstacles arose, you worked until it they were resolved."

O. Soni

Hauppauge, N.Y.

"You have always been extremely courteous, efficient, and honorable to deal with. You've showed a true concern for our interest and function with good judgment and integrity."

C. Rieders, Esq.

Williamsport, Pa.

"Thanks for all your help with this transaction. I am still not certain how you were able to negotiate such a deal in our Atlanta market."

T. Platford

Atlanta, Ga.

"*I received your latest document and it appears that you have finally put together a workable deal. I want to compliment you on your perseverance.*"

H. Sickler, Jr., CPA

Tyrone, Pa.

"*Mr. Poorman saved my Company a substantial sum because of his involvement and his contacts with people in government. More importantly, he quickly resolved a serious and complicated problem.*"

F. Vognet, Valley Marketing

Williamsport, Pa.

Mr. Poorman talks with Lock Haven University students outside of the College of Business Building.

The Haven Advantage...
Transferring Theory Into Practice

The **Stephen Poorman College of Business, Information Systems and Human Services** is focused on learning both in the classroom, through its Scholar-in-Residence speakers and exposure to real-life business situations... allowing students to develop new skills, attitudes and ways of thinking.

Visit our campus today to learn for yourself why students fall in love with **The Haven**!

LOCK
HAVEN
UNIVERSITY

lockhaven.edu/visit | 570•484•2027
admissions@lockhaven.edu

INDEX

Index